Volatility as an Asset Class

Volatility as an Asset Class
A guide to buying, selling and trading third-generation volatility products

Edited by Israel Nelken

Published by Risk Books, a Division of Incisive Financial Publishing Ltd

Haymarket House
28–29 Haymarket
London SW1Y 4RX
Tel: +44 (0)20 7484 9700
Fax: +44 (0)20 7484 9800
E-mail: books@incisivemedia.com
Sites: www.riskbooks.com
       www.incisivemedia.com

Every effort has been made to secure the permission of individual copyright holders for inclusion.

© Incisive Media 2007

ISBN 978 1 904 339 71 7

British Library Cataloguing in Publication Data
A catalogue record for this book is available from the British Library

Publisher: Clare Beesley
Assistant Editor: Jennifer Gibb

Typeset by Sunrise Setting Ltd, Torquay, UK

Printed and bound in Spain by Espacegrafic, Pamplona, Navarra

Conditions of sale
All rights reserved. No part of this publication may be reproduced in any material form whether by photocopying or storing in any medium by electronic means whether or not transiently or incidentally to some other use for this publication without the prior written consent of the copyright owner except in accordance with the provisions of the Copyright, Designs and Patents Act 1988 or under the terms of a licence issued by the Copyright Licensing Agency Limited of 90, Tottenham Court Road, London W1P 0LP.

Warning: the doing of any unauthorised act in relation to this work may result in both civil and criminal liability.

Every effort has been made to ensure the accuracy of the text at the time of publication, this includes efforts to contact each author to ensure the accuracy of their details at publication is correct. However, no responsibility for loss occasioned to any person acting or refraining from acting as a result of the material contained in this publication will be accepted by Incisive Financial Publishing Ltd.

Many of the product names contained in this publication are registered trade marks, and Risk Books has made every effort to print them with the capitalisation and punctuation used by the trademark owner. For reasons of textual clarity, it is not our house style to use symbols such as TM, ®, etc. However, the absence of such symbols should not be taken to indicate absence of trademark protection; anyone wishing to use product names in the public domain should first clear such use with the product owner.

Contents

About the Editor   vii

About the Authors   ix

Introduction   xv
Israel Nelken
Super Computer Consulting, Inc.

PART I: NOVEL USES OF VOLATILITY, IN A TRADITIONAL FRAMEWORK

1   Building Implied Volatility Surfaces from the Available Market Quotes: A Unified Approach   3
Antonio Castagna; Fabio Mercurio
Banca Profilo; Banca IMI

2   Shedding Light on Alternative Beta: A Volatility and Fixed Income Asset Class Comparison   61
David E. Kuenzi
Glenwood Capital Investments, LLC

3   Trend Following as a Long Volatility Strategy   83
Patrick Kremer; Hari P. Krishnan; Marc Malek
Conquest Capital Group LLC; Heptagon Capital; Conquest Capital Group LLC

4   Basket Volatility and Correlation   95
Matthias R. Fengler, Kay F. Pilz, Peter Schwendner
Sal. Oppenheim

5   Rethinking Volatility in the Era of Markov Processes, Fractal Geometry and Guided Random Walks   133
Peter Krause
Krause Financial Systems

PART II: THE VIX

6   Construction and Interpretation of Model-free Implied Volatility   141
Torben G. Andersen; Oleg Bondarenko
Kellogg School of Management, Northwestern University, IL; University of Illinois at Chicago, IL

CONTENTS

PART III: NEW PRODUCTS RELATED TO TRADING VOLATILITY

7   Second-Generation Volatility Products   185
    Nicolas Mougeot
    Deutsche Bank

8   Exchange-traded Volatility: CBOE and CFE VIX and
    Variance Derivatives   233
    John Hiatt, Catherine Shalen
    CBOE

9   Investment Strategies Using the Volatility Index
    (case study of the Korean market)   251
    Chul Min Kim
    Hyundai Securities

10 Risk Premium, Pricing and Hedging for Variance Swaps   259
    Srdjan D. Stojanovic
    University of Cincinnati

11 Corridor Variance Swaps   287
    Peter Carr; Keith Lewis
    Bloomberg/NYU; KALX, LLC

    Index   307

About the Editor

Israel Nelken is president of Super Computer Consulting, Inc. in Northbrook, Illinois. Super Computer Consulting, Inc. specialises in complex derivatives, structured products, risk management and hedge funds. He holds a PhD in computer science from Rutgers University and was on the faculty at the University of Toronto. Israel's firm has many consulting clients including several regulatory bodies, major broker-dealers, large and medium-sized banks as well as hedge funds. He is a lecturer at the prestigious mathematics department at the University of Chicago and teaches numerous courses and seminars around the world on a variety of topics. Israel's seminars are known for being non-mathematical. Instead they combine cutting edge analytics with real-world applications and intuitive examples. He is a member of the Chicago Board Options Exchange New Products Committee.

About the Authors

Torben G. Andersen is the Nathan S. and Mary P. Sharp Distinguished Professor of finance at the Kellogg School of Management, Northwestern University, and Research Associate at the National Bureau of Economic Research, Cambridge, MA, and CREATES in Aarhus, Denmark. He holds a PhD in economics from Yale University and a Master's degree from the University of Aarhus, Denmark. He has published widely within financial econometrics and, in particular, on return volatility modelling and risk management. He has been editor of *Journal of Business and Economic Statistics* and is editor of the forthcoming *Handbook of Financial Time Series* from Springer-Verlag He has also served on the editorial boards of *Journal of Finance, Review of Financial Studies* and *Management Science* amongst others. Torben is currently the director of the International Business and Markets Program and the International Business and Markets Research Center at the Kellogg School. He is the recipient of a Fulbright Fellowship and he has received multiple National Science Foundation and Q-Group research grants, given invited lectures worldwide and consults widely for financial firms, central banks and policy organisations.

Oleg Bondarenko is an associate professor of finance at the University of Illinois at Chicago. He holds a PhD in social sciences from the California Institute of Technology, an MS in banking and finance from the International University in Moscow and an MS in applied mathematics from the Moscow Institute of Physics and Technology. He has published in areas of option pricing, rationality of financial markets and market microstructure. Oleg has made invited presentations at numerous academic and practitioner conferences. His recent research focuses on understanding the role of the volatility risk and performance of hedge funds.

Peter Carr has over 10 years of experience in the derivatives industry. For the past three years, he has headed Quantitative Financial Research at Bloomberg and the Masters in Mathematical Finance programme at NYU's Courant Institute. Prior to Peter's current positions, he headed equity derivative research groups at two major banks and was a finance professor for eight years at Cornell University. Conducting research in the interface between academia and industry, Peter has published extensively in both academic and industry-oriented journals. He is currently the treasurer of the Bachelier Finance Society and an associate editor for eight journals related to mathematical finance. A plenary speaker at many practitioner conferences, Peter has recently won awards from Wilmott Magazine for Cutting Edge Research and from *Risk* Magazine for "Quant of the Year". In ICBI's 2006 survey of contributions to the derivatives industry, he was ranked as a leading academic and practitioner, the only person to appear in the top three in both categories.

Antonio Castagna is currently head of the Structured Products Desk and of the Quantitative Department in Banca Profilo, Milan. He was previously at Banca IMI, Milan, from 1999 to 2006. Antonio was first a market maker of cap/floors and swaptions, and then he set up the foreign exchange options desk and ran the book of plain vanilla and exotic options on the major currencies, also being responsible for the entire foreign exchange volatility trading. Antonio has written papers on different issues, including credit derivatives, managing of exotic options risks and volatility smiles. He is often invited to academic and post-graduate courses.

Matthias R. Fengler is a senior quantitative analyst for exotic equity derivatives at Sal. Oppenheim, Frankfurt. He earned his PhD in quantitative finance from the Humboldt-Universität zu Berlin and published, *inter alia*, in *Computational Statistics*, the *Review of Derivatives Research*, the *Journal of Derivatives* and the *Journal of Financial Econometrics*. Matthias is author of the textbook *Semiparametric Modelling of Implied Volatility* edited by Springer-Verlag.

John Hiatt is a director in the Product Development Group of the Chicago Board Options Exchange. He has worked for the CBOE since March 1994. He received an MS degree in Finance from DePaul University and a BS in Aerospace Engineering from the Illinois Institute of Technology. He is also a CFA charterholder.

Chul Min Kim is a quantitative analyst at Hyundai Securities in Seoul, Korea. He specialises in developing and backtesting equity investment strategies and assessing the performance. With his experience in both IT and research, he helps local institutional investors grab excess returns using various quantitative methods. This includes stock screening, enhanced index methodology and sector rotation strategy. He publishes a monthly style investment guide and speaks frequently at investment conferences.

Peter Krause has worked in the Chicago derivatives community for over 20 years, in numerous capacities, ranging from floor clerk to portfolio manager. Spearheading Krause Financial Systems, he developed market making and risk management systems for LETCO from 1990 until 2001, helping LETCO grow into one of the highest volume equity options specialists in the world. Since then, he has worked on statistical arbitrage systems, a hidden-markov model based market tone oriented stock forecasting system, equity and option execution algorithms and numerous other projects for many clients, ranging from hedge funds to brokerage firms to money centre banks. This article is the first thing he has ever published relating to financial markets or options theory.

ABOUT THE AUTHORS

Patrick Kremer is vice president at Conquest Capital Group LLC. He originally joined Conquest as a quantitative analyst after having begun his career in the Government Analytics group at Lehman Brothers. He graduated from the Massachusetts Institute of Technology with a BSc in mathematics with computer science and a BSc in management science.

Hari P. Krishnan is a director at Heptagon Capital in London, where he manages the internal derivatives trading and fund of funds platforms. Previously he was an executive director at Morgan Stanley and a senior economist at the Chicago Board of Trade. Hari holds a PhD in applied math from Brown University and was a postdoctoral research scientist at Columbia University.

David E. Kuenzi is head of risk management and quantitative research at Glenwood Capital Investments, LLC, a US$6 billion hedge fund of funds and a member of the Man Group. In his current role he is responsible for risk management activities and for the development of quantitative techniques for assessing hedge funds and hedge fund portfolios. Prior to joining Glenwood, David was a vice president at Nuveen Investments where he held a number of roles, most recently in research, development and risk management. Prior to joining Nuveen in 1996, he was a small-cap stock analyst at Perritt Capital Management. David received a BA from Western Michigan University, an MFA from the University of Iowa, an MBA in Analytic Finance and International Business from the University of Chicago, and an MS in Financial Mathematics from the University of Chicago. He is also a Chartered Financial Analyst (CFA). His articles on investing, risk management and derivatives have appeared in *The Journal of Alternative Investments*, *The Journal of Portfolio Management*, *The Journal of Investing*, *The Journal of Performance Measurement* and the "Cutting Edge" section of *Risk*.

Keith Lewis is the managing member of KALX, LLC, a New York consulting firm that provides quantitative and technology solutions to financial companies. KALX was founded in 2002 to produce high-quality software tools and analytic libraries like those used by large investment banks for trading and risk management using a tried and tested methodology for reducing the time required to turn quantitatively demanding business requirements into production quality software.

Marc Malek is managing partner at Conquest Capital Group LLC. He started his career in 1992 at Salomon Brothers in New York as a financial analyst in the Financial Strategy Group. From Salomon, he was hired in 1993 to KB Currency Advisors (KB), a US$400 million hedge fund and financial advisory firm. For the next two years, Marc traded currency options, worked on developing proprietary trend following trading systems and dealt with currency overlay customers. He joined UBS in 1995, where he held various senior level positions within the foreign exchange department at UBS in New York, London and Tokyo. Marc was the worldwide head of the Exotic Foreign Exchange Derivatives Group, and by the time he left the bank in 1998, he held the post of executive director in charge of foreign exchange proprietary trading in Europe. He was a principal in Avalon Asset Management, which ran The Enterprise Fund and the Falcon Fund of Funds commencing in 1999. Marc graduated with honours from the California Institute of Technology (Caltech) with a BS in engineering and applied science, and holds a BA in mathematics from Reed College. While at Caltech, Marc did extensive research on neural networks and decision support systems, and was awarded a grant from the Pentagon through the Caltech Summer Undergraduate Research Fellowship to conduct research on computer-based decision systems.

Fabio Mercurio is the head of financial engineering at Banca IMI, Milan. He holds a BSc in applied mathematics from the University of Padua and a PhD in mathematical finance from the Erasmus University of Rotterdam. Fabio's recent scientific interests include interest rate modelling for pricing and hedging exotics, the pricing of hybrids and the smile modelling for the equity, foreign exchange and interest rate markets. He has published several articles in journals such as *Mathematical Finance*, *Quantitative Finance*, *Finance and Stochastics* and *Risk*. He has also co-authored the book *Interest Rate Models: Theory and Practice*, published by Springer.

Nicolas Mougeot is head of European equity derivatives strategy at Deutsche Bank. His current role involves advising the bank's clients on new volatility products as well as defining quantitative volatility strategies. Prior to Deutsche Bank, Nicolas held senior positions at BNP Paribas, Salomon Smith Barney and Lehman Brothers. He is a regular guest speaker at international conferences on topics such as volatility or correlation trading. His research has been published in various academic and practitioner's journals such as *Risk* or the *Journal of Banking and Finance*. Nicolas holds a maitrise in econometrics from the University of Strasbourg and a MSc in banking and finance and a PhD in finance from the University of Lausanne.

Kay F. Pilz is working as a quantitative analyst for Sal. Oppenheim in Frankfurt. His work and research interests focus mainly on the development and implementation of equity as well as commodity models for pricing and hedging derivative securities. Kay graduated in mathematics from the University of Frankfurt and holds a PhD in mathematical statistics from the University of Bochum.

Peter Schwendner heads the Quantitative Research group at the Trading and Derivatives division of Sal. Oppenheim. His group develops the models for pricing and hedging across all relevant asset classes. Peter holds a PhD in physics from the University of Göttingen.

ABOUT THE AUTHORS

Catherine Shalen has been director of research in the Product Development Group of the Chicago Board Options Exchange since 2002. She previously worked as senior economist in the Research Departments of the Chicago Board of Trade and the Chicago Mercantile Exchange. Prior to her life at the Chicago exchanges, she was an assistant professor of finance at the University of Illinois in Chicago. She holds a PhD and an MBA from Columbia University Graduate School of Business and a BA in mathematics from Harvard University. She has published in the *Review of Financial Studies* and the *Journal of Futures Markets*, as well as in financial industry periodicals and books.

Srdjan D. Stojanovic is full professor of mathematics at the University of Cincinnati, where he leads the research group in computational finance. Srdjan is a frequent speaker at academic and industry quant conferences. He is an author of numerous research articles in applied and financial mathematics journals, and also author of *Computational Financial Mathematics using Mathematica*, published in 2002 by Birkhäuser, Boston. His recent research is in the area of optimal portfolio theory approach to risk premium, pricing and hedging of financial contracts in multi-dimensional incomplete markets, with special emphasis on foreign exchange, equity and volatility. Srdjan holds a PhD degree in mathematics from Northwestern University.

Introduction

Israel Nelken
Super Computer Consulting, Inc.

It gives me great pleasure to be the editor of this collection of important essays on volatility. In the last few years (2002–2006), volatility has, for the most part, been on a steady decline. As this introduction is being written (August 2007), volatility has been on a steep rise. This is, of course, due to the sub-prime mortgage issues in the US and the problems associated with it. Many in the markets are trying to guess what will happen next. One thing is for sure, the financial markets are always very interesting.

This book was motivated in large part by my work at the CBOE New Products Committee. One of the most successful products has been options on the implied volatility index (VIX options). A car is a solid structure – you feel it if it hits you. There is a company that makes the car; there is a stock on the company that makes the car. There is a stock index (eg, SPX) that is composed by many companies; there are options on the stock index. We can speak about the implied volatility skew of those options. We can even quantify the entire skew with one number (say VIX). Finally, we have options whose underlying is the measure of the skew of the options on the stock index. All in all, options on implied volatility are many levels removed from anything "tangible". Yet they have been trading in very large volumes.

The history of the VIX product is quite fascinating. In 1995 I was asked to edit the *Handbook of Exotic Options*, in which Anthony Neuberger of the London Business School wrote a chapter on "log options". These are options whose payout relates to the natural logarithm of the stock price. The conclusion was that "the log contract provides a much easier and more reliable way of betting on volatility". In 1995 this was a purely theoretical result which was not much use to practitioners. During the LTCM meltdown of 1997–1998, volatility levels rose to unprecedented heights. It was at that time that the first transactions in volatility swaps occurred. In March 1999 Emanuel Derman and his colleagues from Goldman

Sachs released a paper titled "More than you ever wanted to know about volatility swaps but less than can be said", which laid the groundwork to the way the CBOE constructs the VIX. It just so happens that Derman also wrote a chapter in my *Handbook of Exotic Options* book. Several years later he used the Neuberger chapter as the basis of his volatility paper. The Neuberger chapter, which was written as a purely academic exercise, was turned by Derman and his colleagues into a practical recipe that was later used by the CBOE to construct the VIX.

Much has happened since the publication of that book. At that time, the trend was to create exotic options (eg, lookback, chooser, compound, etc) on vanilla underlying instruments (eg, SP500, currency rates, etc). Nowadays, the trend is to create vanilla options on exotic or esoteric underlying instruments. The VIX options are an example of a simple derivative instrument on a pretty complicated underlying instrument. So we have gone from "exotic options on vanilla underlying instruments" to "vanilla options on exotic underlying instruments" – it is difficult to predict the future, but perhaps we will see "exotic options on exotic underlying instruments".

Options on the VIX are just one of the new and exciting ways to trade volatility. Indeed, volatility has become an asset class all by itself. It can be traded much like any other market. In this book, we asked a world-spanning collection of luminaries to unravel the mysteries surrounding volatility.

The 11 chapters before you are organised as follows: the first five chapters describe how volatility can be measured among various underlying products, what it means and how it can be used. In Chapter 1, Antonio Castagna and Fabio Mercurio write about building volatility surfaces. In Chapter 2 David Keunzi compares volatility and fixed income asset classes. Patrick Kremer, Hari Krishnan and Marc Malek describe trend following in terms of a volatility strategy in Chapter 3. Chapter 4 is a discussion by Matthias Fengler, Kay Pilz and Peter Schwendner on basket volatility and correlation. Peter Krause writes about using some new tools to understand volatility in Chapter 5.

In Chapter 6 Torben Andersen and Oleg Bondarenko examine the reliability of the VIX.

The last five chapters are devoted to the new financial products designed to trade volatility. Chapter 7 is an exposition by Nicolas Mougeot of second-generation volatility products. In Chapter 8, John Hiatt and Catherine Shalen describe the VIX and other CBOE-traded volatility products. Chapter 9 is a Korean case study of using the volatility index by Chul Min Kim. Srdjan Stojanovic writes about pricing and hedging variance swaps in Chapter 10. In Chapter 11 Peter Carr and Keith Lewis write about corridor variance swaps.

My sincere thanks are given to all the contributors who participated and to Laurie Donaldson and Jennifer Gibb of Risk Books for all their good work. Finally, I want to express my heartfelt thanks to you – the reader.

Part I

Novel Uses of Volatility, in a Traditional Framework

1

Building Implied Volatility Surfaces from the Available Market Quotes: A Unified Approach

Antonio Castagna; Fabio Mercurio

Banca Profilo; Banca IMI

INTRODUCTION

The volatility surface, or matrix (we will use the two terms without any distinction), is the map of the implied volatilities quoted by the market for plain vanilla options struck at different levels and expiring at different dates. Implied volatility is the parameter σ to plug into the Black–Scholes (BS) formula to calculate the price of an option.

In practice, the matrix is built according to three main conventions, each prevailing as a standard in the market according to the traded underlying: the sticky strike; the sticky Delta; and, finally, the sticky absolute. These are simple rules used to conveniently quote and trade options written on different assets and, as such, are not intended to model the evolution of the volatility surface.

When the sticky strike rule is effective, implied volatilities are mapped, for each expiry, with respect to the strike prices; this is the rule usually adopted in official markets (eg, equity options and futures options). The name sticky strike refers to the fact that implied volatilities do not change if the underlying asset's price changes. Clearly, that almost never happens since the volatility matrix is not at all constant in reality. Nevertheless, the assumption is believed to be in force for small movements of the underlying asset. Accordingly, traders quote option prices for specific strikes, and usually in terms of premiums, so that one has to back out the implied volatility from those.

If the sticky Delta rule is adopted, implied volatilities are mapped, for each expiry, with respect to the Delta[1] of the option; this rule is usually used in over-the-counter (OTC) markets (eg, foreign exchange (FX) options). The underpinning assumption is that options are priced depending on their Delta, so that when the underlying asset's price moves and the Delta of an option changes accordingly, a different implied volatility has to be plugged into the formula.

Lastly, the sticky absolute rule produces matrices with implied volatilities mapped, for each expiry, in terms of absolute distance, measured in some units of price, from the at-the-money (ATM) strike.[2] This rule, which is in some way a mix of the two described above, prevails in some OTC markets, such as those for swaptions and for bond options. It implies that the implied volatility for a given strike changes along movements in the underlying asset's price, since the absolute distance from the ATM is also different.[3]

Whichever rule is prevailing, the main problem a market maker has to cope with is building a consistent volatility surface for a wide range (in terms of expiries and strikes) of options, given the knowledge of a few prices. The problem is twofold. First, they need a tool to interpolate/extrapolate implied volatilities amongst strikes for a given expiry. Second, they face the problem of the interpolation amongst available expiries. To address the former issue, we introduce the Vanna–Volga (VV) method, which is commonly employed in the FX option market, where three main volatility quotes are typically available for a given conventional maturity. We will see that the method can also be extended effectively to other markets. The latter issue is instead tackled by proposing a weighting scheme to consistently include working days, eventful days and holidays.

Before analysing both issues, we first have to choose how to represent and handle a volatility surface in an efficient, intuitive and convenient way, capable of satisfying different instances presented by a financial institution. This is explained in the following section.

CRITERIA FOR AN EFFICIENT AND CONVENIENT REPRESENTATION OF THE VOLATILITY SURFACE

The representation of the volatility surface is not directly related to the specific conventions of the reference market. Actually, not all of the rules we have described in the previous section grant and imply a convenient way to handle the volatility matrix. We now list some critical features that the representation should have.

- *Parsimony*: the representation contains the smallest amount of information needed to retrieve the entire volatility surface for all strikes and expiries.
- *Consistency*: the information contained in the representation is consistently organised along the expiries and strikes, so as to make the integration of missing points, either by interpolation or extrapolation, easily possible.
- *Intuitiveness*: the information provides the user with a clear picture about the shape of the volatility surface, and each piece of the information distinctly affects one specific trait of the volatility surface.

The representation is parsimonious if one can devise a suitable interpolation/extrapolation scheme amongst strikes and expiries, which requires only a few points as input. In principle, this seems a hard task to achieve, because for each given expiry, a volatility smile has as many degrees of freedom as considered strikes. However, from an empirical point of view, volatilities do not move independently of each another, and one may reasonably assume that there are only three degrees of freedom: (i) level, (ii) slope and (iii) convexity. In fact, as a principal component analysis can show, most of shape variations can be explained by a parallel shift of the smile, by a tilt to the right or to the left, or by a relative change of the wings with respect to the central strike. Therefore, for each expiry, a minimum of three points are needed to represent these stylised movements: the volatility for the ATM strike, that for an out-of-the-money call and that for an out-of-the-money put.[4]

These strike triplets, one for each expiry, must also be chosen in such a way that the resulting representation is consistent. To make things clear let us think of a very simple volatility surface with only two expiries: one week and 10 years. For both expiries, one of the three strikes to choose may be set equal to the current price of the underlying asset (ATM spot). This choice is reasonable but not necessarily the best. In fact, it would be better to replace the two ATM spot values with the forward prices at the two expiries, which can be viewed as expected values of the future underlying asset under suitable measures (the corresponding forward risk-adjusted measures).

Things can even be worse for the other two points, because a meaningful selection criterion likely leads to different values for the two expiries: two chosen strikes may convey a good amount of information regarding the smile for the one-week expiry, but may be not so informative for the 10-year expiry. In fact, what matters (from a probabilistic point of view) is the relative distance of a strike from the central strike, possibly expressed in volatility units, which makes the chosen strikes, and their corresponding implied volatilities, comparable throughout the entire range of expiries. A meaningful distance measure, familiar to practitioners, is provided by the Delta of an option (in absolute terms), because it is a common indicator used in the market and has the same signalling power as the relative distance from the ATM (in units of total standard deviation). For this reason, we will select, for each expiry, the volatility for the ATM and the 25Δ call and the 25Δ put.[5] These two Delta levels are introduced because they are almost midway between the centre of the smile and the extreme wings (0Δ put and 0Δ call) and also because they are the strikes associated with high Volga,[6] thus containing a good deal of information on the underlying asset's fourth moment, and hence on the curvature of the smile.

Finally, the representation is intuitive if it is directly expressed in terms of three qualitative features of the surface, instead of three implied volatilities. These features, already mentioned above, are the level, the steepness and the convexity of the smile for each maturity. The level is correctly measured by the ATM volatility. As for the steepness, we can use the difference between the 25Δ call and the 25Δ put, which in the market lore is called risk reversal (or collar). A good indicator for the convexity is the average level of the volatility for the two 25Δ wings, with respect to the ATM level: in the market jargon it is referred to as the butterfly.[7] In a representation such as this, a user is able to change the shape of the volatility surface by simply changing these three indicators.

BUILDING IMPLIED VOLATILITY SURFACES FROM THE AVAILABLE MARKET QUOTES

Table 1.1 Stylised representation of a volatility surface in the compact form.

Expiry	ATM	25Δ risk reversal	25Δ butterfly
τ_1	σ_1	rr_1	fly_1
τ_2	σ_2	rr_2	fly_2
τ_3	σ_3	rr_3	fly_3
τ_4	σ_4	rr_4	fly_4
τ_5	σ_5	rr_5	fly_5
τ_6	σ_6	rr_6	fly_6

As for the set of expiries, a fixed number of maturities expressed as a fraction or multiple of years (and not as a fixed date) is the most intuitive and consistent choice to represent the volatility surface. This makes it easier to compare times in the matrix and is more respondent to the requirements of intuitiveness and consistency.

To sum up the considerations above, a convenient and efficient way to represent the volatility surface can be obtained by organising the information as follows: for each expiry (expressed as time to maturity and in year units) store the ATM volatility, the risk reversal and the butterfly for the 25Δ call and put. The ATM is referred to a strike set equal to the forward price for each expiry. One could also choose the ATM 0Δ straddle, the definition of which is given below. Practitioners accustomed with FX options will easily realise that this representation coincides with the standard way to handle a volatility matrix in the FX market. An example of such a representation, in a stylised form, is provided in Table 1.1.

COMMONLY ADOPTED APPROACHES TO BUILD A VOLATILITY SURFACE

Several recipes have been proposed in the literature for the manufacture of a volatility surface, considering the availability of a limited number of options prices. Some of them are simply very general interpolation/smoothing schemes, capable of fitting almost all available data perfectly, provided that no-arbitrage conditions of the resulting matrix are preserved (see, for instance, Fengler (2005) and the references therein). These tools produce good results but they may require many prices to work efficiently, because they are not founded on any valuation model but just on mere no-arbitrage restrictions.

A simpler interpolation method that enjoyed some popularity, both among practitioners and academics, is the second-order polynomial function (in Delta) proposed by Malz (1997), which, like the VV approach, needs three basic volatilities in input:

$$\sigma_{\Delta\text{put}} = \sigma_{\text{ATM}} + 2(\sigma_{75\Delta\text{put}} - \sigma_{25\Delta\text{put}})(\Delta\text{put} - 0.5)$$
$$+ 16\left(\frac{\sigma_{75\Delta\text{put}} + \sigma_{25\Delta\text{put}}}{2} - \sigma_{\text{ATM}}\right)(\Delta\text{put} - 0.5)^2 \quad (1.1)$$

This method has been specifically devised for the FX options market, but it can be rather easily extended to other markets. Its main flaws are due to the simplifying assumptions underpinning the expression above, ie, the Delta of the call is equal to one minus the Delta of the put (which is true only in a zero foreign rates environment, in the FX case considered), and the ATM volatility is 50Δ. However, without regards to this criticism, the interpolation (1.1) fits the three provided points and performs quite well in interpolating amongst them; nevertheless Malz's formula usually underestimates implied volatilities both for low and high put Deltas: we will clearly see this later on, when we apply the VV approach to different markets and compare it with other methods. In addition, there is no real financial justification for a second-order interpolation amongst the three volatilities, except for the mathematical fact that this is the simplest form fitting them perfectly.

A different approach involves the calibration of a stochastic volatility model to available prices: then the entire volatility surface can be built. For instance, in equity markets, a widely adopted choice is the Heston (1993) model, with constant or time-dependent parameters; in the swaptions market a popular model is the SABR (stochastic alpha, beta, rho) model, by Hagan et al (2002), which is used to generate volatility smiles for any expiry and tenor. This model is quite appealing since in its framework the authors derive an explicit function for equivalent BS implied volatilities:

$$\sigma(K) \simeq \alpha \left\{ (S_{a,b}(0)K)^{(1-\beta)/2} \left[1 + \frac{(1-\beta)^2}{24} \ln^2\left(\frac{S_{a,b}(0)}{K}\right)\right.\right.$$
$$\left.\left. + \frac{(1-\beta)^4}{1920} \ln^4\left(\frac{S_{a,b}(0)}{K}\right)\right]\right\}^{-1} \frac{z}{x(z)} \Gamma(K) \quad (1.2)$$

where

$$\Gamma(K) := 1 + \left[\frac{(1-\beta)^2 \alpha^2}{24(S_{a,b}(0)K)^{1-\beta}} + \frac{\rho \beta \epsilon \alpha}{4(S_{a,b}(0)K)^{(1-\beta)/2}} + \epsilon^2 \frac{2-3\rho^2}{24} \right] T_a$$

$$z := \frac{\epsilon}{\alpha} (S_{a,b}(0)K)^{(1-\beta)/2} \ln\left(\frac{S_{a,b}}{K}\right)$$

$$x(z) := \ln\left[\frac{\sqrt{1-2\rho z + z^2} + z - \rho}{1-\rho}\right]$$

with the particular case

$$\sigma(K = S_{a,b}(0)) \simeq \frac{\alpha}{S_{a,b}^{1-\beta}(0)} \Gamma(S_{a,b}(0))$$

for the ATM volatility.

Similarly to the first approach, the stable calibration of a stochastic volatility model demands many prices and they may not always be available.

Instead, we introduce a different approach: the aforementioned VV method, which is extensively studied in the next section and in Appendix A. This approach has several advantages. First it has a clear financial rationale supporting it, based on a hedging argument leading to its definition: this is shared with other stochastic volatility models, but not with the pure interpolation/smoothing schemes. Second, it requires just three prices per maturity to generate a complete (ie, for any strike) and consistent smile. Finally, it allows for an automatic calibration to the three input volatilities (derived from market prices), being an explicit function of them. To the best of our knowledge, no other functional form enjoys the same features. In addition, we show that it enjoys some interesting properties which make it very useful for practical purposes.

The interpolation implied by the VV method also yields a very good approximation of the induced smile, after calibration to three available prices, by a stochastic volatility model, especially within the range delimited by the two extreme strikes. A confirmation of this statement will be provided later, where we compare the VV approach with the SABR functional form and with the Heston model. This further supports the choice of the method, because it attains very similar results to those produced by renowned stochastic volatility models, but with reduced effort and fewer input data required.

SMILE INTERPOLATION AMONG STRIKES

The VV method is a known empirical procedure that can be used to infer an implied-volatility smile from three available quotes for a given maturity.[8] It is based on the construction of locally replicating portfolios whose associate hedging costs are added to corresponding BS prices so as to produce smile-consistent values. In addition to being intuitive and easy to implement, this procedure has a clear financial interpretation, which further supports its use in practice.

In this section, we describe the main features of the VV approach, showing how to construct an implied-volatility smile from three given market quotes. Further motivations and descriptions of the approach are provided in Appendix A.[9]

The VV approach

We consider an option market where, for a given maturity T, three basic options are quoted. We denote the corresponding strikes by K_i, $i = 1, 2, 3$, $K_1 < K_2 < K_3$, and set $\mathcal{K} := \{K_1, K_2, K_3\}$. The market implied volatility associated to K_i is denoted by σ_i, $i = 1, 2, 3$.

The VV method serves the purpose of defining an implied-volatility smile that is consistent with the basic volatilities σ_i. The rationale behind it stems from a replication argument in a flat-smile world where the constant (through strikes) level of implied volatility varies stochastically over time. This argument is presented hereafter, where for simplicity we consider the same type of options, namely calls.

It is well known that, in the BS model, the payout of a European call with maturity T and strike K can be replicated by a dynamic Δ-hedging strategy, whose value (comprehensive of the bank account part) matches, at every time t, the option price $C^{\text{BS}}(t; K)$ given by

$$C^{\text{BS}}(t;K) = S_t e^{-\delta \tau} \Phi\left(\frac{\ln(S_t/K) + (r^d - \delta + \frac{1}{2}\sigma^2)\tau}{\sigma\sqrt{\tau}}\right)$$
$$- K e^{-r^d \tau} \Phi\left(\frac{\ln(S_t/K) + (r^d - \delta - \frac{1}{2}\sigma^2)\tau}{\sigma\sqrt{\tau}}\right) \quad (1.3)$$

where S_t denotes the underlying asset's price at time t, $\tau := T - t$, r^d and δ denote, respectively, the domestic risk-free rate and the continuous cashflow yielded by the asset,[10] σ is the constant BS implied volatility and Φ denotes the cumulative standard normal distribution function. In real financial markets, however, volatility is stochastic and traders hedge the associated risk by constructing portfolios that are Vega-neutral in a BS (flat-smile) world.

Maintaining the assumption of flat but stochastic implied volatilities, the presence of three basic options in the market even makes it possible to build a portfolio that zeros partial derivatives up to the second order. The first step in the VV procedure is the derivation of such a hedging portfolio for the above call with maturity T and strike K. To this end, we set $t = 0$, dropping the argument t in the call prices, and start by finding time-0 weights $x_1(K)$, $x_2(K)$ and $x_3(K)$ such that the resulting portfolio of European calls with maturity T and strikes K_1, K_2 and K_3, respectively, hedges the price variations of the call with maturity T and strike K, up to the second order in the underlying and the volatility. Assuming a Δ-hedged position and given that, in the BS world, portfolios of plain-vanilla options (with the same maturity) that are Vega-neutral are also Gamma-neutral, the weights $x_1(K)$, $x_2(K)$ and $x_3(K)$ can be found by imposing that the "replicating" portfolio has the same Vega, $\partial \text{Vega}/\partial \text{Vol}$ and $\partial \text{Vega}/\partial \text{Spot}$ as the call with strike K:[11]

$$\frac{\partial C^{BS}}{\partial \sigma}(K) = \sum_{i=1}^{3} x_i(K) \frac{\partial C^{BS}}{\partial \sigma}(K_i)$$

$$\frac{\partial^2 C^{BS}}{\partial \sigma^2}(K) = \sum_{i=1}^{3} x_i(K) \frac{\partial^2 C^{BS}}{\partial \sigma^2}(K_i) \quad (1.4)$$

$$\frac{\partial^2 C^{BS}}{\partial \sigma \partial S_0}(K) = \sum_{i=1}^{3} x_i(K) \frac{\partial^2 C^{BS}}{\partial \sigma \partial S_0}(K_i)$$

The weights can then be obtained by numerically solving this system. An explicit formula for them can also be derived, see Appendix A.

We can now proceed to the definition of the VV price, which is consistent with the market prices of the basic options. The VV price for the call with strike K is obtained by adding to the BS price the cost of implementing the above hedging strategy at prevailing market prices. In formulae,

$$C(K) = C^{BS}(K) + \sum_{i=1}^{3} x_i(K)[C^{MKT}(K_i) - C^{BS}(K_i)] \quad (1.5)$$

This price depends on the volatility parameter σ. In practice, the typical choice is to set $\sigma = \sigma_{ATM}$.

The new option price is thus defined by adding to the "flat-smile" BS price the cost difference of the hedging portfolio induced by the market implied volatilities with respect to the constant volatility σ. A possible justification for such a definition is given in Appendix A.

When $K = K_j$, $C(K_j) = C^{MKT}(K_j)$, because $x_i(K) = 1$ for $i = j$ and zero otherwise. Therefore, (1.5) defines a rule for either interpolating or extrapolating prices from the three option quotes $C^{MKT}(K_1)$, $C^{MKT}(K_2)$ and $C^{MKT}(K_3)$. An analogous interpretation holds for the corresponding implied volatilities $\varsigma(K)$, which can be obtained by inverting (1.5), for each considered K, through the BS formula. As, by construction, $\varsigma(K_i) = \sigma_i$, the function $\varsigma(K)$ yields an interpolation/extrapolation tool for the market implied volatilities.

Limit and no-arbitrage conditions

The VV option price has several interesting features that we analyse in the following.

The option price $C(K)$, as a function of the strike K, is twice differentiable and satisfies the following (no-arbitrage) conditions:

(i) $\lim_{K \to 0^+} C(K) = S_0 e^{-\delta T}$ and $\lim_{K \to +\infty} C(K) = 0$;
(ii) $\lim_{K \to 0^+} (dC/dK)(K) = -e^{-r^d T}$ and $\lim_{K \to +\infty} K(dC/dK)(K) = 0$.

These properties, which are trivially satisfied by $C^{BS}(K)$, follow from the fact that, for each i, both $x_i(K)$ and $dx_i(K)/dK$ go to zero for $K \to 0^+$ or $K \to +\infty$.

To avoid arbitrage opportunities, the option price $C(K)$ should also be a convex function of the strike K, ie, $d^2C(K)/dK^2 > 0$ for each $K > 0$. This property, which is not true in general,[12] holds however for typical market parameters, so that (1.5) indeed leads to prices that are arbitrage-free in practice.

Unfortunately, there is no guarantee that VV price is always positive. In fact, for quite steep smiles, namely for extremely large risk-reversal values, (1.5) may become negative. In these situations, which may occur in the current equity markets at extreme strikes, the VV procedure must be handled with care as far as the valuation of the wings is concerned. In most common cases, however, the VV approach yields robust and reliable option prices and volatilities.

Approximating implied volatilities

The specific expression of the VV option price, combined with our analytical formula (A.6) for the weights, allows for the derivation of a straightforward approximation for the VV implied volatility $\varsigma(K)$. In fact, by expanding both members of (1.5) at first order in $\sigma = \sigma_2$, one has

$$C(K) \approx C^{BS}(K) + \sum_{i=1}^{3} x_i(K)\mathcal{V}(K_i)[\sigma_i - \sigma]$$

which, remembering (A.6) and the fact that $\sum_{i=1}^{3} x_i(K)\mathcal{V}(K_i) = \mathcal{V}(K)$, leads to

$$C(K) \approx C^{BS}(K) + \mathcal{V}(K)\left[\sum_{i=1}^{3} y_i(K)\sigma_i - \sigma\right] \quad (1.6)$$

where

$$y_1(K) = \frac{\ln(K_2/K)\ln(K_3/K)}{\ln(K_2/K_1)\ln(K_3/K_1)}, \quad y_2(K) = \frac{\ln(K/K_1)\ln(K_3/K)}{\ln(K_2/K_1)\ln(K_3/K_2)}$$

$$y_3(K) = \frac{\ln(K/K_1)\ln(K/K_2)}{\ln(K_3/K_1)\ln(K_3/K_2)}$$

Comparing (1.6) with the first-order Taylor expansion

$$C(K) \approx C^{BS}(K) + \mathcal{V}(K)[\varsigma(K) - \sigma]$$

one immediately has the following.

Proposition 1 *The implied volatility $\sigma(K)$ for the above option with price $C(K)$ is approximately given by*

$$\varsigma(K) \approx \varsigma_1(K) := \frac{\ln(K_2/K)\ln(K_3/K)}{\ln(K_2/K_1)\ln(K_3/K_1)}\sigma_1 + \frac{\ln(K/K_1)\ln(K_3/K)}{\ln(K_2/K_1)\ln(K_3/K_2)}\sigma_2$$
$$+ \frac{\ln(K/K_1)\ln(K/K_2)}{\ln(K_3/K_1)\ln(K_3/K_2)}\sigma_3 \quad (1.7)$$

The implied volatility $\varsigma(K)$ can thus be approximated by a linear combination of the basic volatilities σ_i, with combinators $y_i(K)$ that sum up to one (as tedious but straightforward algebra shows). It is also easily seen that the approximation is a quadratic function of $\ln K$, meaning that one can resort to a simple parabolic interpolation when log coordinates are used.

A graphical representation of the goodness of the approximation (1.7) is shown in Figure 1.1, where we show, as an example, the

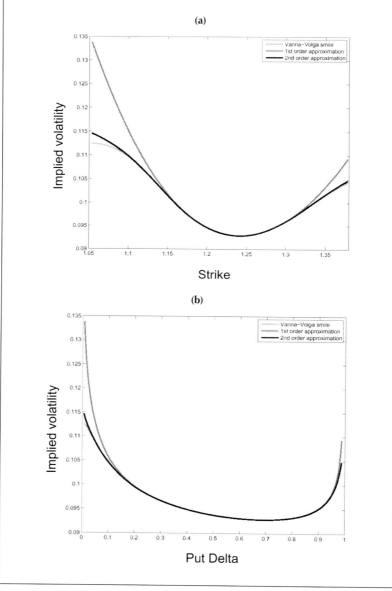

Figure 1.1 Implied volatilities and their approximations of the exchange rate euro/US dollar, plotted both against (a) strikes and (b) put Deltas (in absolute value).

smile for the exchange rate euro/US dollar, produced by using the following data: $T = 3m$ ($= 94$ days), $S_0 = 1.205$, $\sigma_{\text{ATM}} = 9.05\%$, $\sigma_{\text{RR}} = -0.50\%$, $\sigma_{\text{VWB}} = 0.13\%$, which lead to $\sigma_{25\Delta c} = 8.93\%$, $\sigma_{50\Delta c} = 9.05\%$, $\sigma_{25\Delta p} = 9.43\%$, $K_{\text{ATM}} = 1.2114$, $K_{25\Delta p} = 1.1733$ and $K_{25\Delta c} = 1.2487$. This is the same data set we will use in the next section, where we show practical examples for several markets: see also Table 1.4 for the discount factors used.

The approximation (1.7) is extremely accurate inside the interval $[K_1, K_3]$. The wings, however, tend to be overvalued. In fact, as the functional form is quadratic in the log-strike, the no-arbitrage conditions derived by Lee (2004) for the asymptotic value of implied volatilities are violated here. This drawback is addressed by a second, more precise, approximation, which is asymptotically constant at extreme strikes, and is obtained by expanding both members of (1.5) at second order in $\sigma = \sigma_2$:

$$C(K) \approx C^{\text{BS}}(K) + \sum_{i=1}^{3} x_i(K) \left[\mathcal{V}(K_i)(\sigma_i - \sigma) + \frac{1}{2} \frac{\partial^2 C^{\text{BS}}}{\partial^2 \sigma}(K_i)(\sigma_i - \sigma)^2 \right]$$

Comparing this expression with the second-order Taylor expansion

$$C(K) - C^{\text{BS}}(K) \approx \mathcal{V}(K)(\varsigma(K) - \sigma) + \frac{1}{2} \frac{\partial^2 C^{\text{BS}}}{\partial^2 \sigma}(K)(\varsigma(K) - \sigma)^2$$

one can write

$$\mathcal{V}(K)(\varsigma(K) - \sigma) + \frac{1}{2} \frac{\partial^2 C^{\text{BS}}}{\partial^2 \sigma}(K)(\varsigma(K) - \sigma)^2$$
$$\approx \sum_{i=1}^{3} x_i(K) \left[\mathcal{V}(K_i)(\sigma_i - \sigma) + \frac{1}{2} \frac{\partial^2 C^{\text{BS}}}{\partial^2 \sigma}(K_i)(\sigma_i - \sigma)^2 \right]$$

Solving this algebraic second-order equation in $\varsigma(K)$ then leads to the following.

Proposition 2 *The implied volatility $\varsigma(K)$ can be better approximated as*

$$\varsigma(K) \approx \varsigma_2(K)$$
$$:= \sigma_2 + \frac{-\sigma_2 + \sqrt{\sigma_2^2 + d_1(K)d_2(K)(2\sigma_2 D_1(K) + D_2(K))}}{d_1(K)d_2(K)} \quad (1.8)$$

where

$$D_1(K) := \varsigma_1(K) - \sigma_2$$
$$D_2(K) := \frac{\ln(K_2/K)\ln(K_3/K)}{\ln(K_2/K_1)\ln(K_3/K_1)}d_1(K_1)d_2(K_1)(\sigma_1 - \sigma_2)^2$$
$$+ \frac{\ln(K/K_1)\ln(K/K_2)}{\ln(K_3/K_1)\ln(K_3/K_2)}d_1(K_3)d_2(K_3)(\sigma_3 - \sigma_2)^2$$

As we can see from Figure 1.1, the approximation (1.8) is extremely accurate also in the wings, even for extreme values of put Deltas. Its only drawback is that it may not be defined due to the presence of a square-root term. The radicand, however, is positive in most practical applications.

We make use of this second approximation in our examples concerning the equity and interest rate markets below.

SMILE INTERPOLATION AMONG EXPIRIES: IMPLIED VOLATILITY'S TERM STRUCTURE

In the options market a set of maturities are actively traded and provide the market makers with a guide to price options with any expiry. One could first try to use some function fitting, more or less accurately, the given expiries, and then interpolate/extrapolate by means of it. For example, a form of the Heston type for the instantaneous variance of the underlying asset

$$\eta^2(t) = \sigma_\infty^2 + (\eta_0^2 - \sigma_\infty^2)e^{-\kappa t} \tag{1.9}$$

has been proposed to fit the FX options volatility term structure of ATM volatilities. This expression could also be used in other markets, such as the equity or commodity options markets. In (1.9), the instantaneous variance $\eta^2(t)$ evolves towards a long-term average level σ_∞^2 by a mean-reversion speed measured by the parameter κ, starting from an initial level η_0^2. In order to retrieve the implied volatility for a given expiry, one has to integrate Equation (1.9), divide the result by the time to the expiry T and take the square root:

$$\varsigma(T) = \sqrt{\frac{\int_0^T \eta^2(t)\,dt}{T}} = \sqrt{\sigma_\infty^2 + (\eta_0^2 - \sigma_\infty^2)\frac{1 - e^{-\kappa T}}{\kappa T}} \tag{1.10}$$

Usually, although (1.9) is qualitatively appealing, the fitting to the market data is not completely satisfactory, and one must resort to some time-dependency of the parameters (or to the introduction of a free extra parameter) in order to improve the performance.

As far as interest rates are concerned, formula (1.9) is typically not flexible enough to recover the specific shape of the volatility term structure observed in the market, so that one has to devise a more suitable formulation. A possible example is given by the following function, which has been proposed for modelling the instantaneous volatility of forward (LIBOR) rates expiring at time T_i (see, for example, Brigo and Mercurio (2006)):

$$\eta_i(t) = (a(T_i - t) + b)e^{-b(T_i - t)} + d$$

leading to the implied volatility:

$$\varsigma_i(T) = \sqrt{\frac{\int_0^T ((a(T_i - t) + b)e^{-b(T_i - t)} + d)^2 \, dt}{T}} \qquad (1.11)$$

Also, this function, although richer than the first one above, is seldom able to perfectly fit the available market quotes simultaneously.

Functions (1.10) and (1.11) are examples of parametric forms that can be chosen to fit the ATM volatilities in a given options market. However, the problem of finding a suitable parametrisation is not fundamental by itself, because one may reasonably accept the term structures provided by the market as a matter of fact (unless they engender an arbitrage) and simply interpolate between consecutive maturities.[13]

The volatility interpolation between two given expiries needs to be correctly implemented by taking into account the daily variations, and weighing the days with sensible factors. Focusing on the interpolation issue, we would like to stress that the interpolation of the term structure refers only to the ATM volatility, thus only concerning the level of the surface.

Let us start with a set of M standard traded expiries $\mathcal{T} = \{T_1, T_2, \cdots, T_M\}$. Our problem is how to devise a method to consistently interpolate between two contiguous dates. Let T be an expiry date between two dates $T_i \leq T \leq T_{i+1}$ and $\eta(t)$ be the instantaneous volatility of the spot process. The squared implied volatility for expiry T, in a BS world, is given by

$$\varsigma^2(T) = \frac{1}{T} \int_0^T \eta^2(t) \, dt$$

Such a volatility can be obtained by linearly interpolating the mean variance

$$V(T) = \int_0^T \eta^2(t)\,dt = T\varsigma^2(T)$$

between its time T_i and time T_{i+1} values. We obtain

$$\begin{aligned}\int_0^T \eta^2(t)\,dt &= \frac{V(T_{i+1}) - V(T_i)}{T_{i+1} - T_i}(T - T_i) + V(T_i) \\ &= \frac{T_{i+1}\varsigma^2(T_{i+1}) - T_i\varsigma^2(T_i)}{T_{i+1} - T_i}(T - T_i) + T_i\varsigma^2(T_i) \\ &= \frac{T - T_i}{T_{i+1} - T_i}T_{i+1}\varsigma^2(T_{i+1}) + \frac{T_{i+1} - T}{T_{i+1} - T_i}T_i\varsigma^2(T_i)\end{aligned}$$

and, hence,

$$\varsigma(T) = \sqrt{\frac{T - T_i}{T_{i+1} - T_i}\frac{T_{i+1}}{T}\varsigma^2(T_{i+1}) + \frac{T_{i+1} - T}{T_{i+1} - T_i}\frac{T_i}{T}\varsigma^2(T_i)} \quad (1.12)$$

This is what we call the total variance interpolation method.

As a subsequent step, we then take into account the weighting of the days entering in the interpolation, because holidays and other events may have a major effect on the daily volatility. One simple way to account for different weighting of the days is as follows.

- Calculate the number of days N_1 occurring between T_i and T and the number of days N_2 occurring between T_i and T_{i+1}.
- Associate each day with a proper weight w_i:
  - $w_i = 1$ for a normal business day;
  - $w_i < 1$ for holidays in the underlying markets (eg, in the FX market, it can be set equal to 0.5 if the day is a holiday in one of the two countries involved in the exchange rate, or it can set at 0 for weekends);
  - $w_i > 1$ for days when special events are expected (eg, key economic figures are released).
- Set

$$\tau_1 = \frac{\sum_{i=1}^{N_1} w_i}{N_y}, \quad \tau_2 = \frac{\sum_{i=1}^{N_2} w_i}{N_y}$$

where N_y is the total number of days in the year ($N_y = 365$ or $N_y = 366$).

- Replace $T - T_i$ with τ_1 and $T_{i+1} - T_i$ with τ_2 in the interpolation formula (1.12):

$$\varsigma(T) = \sqrt{\frac{\tau_1}{\tau_2}\frac{T_{i+1}}{T}\varsigma^2(T_{i+1}) + \frac{\tau_2 - \tau_1}{\tau_2}\frac{T_i}{T}\varsigma^2(T_i)} \qquad (1.13)$$

The weighting has tangible effects for expiries up to one year. After that, it is quite immaterial to use either (1.12) or (1.13).

As mentioned before, the interpolation is used only for the ATM volatilities. If the implied volatility of an out-of-the-money option has to be recovered, then first one interpolates by means of (1.13) the ATM volatility, then they may use a simple linear interpolation for the risk reversal and butterfly (so to find out the slope and the convexity for the intermediate expiry) and finally use the method explained in the section "Smile interpolation among strikes" to obtain the consistent volatility for the given strike. The rationale behind it is the following: while the daily volatility (ie, the second moment of the price returns' distribution) can be affected by the related market activity (so that it changes according to the holidays, the release of economic figures, etc), the higher order moments (ie, skewness and kurtosis) are more stable and smoothly changing between expiries. This justifies the weighted interpolation for the ATM volatility, which has an impact on the level of the volatility surface and, hence, the second moment of the price returns' distribution; it also justifies the linear interpolation for the risk reversal and the butterfly, which measure, respectively, the slope and the convexity of the volatility surface and, hence, the skewness and the kurtosis of the returns' distribution.

Clearly, in any case and whatever interpolation is used to retrieve the implied volatility for a given strike, the volatility surface must be arbitrage-free. This means that, for every strike K and time to maturity T,

$$\frac{\partial \mathcal{O}(T, K)}{\partial T} > 0 \qquad (1.14)$$

where we denote by $\mathcal{O}(T, K)$ the price of an option struck at K and expiring in T.

It is worth giving a brief explanation for the last condition. The Theta of an option is normally a positive function of the time to maturity, and this is exactly what has been expressed

Table 1.2 Term structure of ATM implied volatilities traded on 29 March, 2004.

Expiry	ATM volatility (%)
5 April 2004	12.40
12 April 2004	11.50
28 April 2004	11.70
26 May 2004	11.55
28 June 2004	11.27
28 September 2004	11.20
29 December 2004	11.14
29 March 2005	11.10

in the condition above. Nevertheless, sometimes for deep-in-the-money options, and when there is a huge difference between the spot and the forward price of the underlying asset, the Theta can become negative. To avoid this kind of problem, one should check the admissibility of the volatility surface with out-of-the-money options, for which condition (1.14) is always a bounding constraint.

We finally present an application of the weighted interpolation based on real market data as of 29 March, 2004, for the euro/US dollar exchange rate. The ATM volatility for a set of standard maturities is provided in Table 1.2 whereas Figure 1.2 shows the two interpolations obtained by means of (1.12) and (1.13). The effect of the weighting is quite remarkable, considering also that the Easter holidays occurred between the one and two-week expiries, with almost four closed market days in a row. Generally one can note that the weighted interpolation produces a sawtooth function, with a collapse of the implied volatility that is usually experienced on Mondays because weekends are weighted by zero. Short-dated options are mostly affected by the weighting and its impact could be even wider than the usual bid–ask spreads.

BUILDING A VOLATILITY SMILE IN PRACTICE

After the description of the methods to efficiently interpolate amongst strikes and between expiries, we now focus on how to practically build a volatility surface. We choose three paradigmatic markets, each following one of the three rules that can be adopted in quoting options. More specifically, we start with the FX market, where the sticky Delta rule prevails; afterwards, we move to the

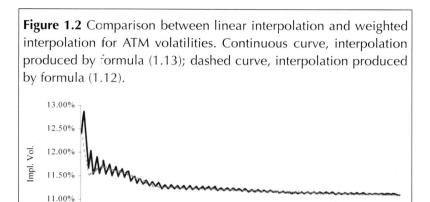

Figure 1.2 Comparison between linear interpolation and weighted interpolation for ATM volatilities. Continuous curve, interpolation produced by formula (1.13); dashed curve, interpolation produced by formula (1.12).

equity index market, where the sticky strike rule is adopted; finally, we show an application in the swaption market, where quotes are provided according to the sticky absolute rule. In each case we briefly describe the market and then we show how to exploit market data to consistently build a volatility surface.

The FX market

In the FX option market, the volatility matrix is built according to the sticky Delta rule. The underlying assumption is that options are priced depending on their Delta, so that when the underlying asset price moves and the Delta of an option changes accordingly, a different implied volatility has to be plugged into the pricing formula.

The FX option market is very liquid, up to relatively long-dated expiries (two years, at least for the euro/US dollar exchange rate). The ATM volatility is readily available, and the risk reversal (RR) for 25Δ call and put and the (Vega-weighted) butterfly (VWB) with 25Δ wings are also commonly traded. From this data one can easily infer three basic implied volatilities, from which one can then build the entire smile for the range running from a 5Δ put to a 5Δ call by means of the VV method.

We denote by S_t the value of a given exchange rate at time t and assume constant domestic and foreign risk-free rates, which will be denoted by r^d and δ, respectively. We then consider a market maturity T and define the related quotes in the following.[14]

The ATM volatility quoted in the FX market is that of a 0Δ straddle, whose strike, for each given expiry, is chosen so that a put and a call have the same Δ but with different signs (no Δ hedge is needed when trading this straddle).

Denoting by σ_{ATM} the ATM volatility for the expiry T, the ATM strike K_{ATM} must then satisfy

$$e^{-\delta T}\Phi\left(\frac{\ln(S_0/K_{\text{ATM}})(r^d - \delta + \frac{1}{2}\sigma_{\text{ATM}}^2)T}{\sigma_{\text{ATM}}\sqrt{T}}\right)$$
$$= e^{-\delta T}\Phi\left(-\frac{\ln(S_0/K_{\text{ATM}}) + (r^d - \delta + \frac{1}{2}\sigma_{\text{ATM}}^2)T}{\sigma_{\text{ATM}}\sqrt{T}}\right)$$

Straightforward algebra leads to:[15]

$$K_{\text{ATM}} = S_0 e^{(r^d - \delta + \frac{1}{2}\sigma^2)T} \tag{1.15}$$

The RR is a typical structure made up by buying a call and selling a put with a symmetric Δ. The RR is quoted as the difference between the two implied volatilities, $\sigma_{25\Delta c}$ and $\sigma_{25\Delta p}$ to plug into the BS formula for the call and the put, respectively. Denoting such a price, in volatility terms, by σ_{RR}, we have:[16]

$$\sigma_{\text{RR}} = \sigma_{25\Delta c} - \sigma_{25\Delta p} \tag{1.16}$$

The VWB is built up by selling an ATM straddle and buying a 25Δ strangle. To be Vega-weighted, the quantity of the former has to be smaller than the quantity of the latter, because the Vega of the straddle is greater than the Vega of the strangle. The butterfly's price in volatility terms, σ_{VWB}, is then defined by

$$\sigma_{\text{VWB}} = \frac{\sigma_{25\Delta c} + \sigma_{25\Delta p}}{2} - \sigma_{\text{ATM}} \tag{1.17}$$

For the given expiry T, the two implied volatilities $\sigma_{25\Delta c}$ and $\sigma_{25\Delta p}$ can be immediately identified by solving a linear system. We obtain

$$\sigma_{25\Delta c} = \sigma_{\text{ATM}} + \sigma_{\text{VWB}} + \tfrac{1}{2}\sigma_{\text{RR}} \tag{1.18}$$
$$\sigma_{25\Delta p} = \sigma_{\text{ATM}} + \sigma_{\text{VWB}} - \tfrac{1}{2}\sigma_{\text{RR}} \tag{1.19}$$

The two strikes corresponding to the 25Δ put and 25Δ call can be derived, after straightforward algebra, by remembering their respective definitions. For instance, for a 25Δ put we must have that

$$-e^{-\delta T}\Phi\left(-\frac{\ln(S_0/K_{25\Delta p}) + (r^d - \delta + \frac{1}{2}\sigma_{25\Delta p}^2)T}{\sigma_{25\Delta p}\sqrt{T}}\right) = -0.25$$

which immediately leads to

$$K_{25\Delta p} = S_0 e^{-\alpha\sigma_{25\Delta p}\sqrt{T} + (r^d - \delta + \frac{1}{2}\sigma_{25\Delta p}^2)T} \qquad (1.20)$$

where $\alpha := -\Phi^{-1}(\frac{1}{4}e^{\delta T})$ and Φ^{-1} is the inverse normal distribution function. Similarly, one also obtains

$$K_{25\Delta c} = S_0 e^{\alpha\sigma_{25\Delta c}\sqrt{T} + (r^d - \delta + \frac{1}{2}\sigma_{25\Delta c}^2)T} \qquad (1.21)$$

We stress that, for typical market parameters and for maturities up to two years, $\alpha > 0$ and

$$K_{25\Delta p} < K_{ATM} < K_{25\Delta c}$$

The way of quoting prices in the FX market (according to the sticky Delta rule) and the price of the most actively traded options provide us with all of the information we need to express the volatility matrix in the compact form we suggested in the section "Criteria for an efficient and convenient representation of the volatility surface", in terms of ATM volatilities, 25Δ risk reversals and 25Δ butterflies. Basically, in this case, all we have to do is to simply take the data available via market makers and brokers, and we are done. In Table 1.3 we show the market volatility surface for the euro/US dollar exchange rate, as of 1 July, 2005.

As an example, we calculate the entire volatility smile for a single expiry, namely the three-month expiry. The following euro/US dollar data is used: $T = 3M$,[17] $S_0 = 1.2050$, and the other data needed is provided in Tables 1.4 and 1.5. We use the formulae provided above to retrieve the three main strikes and related volatilities; then we apply the VV approach to calculate the implied volatilities for other strikes.

In Figure 1.3 we compare the volatility smiles yielded by the VV price (1.5), the Malz (1997) quadratic interpolation and the SABR functional form,[18] plotting the respective implied volatilities

Table 1.3 ATM volatilities for the exchange rate euro/US dollar, 25Δ risk reversals and butterflies for main expiries, as of 1 July, 2005. (Source: Bloomberg.)

	ATM volatility (%)	25Δ RR (%)	25Δ VWB (%)
One day	6.25	−0.63	0.13
One week	10.33	−0.63	0.13
Two weeks	9.60	−0.55	0.13
One month	9.33	−0.65	0.15
Two months	9.43	−0.55	0.15
Three months	9.37	−0.50	0.17
Six months	9.40	−0.33	0.17
Nine months	9.45	−0.27	0.17
One year	9.55	−0.23	0.17
Two years	9.55	−0.18	0.17
Five years	9.75	−0.10	0.20

both against strikes and against put Deltas. The three graphs are obtained after calibration to the three basic quotes $\sigma_1 = \sigma_{25\Delta p}$, $\sigma_2 = \sigma_{ATM}$, $\sigma_3 = \sigma_{25\Delta c}$.

Once the three functional forms are calibrated to the liquid quotes $\sigma_1, \sigma_2, \sigma_3$, one may then compare their values at extreme strikes with the corresponding quotes possibly provided by brokers or market makers. To this end, in Figure 1.3 we also report the implied volatilities of the 10Δ put and call options (respectively equal to 10.46% and 9.49%, again provided by Bloomberg) to show that the Malz's quadratic function (1.1) is typically not consistent with the quotes for strikes outside the basic interval $[K_1, K_3]$.

We repeat the same procedure for each expiry, first by calculating the three implied volatilities and the related strikes, then deriving the smile in terms of put Delta (in absolute terms) for a range running from zero to the Delta corresponding to the ATM 0Δ strike, and then for this to zero, in terms of call Delta. The whole surface, up to the five-year expiry, is shown in Figure 1.4.

The equity market
In the equity market, options are traded on indexes and on single stocks. Most options on the main indices are listed, whereas single stock options are mainly traded OTC, although major stocks also have options traded in official markets. Here we focus on the building of a volatility surface for an index, namely the Eurostoxx50,

Figure 1.3 Implied volatilities, plotted both against (a) strikes and (b) put Deltas (in absolute value), calibrated to the three basic euro/US dollar quotes (open points) and compared with the 10Δ (put and call) volatilities (full points). (Source: Bloomberg.)

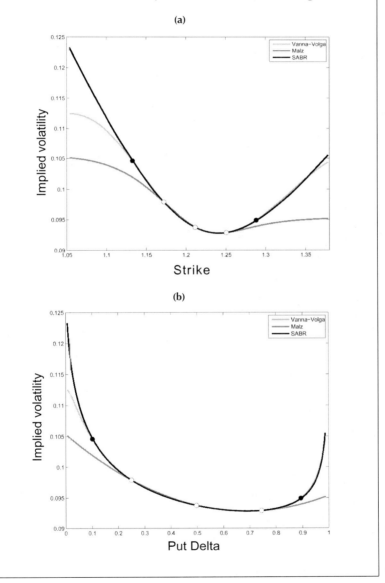

Figure 1.4 Implied volatility surface for the euro/US dollar exchange rate, plotted against put Deltas (in absolute value), on the left-hand side of the x-axis, and of call Deltas, on the right-hand side of the x-axis. The centre of the x-axis is the ATM 0Δ strike. The surface is derived from the three basic euro/US dollar quotes for each expiry, as of 1 July, 2005. (Source: Bloomberg.)

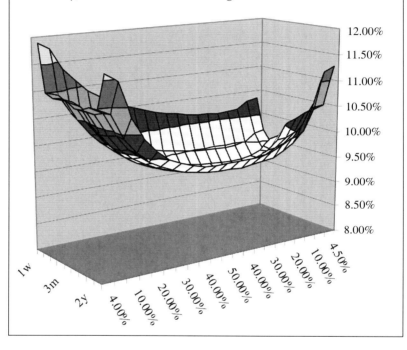

Table 1.4 Discount factors as of 1 July, 2005.

	Expiry	US$	€
One week	8 July 2005	0.999359943	0.999596629
Two weeks	15 July 2005	0.998722162	0.999192507
One month	1 August 2005	0.997172831	0.998209720
Two months	1 September 2005	0.994200158	0.996422682
Three months	3 October 2005	0.990275201	0.994585501
Six months	2 January 2006	0.981432457	0.989469460
Nine months	31 March 2006	0.971922580	0.984507154
One year	1 July 2006	0.962184069	0.979390945
Two year	1 July 2007	0.922537377	0.957453505
Five years	30 June 2010	0.810104943	0.876048376

Table 1.5 Strikes and volatilities corresponding to the three main Deltas, as of 1 July, 2005.

Delta	Strike	Volatility (%)
25Δ put	1.1720	9.79
ATM	1.2115	9.37
25Δ call	1.2504	9.29

whose listed options market is one of the most liquid. Listed options are typically quoted according to the sticky strike rule, and expiries are given in terms of fixed dates (determined according to specific rules), differently from OTC markets where expiries are usually quoted in terms of fixed time to maturity (even though any other expiry date can be quoted on request).

Let us start by presenting actual market data for the Eurostoxx50, as of 23 February, 2007, which we show in Table 1.6 and Figure 1.5, when the level of the index was 4,242. Table 1.6 is organised so that for each expiry, volatilities are provided for a range of strikes. The actual number of tradeable strikes is larger than that included in the table, but for the sake of clarity we pruned it. The tradeable expiries are determined according to the regulation published by the stock exchange (in this case, the Eurex). Finally, the discount factors for the euro currency and for the continuous dividend yield on the index (they are derived from the quoted options prices via the put–call parity) are shown in Table 1.7.[19]

We have already mentioned that representing a volatility matrix in such a fashion does not match the requirements listed in the section "Criteria for an efficient and convenient representation of the volatility surface". It is very hard to compare data along the strikes and for different maturities as time elapses. Moreover, the information is not consistently organised.

We propose to represent the volatility matrix in the same compact form as in the FX case, providing, for each expiry, the ATM 0Δ strike volatility and the 25Δ risk reversal and butterfly. To this end, one should implement the following procedure.

1. For each listed expiry, detect the traded strike K_2 nearest to the forward price and back out its implied volatility σ_2.
2. Pick up two strikes, K_1 lower and K_3 higher than K_2, such that they, respectively, yield a put Delta and a call Delta as near as

Table 1.6 Implied volatility surface for Eurostoxx50. The surface shows implied volatilities derived from the listed options quotes at the Eurex exchange for available expiries, as of 23 February, 2007. A missing quote is set equal to that of the nearest available strike. (Source: Bloomberg.)

	3,800	3,900	4,000	4,100	4,150	4,200	4,300	4,400	4,500	4,600
16 March 2007	23.25%	20.51%	17.97%	15.50%	14.28%	12.98%	11.01%	10.39%	11.26%	13.58%
20 April 2007	19.31%	17.88%	16.47%	14.98%	14.21%	13.50%	12.14%	11.13%	10.66%	10.63%
18 May 2007	17.40%	17.40%	16.10%	14.93%	14.29%	13.71%	12.66%	11.84%	11.30%	11.15%
15 June 2007	18.17%	17.22%	16.14%	15.12%	14.60%	14.10%	13.19%	12.46%	11.94%	11.77%
21 September 2007	18.42%	17.63%	16.84%	16.12%	15.73%	15.36%	14.67%	14.03%	13.46%	13.02%
21 December 2007	18.53%	17.92%	17.25%	16.65%	16.34%	16.03%	15.43%	14.88%	14.30%	13.90%
20 June 2008	18.24%	17.69%	17.47%	16.99%	16.74%	16.50%	16.02%	15.56%	15.08%	11.63%
19 December 2008	18.28%	18.28%	17.95%	17.61%	17.40%	17.19%	16.77%	16.38%	15.85%	15.85%
19 June 2009	18.19%	18.19%	18.19%	17.98%	17.79%	17.60%	17.23%	16.88%	16.68%	16.36%
18 December 2009	18.75%	18.75%	18.75%	18.58%	18.41%	18.24%	17.90%	17.58%	17.25%	16.96%
17 December 2010	20.40%	20.40%	20.40%	19.71%	19.39%	19.07%	18.46%	17.90%	17.63%	17.21%
16 December 2011	20.94%	20.94%	20.94%	20.43%	20.15%	19.88%	19.35%	18.89%	18.67%	18.67%

Figure 1.5 Implied volatility surface for Eurostoxx50, plotted against strikes. The surface is derived from the listed options quotes at the Eurex exchange for available expiries, as of 23 February, 2007. A missing quote is set equal to that of the nearest available strike. (Source: Bloomberg.)

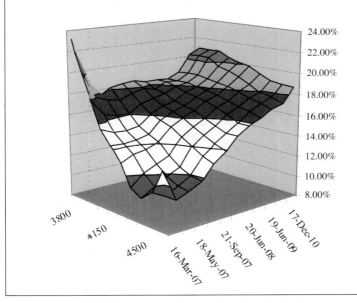

Table 1.7 Discount factors for the euro currency and for the continuous dividend yield on the Eurostoxx50, as of 23 February, 2007.

	Discount factor	
Expiry	€ currency	Dividend yield
16 March 2007	0.999815	0.997890
20 April 2007	0.997566	0.994198
18 May 2007	0.985432	0.991208
15 June 2007	0.975925	0.988184
21 September 2007	0.971316	0.977318
21 December 2007	0.967972	0.967242
20 June 2008	0.941159	0.947388
19 December 2008	0.933080	0.927848
19 June 2009	0.907050	0.908792
18 December 2009	0.898592	0.890263
17 December 2010	0.865026	0.854121
16 December 2011	0.831872	0.819382

possible to 25% (absolute value). Back out the corresponding implied volatility σ_1 and σ_3.

3. Calculate the ATM 0Δ strike, by Equation (1.15) and by an iterative procedure (three or four iterations are usually enough to get the result) to retrieve the related implied volatility. In the iterative procedure, Equation (1.5) is employed and the constant volatility σ is set initially equal to the implied volatility of the central strike ($\sigma = \sigma_2$), and it will be the final result of the iteration. A sketch of this iterative procedure is as follows:

(i) $\sigma = \sigma_2$;

(ii) $K_{\text{ATM}}^i = S_0 e^{(r^d - \delta + \frac{1}{2}\sigma^2)T}$ (ATM strike at the ith iteration);

(iii) $C(K_{\text{ATM}}^i) = C^{\text{BS}}(K_{\text{ATM}}^i) + \sum_{j=1}^{3} x_j(K_{\text{ATM}}^i)[C^{\text{MKT}}(K_j) - C^{\text{BS}}(K_j)]$, with the BS price calculated by plugging in the BS formula the constant level σ;

(iv) $\sigma = (C^{\text{BS}})^{-1}(C(K_{\text{ATM}}^i))$ (volatility level that plugged into the BS formula gives $C(K_{\text{ATM}}^i)$);

(v) iterate from point (ii) until $K_{\text{ATM}}^i - K_{\text{ATM}}^{i-1} < \epsilon$, ϵ suitably small;

(vi) the final result is the ATM 0Δ strike K_{ATM} with its implied volatility $\sigma_{\text{ATM}} = \sigma$.

4. Calculate the 25Δ call and put strikes, using Equations (1.20) and (1.21), and an iterative procedure (again, three or four iterations will suffice to get a result within an acceptable degree of accuracy). The sketch of this procedure is as follows:

(i) $\sigma_{25\Delta p} = \sigma_1$; $\sigma_{25\Delta c} = \sigma_3$;

(ii) $K_{25\Delta p}^i = S_0 e^{-\alpha \sigma_{25\Delta p}\sqrt{T} + (r^d - \delta + \frac{1}{2}\sigma_{25\Delta p}^2)T}$
(the superscript i denotes the iteration number);

(iii) $K_{25\Delta c}^i = S_0 e^{\alpha \sigma_{25\Delta c}\sqrt{T} + (r^d - \delta + \frac{1}{2}\sigma_{25\Delta c}^2)T}$;

(iv) $C(K_{25\Delta p}^i) = C^{\text{BS}}(K_{25\Delta p}^i) + \sum_{j=1}^{3} x_j(K_{25\Delta p}^i)[C^{\text{MKT}}(K_j) - C^{\text{BS}}(K_j)]$;

(v) $C(K_{25\Delta c}^i) = C^{\text{BS}}(K_{25\Delta c}^i) + \sum_{j=1}^{3} x_j(K_{25\Delta c}^i)[C^{\text{MKT}}(K_j) - C^{\text{BS}}(K_j)]$; in the last two equations, the BS price is calculated by plugging in the BS formula the constant level σ_{ATM} found before;

(vi) $\sigma_{25\Delta p} = (C^{\text{BS}})^{-1}(C(K_{25\Delta p}^i))$; $\sigma_{25\Delta c} = (C^{\text{BS}})^{-1}(C(K_{25\Delta c}^i))$;

(vii) iterate from step (ii) until $K_{25\Delta p}^i - K_{25\Delta p}^{i-1} < \epsilon$ and $K_{25\Delta c}^i - K_{25\Delta c}^{i-1} < \epsilon$, ϵ suitably small;

(viii) the final output is the 25Δ strikes $K_{25\Delta p}$ and $K_{25\Delta c}$ and their implied volatilities $\sigma_{25\Delta p}$ and $\sigma_{25\Delta c}$.

This procedure, repeated for each traded expiry, yields a compact form representation as shown in Table 1.8. The consistency result stated in Proposition A.4 makes sure that, although we change the set of three basic strikes, we still get the same smile as that obtained with the starting strikes (actually taken from the available traded strikes), as long as the implied volatilities of new strikes belong to the smile curve determined by the initial strikes. In other words, Proposition A.4 allows us to express the volatility surface in the most convenient way (in terms of strikes), and in any case we are sure to always be interpolating/extrapolating the same smile. However, we are not finished yet. In fact, we have just built a volatility surface for fixed expiries (those established according to the exchange rules), whereas we want to produce a surface in terms of fixed time-to-maturity periods. To this end, we perform the final step of the building procedure.

5. Define a set of fixed time to maturity expiries and calculate the corresponding dates; then interpolate/extrapolate between the expiries available in the listed market, in the weighted fashion for the ATM volatility and simply linearly for the 25Δ risk reversals and butterflies.

The result of the procedure outlined above is shown in Table 1.9. We defined a set of fixed period expiries, the shortest one being the overnight expiry (ie, the option's life is one business day) and the longest the 10-year expiry. The surface has been derived by interpolating the data in Table 1.8 retrieved from the market; the last actively traded expiry is December 2011, but when the volatility surface is expressed in terms of ATM, risk reversal and butterfly, its basic features are rather easily recognisable. In fact, for expiries longer than 16 December, 2011, we just added a spread of 0.75% per year on the ATM level and kept a decreasing pace on the risk reversal and increasing on the butterfly. The entire volatility surface originating from these parameters is illustrated in Figure 1.6.

As a final issue, one may wonder whether the implicit assumption, underpinning all of the manufacturing of the volatility surface, is well-founded, ie, whether the VV approach is able to reproduce

Table 1.8 Implied volatility surface for Eurostoxx50 expressed in compact form, from the listed options quotes at the Eurex exchange for available expiries, as of 23 February, 2007.

Expiry	ATM (%)	25Δ RR (%)	25Δ VWB (%)
16 March 2007	12.75	−3.38	0.18
20 April 2007	12.78	−3.89	0.42
18 May 2007	13.71	−4.16	0.32
15 June 2007	14.10	−4.14	0.47
21 September 2007	15.00	−4.37	0.51
21 December 2007	15.42	−4.57	0.55
20 June 2008	16.01	−4.69	0.59
19 December 2008	16.36	−4.57	0.48
19 June 2009	17.06	−4.42	0.77
18 December 2009	17.80	−4.63	0.85
17 December 2010	17.89	−4.05	0.93
16 December 2011	19.21	−4.18	0.90

Table 1.9 Implied volatility surface for Eurostoxx50, expressed in compact form and in terms of fixed time to expiry, derived from market data as of 23 February, 2007.

Expiry		ATM (%)	25Δ RR (%)	25Δ VWB (%)
Overnight	27/02/07	12.19	−3.13	0.06
One week	05/03/07	12.70	−3.22	0.11
Two weeks	12/03/07	12.75	−3.32	0.15
One month	26/03/07	12.77	−3.53	0.25
Two months	26/04/07	13.06	−3.95	0.40
Three months	28/05/07	13.88	−4.15	0.37
Six months	27/08/07	14.87	−4.31	0.50
Nine months	26/11/07	15.33	−4.52	0.54
One year	26/02/08	15.64	−4.62	0.56
Two years	26/02/09	16.63	−4.52	0.69
Three years	26/02/10	17.81	−4.52	0.87
Four years	28/02/11	18.15	−4.35	0.92
Five years	27/02/12	19.21	−4.18	0.95
Seven years	26/02/14	19.96	−4.05	0.97
10 years	27/02/17	20.71	−4.00	1.00

Figure 1.6 Implied volatility surface for Eurostoxx50, against put Deltas (in absolute value), on the left-hand side of the x-axis, and of call Deltas, on the right-hand side of the x-axis. The centre of the x-axis is the ATM 0Δ strike. The surface is derived from the data in Table 1.9.

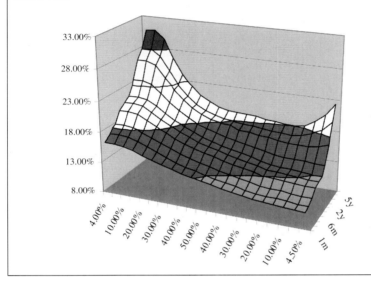

the quoted volatility smile and, hence, reliable ATM, risk reversal and butterfly parameters. Our practical experience is that we can be fairly confident in its ability to capture the traded smile. As a confirmation of this statement, we show in Figure 1.7 the performance of the VV approach, implemented as explained in the procedure above, for the listed options with expiry 19 December, 2008. For comparison purposes, we also show the smile implied by the Heston model (due to its vogue amongst equity options practitioners) after calibration to the market implied volatilities, which are highlighted in the figure. We notice that the VV method performs quite well in replicating the market smile, with similar fitting quality as that implied by the Heston model. This is not surprising given the fact that the VV price function is calibrated to the main degrees of freedom of the volatility surface, and confirms the ability of the VV approach to approximate the smile generated by a stochastic volatility model also in a market such as the equity options one, where the method is not so popular. Considering

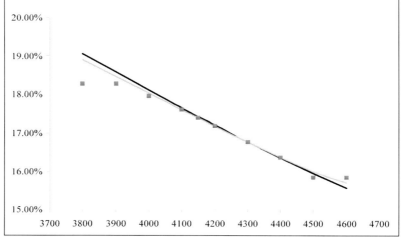

Figure 1.7 Comparison between market-quoted implied volatilities (grey points) and the smile generated by the VV approach (grey curve), for the December 2008 listed options. The smile produced by the Heston model calibrated to market data is also shown (black curve).

the fact that just three quotes are needed to yield a reliable smile and that no calibration is carried out (thus avoiding all of the related problems of instability and global minimum searching), the advantages for using the VV method are rather evident.

The swaption market

As an example of a practical application of the method described above to the interest rate market, we focus on swaptions; we do this for two reasons. On the one hand, in the last few years in the swaption market, the management of the smile has become fairly sophisticated, because the traded volume of exotic options, whose price is highly dependent on the underlying smile, has increased dramatically. On the other hand, this market follows the sticky absolute rule, so that by analysing it, we have a complete picture of all of the conventions used in the volatility markets.

The swaption market is OTC, and transactions are primarily dealt with via brokers. Typically, for a range of expiries running from one week to 30 years, options to enter into a swap contract for a given maturity (this is denominated the tenor) are actively traded.

Table 1.10 ATM volatilities included in the subset of swaptions for which out-of-the-money volatilities are published, as of 27 February, 2007. (Source: Bloomberg.)

ATM	Two years	Five years	10 years	20 years	30 years
Three months	9.60%	11.85%	11.45%	10.85%	10.65%
One year	11.95%	12.70%	12.20%	11.40%	11.15%
Five years	13.20%	12.85%	12.25%	11.35%	11.10%
10 years	11.90%	11.40%	11.15%	10.35%	10.05%
20 years	10.50%	10.15%	10.15%	9.20%	9.05%
30 years	9.90%	9.60%	9.45%	9.05%	8.65%

The most liquid tenors are the two, five and 10 years, whereas the most traded expiries are up to 10 years, the interest of market participants dimming out for longer expiries. The ATM straddle is the basic structure: its strike is set equal to the forward rate of the underlying swap. Out-of-the-money payers and receivers are increasingly quoted, due to the market makers' hedging needs, arising from the exotic products offered to their clients. In particular, constant maturity swap (CMS), CMS cap and floors and CMS spread options boosted, in recent years, the transaction volume on the wings (out-of-the-money strikes).[20]

Quotes for ATM straddles (in terms of implied volatility) are easily found in the broker market and are also provided by major market information sources. In addition, for a subset of expiries and underlying tenors, implied volatilities, expressed as a spread over the ATM value, are usually published for out-of-the-money strikes according to the sticky absolute rule (ie, distance in basis points from the ATM strike):

$$\Delta \sigma_{a,b}^M(\Delta K) = \sigma_{a,b}^M(K_{\text{ATM}} + \Delta K) - \sigma_{a,b}^M(K_{\text{ATM}})$$

where the option has strike K and expiry T_a and is written on a swap maturing in $T_b > T_a$, with payments in $T_{a+1}, \cdots, T_b$. Conventional distances from the ATM are $\Delta K = \pm 200, \pm 100, \pm 50, \pm 25$ basis points. This makes it possible to build a volatility surface for all of the expiries and tenors by means of a proper interpolation/extrapolation scheme.

We start by presenting, as an example, actual market data as of 27 February, 2007. In Table 1.10 we show the ATM volatilities and

Table 1.11 Out-of-the-money volatilities expressed as a spread over the corresponding ATM volatilities, as of 27 February, 2007. The reference strikes are indicated as a distance in basis points from the forward swap rate. (Source: Bloomberg.)

Reference strike		Two years	Five years	10 years	20 years	30 years
−200	Three months	2.34%	6.29%	6.83%	6.61%	6.74%
	One year	4.68%	6.03%	6.56%	6.57%	6.78%
	Five years	4.52%	5.25%	5.40%	5.44%	5.78%
	10 years	3.76%	4.43%	4.81%	5.15%	5.39%
	20 years	3.55%	3.95%	4.60%	4.99%	5.15%
	30 years	3.95%	4.29%	4.61%	5.40%	5.33%
−100	Three months	0.59%	1.99%	2.22%	2.21%	2.35%
	One year	1.39%	1.95%	2.22%	2.30%	2.44%
	Five years	1.47%	1.88%	1.98%	1.99%	2.12%
	10 years	1.29%	1.62%	1.79%	1.91%	1.99%
	20 years	1.23%	1.47%	1.72%	1.83%	1.89%
	30 years	1.33%	1.54%	1.71%	1.98%	1.95%
−50	Three months	0.17%	0.68%	0.76%	0.77%	0.87%
	One year	0.47%	0.71%	0.83%	0.88%	0.96%
	Five years	0.56%	0.76%	0.82%	0.82%	0.87%
	10 years	0.51%	0.67%	0.75%	0.79%	0.82%
	20 years	0.49%	0.62%	0.73%	0.76%	0.79%
	30 years	0.52%	0.63%	0.73%	0.82%	0.81%
−25	Three months	0.06%	0.26%	0.29%	0.29%	0.35%
	One year	0.18%	0.29%	0.34%	0.36%	0.41%
	Five years	0.24%	0.34%	0.37%	0.36%	0.39%
	10 years	0.23%	0.30%	0.34%	0.36%	0.37%
	20 years	0.22%	0.28%	0.34%	0.34%	0.35%
	30 years	0.22%	0.28%	0.33%	0.37%	0.36%

in Table 1.11 we provide the spread over them for out-of-the-money options struck at a given distance from the corresponding forward rate, for the subset of expiries and tenors ordinarily published in the market. The volatility surface expressed in this fashion is not fit for the requirements of the section "Criteria for an efficient and convenient representation of the volatility surface" and we suggest to adopt the representation explained there, in terms of ATM forward volatilities and 25Δ risk reversals and butterflies. To this end we outline the following procedure.

1. For each expiry, retrieve the swaption volatility, $\sigma_{ATM} = \sigma_2$, for the ATM strike $K_{ATM} = K_2$.

Table 1.11 (Continued.)

Reference strike		Two years	Five years	10 years	20 years	30 years
+25	Three months	−0.01%	−0.10%	−0.10%	−0.11%	−0.18%
	One year	−0.08%	−0.16%	−0.19%	−0.22%	−0.26%
	Five years	−0.16%	−0.26%	−0.28%	−0.27%	−0.29%
	10 years	−0.17%	−0.23%	−0.27%	−0.27%	−0.28%
	20 years	−0.16%	−0.23%	−0.27%	−0.27%	−0.20%
	30 years	−0.16%	−0.22%	−0.27%	−0.29%	−0.28%
+50	Three months	0.01%	−0.07%	−0.06%	−0.06%	−0.20%
	One year	−0.08%	−0.21%	−0.26%	−0.29%	−0.38%
	Five years	−0.26%	−0.44%	−0.48%	−0.45%	−0.47%
	10 years	−0.28%	−0.40%	−0.46%	−0.47%	−0.47%
	20 years	−0.28%	−0.41%	−0.34%	−0.46%	−0.47%
	30 years	−0.25%	−0.38%	−0.49%	−0.49%	−0.47%
+100	Three months	0.13%	0.28%	0.38%	0.35%	0.09%
	One year	0.12%	−0.04%	−0.09%	−0.13%	−0.27%
	Five years	−0.29%	−0.61%	−0.66%	−0.58%	−0.60%
	10 years	−0.38%	−0.58%	−0.68%	−0.65%	−0.62%
	20 years	−0.26%	−0.44%	−0.76%	−0.65%	−0.65%
	30 years	−0.29%	−0.55%	−0.76%	−0.68%	−0.63%
+200	Three months	0.54%	1.41%	1.70%	1.65%	1.23%
	One year	0.86%	0.75%	0.83%	0.80%	0.59%
	Five years	0.04%	−0.42%	−0.46%	−0.25%	−0.24%
	10 years	−0.22%	−0.46%	−0.59%	−0.45%	−0.35%
	20 years	−0.23%	−0.45%	−0.84%	−0.51%	−0.49%
	30 years	−0.02%	−0.46%	−0.85%	−0.51%	−0.41%

2. In the subset of tenors and expiries where implied volatilities for the wings are also available, choose two wings K_1 and K_3 (respectively lower and higher than the ATM) such that their Delta (respectively of the receiver and of the payer) is closest to 25% in absolute value. The Black-like formula is the market standard for European swaptions. In the payer's case, it is given by

$$C^{MKT}_{a,b}(K_i) = A(a,b)\,\mathrm{Bl}(K_i, S_{a,b}(0), \sigma_i \sqrt{T_a})$$

$$\mathrm{Bl}(K, S, v) = S\Phi\left(\frac{\ln(S/K) + v^2/2}{v}\right) - K\Phi\left(\frac{\ln(S/K) - v^2/2}{v}\right)$$

$$A(a,b) = \sum_{i=a+1}^{b} \tau_i P(0, T_i), \quad S_{a,b}(0) = \frac{P(0, T_a) - P(0, T_b)}{A(a,b)}$$

where the time notation is the same as used above, $S_{a,b}(0)$ is the underlying forward swap rate at time 0 and $A(a,b)$ its corresponding annuity factor. Receivers can be priced via put–call parity. In calculating the Delta, we suppress the annuity factor (in practice, we calculate the first derivative of $\text{Bl}(K, S, v)$ with respect to S). Having determined the two relevant away-from-the-money strikes, σ_1 and σ_3 are simply set equal to the corresponding implied volatilities.

3. Calculate the 25Δ call and put strikes, using Equations (1.20) and (1.21), and the following iterative procedure:

   (i) $\sigma_{25\Delta p} = \sigma_1$; $\sigma_{25\Delta c} = \sigma_3$;

   (ii) $K^i_{25\Delta p} = S_0 e^{-\alpha \sigma_{25\Delta p} \sqrt{T_a} + \frac{1}{2}\sigma^2_{25\Delta p} T_a}$
   (the superscript i denotes the iteration number);

   (iii) $K^i_{25\Delta c} = S_0 e^{\alpha \sigma_{25\Delta c} \sqrt{T_a} + \frac{1}{2}\sigma^2_{25\Delta c} T_a}$;

   (iv) $C_{a,b}(K^i_{25\Delta p}) = C^{BS}_{a,b}(K^i_{25\Delta p}) + \sum_{j=1}^{3} x_j(K^i_{25\Delta p})[C^{MKT}_{a,b}(K_j) - C^{BS}_{a,b}(K_j)]$;

   (v) $C_{a,b}(K^i_{25\Delta c}) = C^{BS}_{a,b}(K^i_{25\Delta c}) + \sum_{j=1}^{3} x_j(K^i_{25\Delta c})[C^{MKT}_{a,b}(K_j) - C^{BS}_{a,b}(K_j)]$; in the last two equations the BS price is calculated by plugging into the BS formula the constant level σ_{ATM}; it is worth noting that the swaptions' Vega, Vanna and Volga are calculated without considering the annuity factor in the pricing formulae (ie, we just differentiate the function $\text{Bl}(K, S, v)$);

   (vi) $\sigma_{25\Delta p} = (C^{BS})^{-1}(C(K^i_{25\Delta p}))$ (volatility level that plugged into the BS formula gives $C(K^i_{25\Delta p})$;

   (vii) $\sigma_{25\Delta c} = (C^{BS})^{-1}(C(K^i_{25\Delta c}))$;

   (viii) iterate from step (ii) until $K^i_{25\Delta p} - K^{i-1}_{25\Delta p} < \epsilon$ and $K^i_{25\Delta c} - K^{i-1}_{25\Delta c} < \epsilon$, ϵ suitably small;

   (ix) this iteration step yields the 25Δ strikes $K_{25\Delta p}$ and $K_{25\Delta c}$, and their implied volatilities $\sigma_{25\Delta p}$ and $\sigma_{25\Delta c}$.

4. We can express, for each pair of expiries and tenors in the subset, the smile in the compact form of ATM volatilities, 25Δ risk reversals and 25Δ butterflies. The surface of ATM volatilities for a wider range of expiries and tenors is easily retrievable from the market: we can use this data to build a complete swaption volatility cube, by interpolating and extrapolating the levels of risk reversals and butterflies obtained before.

Table 1.12 25Δ risk reversals and butterflies derived from market data, as of 27 February, 2007. (Source: Bloomberg.)

		Two years	Five years	10 years	20 years	30 years
25Δ RR	Three months	−0.04%	−0.23%	−0.25%	−0.25%	−0.33%
	One year	−0.31%	−0.59%	−0.70%	−0.74%	−0.84%
	Five years	−1.05%	−1.64%	−1.75%	−1.62%	−1.66%
	10 years	−1.22%	−1.71%	−1.96%	−1.88%	−1.84%
	20 years	−1.15%	−1.63%	−2.35%	−2.32%	−2.41%
	30 years	−0.53%	−1.54%	−2.24%	−2.18%	−2.15%
25Δ VWB	Three months	0.01%	0.03%	0.04%	0.03%	0.03%
	One year	0.06%	0.09%	0.11%	0.10%	0.10%
	Five years	0.23%	0.22%	0.23%	0.23%	0.24%
	10 years	0.30%	0.30%	0.30%	0.31%	0.32%
	20 years	0.44%	0.37%	0.32%	0.48%	0.50%
	30 years	0.72%	0.44%	0.28%	0.57%	0.57%

From the market data shown in Tables 1.10 and 1.11, following the procedure just described, we obtain the risk reversals and butterfly levels for the 25Δ receivers and payers, as they appear in Table 1.12. We use them, jointly with a more extended ATM volatility surface, to characterise the entire volatility cube, which is plotted in Figures 1.8 (ATM volatilities), 1.9 (risk reversals) and 1.10 (butterflies). We would like to stress how easily and naturally the interpolation and extrapolation of the risk reversals and butterflies allows us to build and manage such a complex object as the swaption volatility cube; in addition, the representation is also very efficient and parsimonious, because only three strikes are needed for each expiry–tenor pair.

As a final check for the procedure we have suggested, we show that the VV approach is actually able to capture the smile typically manifesting in the swaption market. In Figure 1.11 market data is shown for a swaption expiring in 10 years written on a swap maturing in 10 years (a 10Y10Y swaption in market lore). The VV smile is also plotted, compared with the smile engendered by the SABR functional form calibrated to market data. The SABR model has now become a common tool to produce volatility smiles in the swaption market, so that its fitting is quite satisfactory, as it is evident in the figure. Nevertheless the VV approach also generates a very good smile. Actually, the three smiles are undistinguishable for almost any strike (here expressed as the distance in basis points

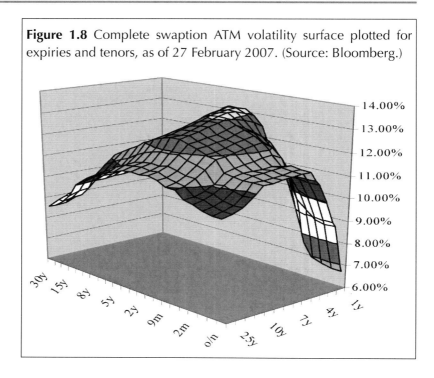

Figure 1.8 Complete swaption ATM volatility surface plotted for expiries and tenors, as of 27 February 2007. (Source: Bloomberg.)

from the forward swap rate). Only for very low strikes, corresponding to extremely low put Delta's, does the VV smile lie below the other two. Anyway, the VV approach yields sufficiently good results for most practical applications.

APPENDIX A. THE VV METHOD IN DETAIL

In this appendix, we illustrate the main features and properties possessed by the VV method. We start by describing the replication argument that the VV procedure is based on and derive closed-form formulae for the weights in the hedging portfolio so as to render the smile construction more explicit. We then derive the hedging error we make by rolling the VV strategy up to long expiries, and comment on the risk-neutral density and smile asymptotics implied by the pricing function. Finally, we test the robustness of the resulting smile by showing that: (i) changing the three initial pairs of strike and volatility consistently eventually produces the same implied volatility curve; (ii) the VV method, if readapted to price European-style claims, is consistent with static-replication

Figure 1.9 Complete swaptions risk reversal surface plotted for all expiries and tenors, obtained by interpolating/extrapolating the data in Table 1.12.

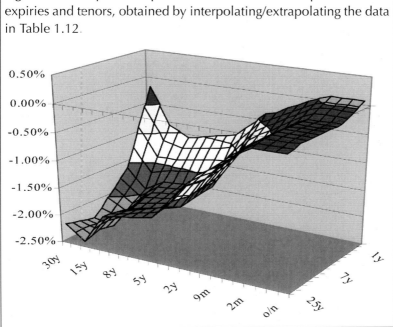

arguments. The latter property is verified under the fundamental case of a variance swap payout.

The replication argument

We consider an option market where, for a given maturity T, three basic options are quoted. We denote the corresponding strikes by K_i, $i = 1, 2, 3$, $K_1 < K_2 < K_3$, and set $\mathcal{K} := \{K_1, K_2, K_3\}$. The market implied volatility associated to K_i is denoted by σ_i, $i = 1, 2, 3$.

The VV method serves the purpose of defining an implied-volatility smile that is consistent with the basic volatilities σ_i. The rationale behind it stems from a replication argument in a flat-smile world where the constant (through strikes) level of implied volatility varies stochastically over time. This argument is presented hereafter, where for simplicity we consider the same type of options, namely calls.

It is well known that in the BS model, the payout of a European call with maturity T and strike K can be replicated by a dynamic Δ-hedging strategy, whose value (comprehensive of the bank account

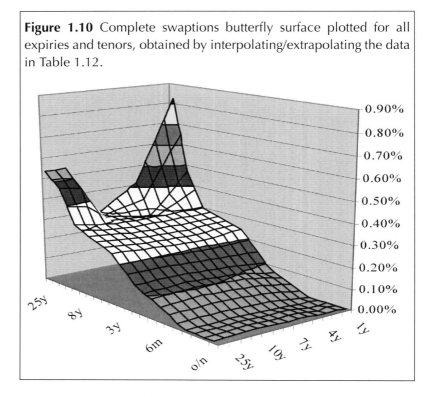

Figure 1.10 Complete swaptions butterfly surface plotted for all expiries and tenors, obtained by interpolating/extrapolating the data in Table 1.12.

part) matches, at every time t, the option price $C^{BS}(t; K)$ given by

$$C^{BS}(t; K) = S_t e^{-\delta \tau} \Phi\left(\frac{\ln(S_t/K) + (r^d - \delta + \frac{1}{2}\sigma^2)\tau}{\sigma\sqrt{\tau}}\right)$$
$$- K e^{-r^d \tau} \Phi\left(\frac{\ln(S_t/K) + (r^d - \delta - \frac{1}{2}\sigma^2)\tau}{\sigma\sqrt{\tau}}\right) \quad (A.1)$$

where the notation of Equation (1.3) is in force. In real financial markets, however, volatility is stochastic and traders hedge the associated risk by constructing portfolios that are Vega-neutral in a BS (flat-smile) world.

Maintaining the assumption of flat but stochastic implied volatilities, the presence of three basic options in the market even makes it possible to build a portfolio that zeros partial derivatives up to the second order. In fact, denoting by Δ_t and x_i the units of underlying asset and options with strikes K_i held at time t, respectively, and setting $C_i^{BS}(t) = C^{BS}(t; K_i)$, under diffusion dynamics both for S_t

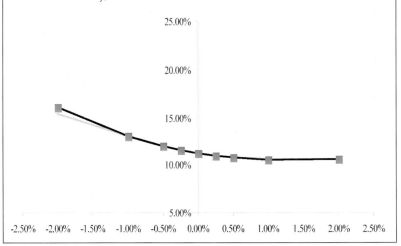

Figure 1.11 Smile for the 10Y10Y swaption generated by the VV method (grey curve), compared with the smile implied by the SABR functional form (black curve) calibrated to market data (grey points), as of 27 February, 2007.

and $\sigma = \sigma_t$, we have by Itô's lemma

$$dC^{BS}(t;K) - \Delta_t\, dS_t - \Delta_t \delta S_t\, dt - \sum_{i=1}^{3} x_i\, dC_i^{BS}(t)$$

$$= \left[\frac{\partial C^{BS}(t;K)}{\partial t} - \sum_{i=1}^{3} x_i \frac{\partial C_i^{BS}(t)}{\partial t} - \Delta_t \delta S_t\right] dt$$

$$+ \left[\frac{\partial C^{BS}(t;K)}{\partial S} - \Delta_t - \sum_{i=1}^{3} x_i \frac{\partial C_i^{BS}(t)}{\partial S}\right] dS_t$$

$$+ \left[\frac{\partial C^{BS}(t;K)}{\partial \sigma} - \sum_{i=1}^{3} x_i \frac{\partial C_i^{BS}(t)}{\partial \sigma}\right] d\sigma_t$$

$$+ \frac{1}{2}\left[\frac{\partial^2 C^{BS}(t;K)}{\partial S^2} - \sum_{i=1}^{3} x_i \frac{\partial^2 C_i^{BS}(t)}{\partial S^2}\right] (dS_t)^2$$

$$+ \frac{1}{2}\left[\frac{\partial^2 C^{BS}(t;K)}{\partial \sigma^2} - \sum_{i=1}^{3} x_i \frac{\partial^2 C_i^{BS}(t)}{\partial \sigma^2}\right] (d\sigma_t)^2$$

$$+ \left[\frac{\partial^2 C^{BS}(t;K)}{\partial S \partial \sigma} - \sum_{i=1}^{3} x_i \frac{\partial^2 C_i^{BS}(t)}{\partial S \partial \sigma}\right] dS_t\, d\sigma_t \qquad \text{(A.2)}$$

Choosing Δ_t and x_i so as to zero the coefficients of dS_t, $d\sigma_t$, $(d\sigma_t)^2$ and $dS_t\, d\sigma_t$,[21] the portfolio made of a long position in the call with strike K, short positions in x_i calls with strike K_i and short the amount Δ_t of the underlying, is locally riskless at time t (no stochastic terms are involved in its differential). Using the BS partial differential equation, we then obtain

$$dC^{BS}(t;K) - \Delta_t\, dS_t - \Delta_t \delta S_t\, dt - \sum_{i=1}^{3} x_i\, dC_i^{BS}(t)$$
$$= r^d \left[C^{BS}(t;K) - \Delta_t S_t - \sum_{i=1}^{3} x_i C_i^{BS}(t) \right] dt \quad (A.3)$$

Therefore, when volatility is stochastic and options are valued with the BS formula, we can still have a (locally) perfect hedge, provided that we hold suitable amounts of three more options to rule out the model risk (the hedging strategy is irrespective of the true asset and volatility dynamics, under the assumption of no jumps).[22]

Remark A.1 The validity of the previous replication argument may be questioned because no stochastic volatility model can produce implied volatilities that are flat and stochastic at the same time. The simultaneous presence of these features, although inconsistent from a theoretical point of view, can be justified, however, on empirical grounds. In fact, the practical advantages of the BS paradigm are so clear that an option trader may choose to run their book by revaluating and hedging according to a BS flat-smile model, with the ATM volatility being continuously updated to the actual market level.[23] This is especially true in the FX market.

The first step in the VV procedure is the construction of the above hedging portfolio, whose weights x_i are explicitly computed in the following section.

Computing the VV weights

In most practical applications, the constant BS volatility is the ATM, and one of the three options will also be chosen so to be struck ATM; thus, we set $\sigma = \sigma_2$ ($=\sigma_{ATM}$) and $K_2 = K_{ATM}$. Anyway, this is not strictly required and one can actually choose any σ as the constant (through strikes) implied volatility. We also assume that $t = 0$, dropping accordingly the argument t in the call prices. From

Equation (A.2), we have that the weights $x_1 = x_1(K)$, $x_2 = x_2(K)$ and $x_3 = x_3(K)$, for which the resulting portfolio of European calls with maturity T and strikes K_1, K_2 and K_3 has the same Vega, $(\partial \text{Vega}/\partial \text{Vol})$ and $(\partial \text{Vega}/\partial \text{Spot})$ as the call with strike K,[24] can be found by solving the following system, see also (1.4):

$$\frac{\partial C^{BS}}{\partial \sigma}(K) = \sum_{i=1}^{3} x_i(K) \frac{\partial C^{BS}}{\partial \sigma}(K_i)$$

$$\frac{\partial^2 C^{BS}}{\partial \sigma^2}(K) = \sum_{i=1}^{3} x_i(K) \frac{\partial^2 C^{BS}}{\partial \sigma^2}(K_i) \qquad (A.4)$$

$$\frac{\partial^2 C^{BS}}{\partial \sigma \partial S_0}(K) = \sum_{i=1}^{3} x_i(K) \frac{\partial^2 C^{BS}}{\partial \sigma \partial S_0}(K_i)$$

Denoting by $\mathcal{V}(K)$ the Vega of a European option with maturity T and strike K,

$$\mathcal{V}(K) = \frac{\partial C^{BS}}{\partial \sigma}(K) = S_0 e^{-\delta T} \sqrt{T} \varphi(d_1(K))$$

$$d_1(K) = \frac{\ln(S_0/K) + (r^d - \delta + \tfrac{1}{2}\sigma^2)T}{\sigma \sqrt{T}} \qquad (A.5)$$

where $\varphi(x) = \Phi'(x)$ is the normal density function, and calculating the second-order derivatives

$$\frac{\partial^2 C^{BS}}{\partial \sigma^2}(K) = \frac{\mathcal{V}(K)}{\sigma} d_1(K) d_2(K)$$

$$\frac{\partial^2 C^{BS}}{\partial \sigma \partial S_0}(K) = -\frac{\mathcal{V}(K)}{S_0 \sigma \sqrt{T}} d_2(K)$$

$$d_2(K) = d_1(K) - \sigma\sqrt{T}$$

we can prove the following.

Proposition A.1 The system (1.4) admits always a unique solution, which is given by

$$x_1(K) = \frac{\mathcal{V}(K)}{\mathcal{V}(K_1)} \frac{\ln(K_2/K) \ln(K_3/K)}{\ln(K_2/K_1) \ln(K_3/K_1)}$$

$$x_2(K) = \frac{\mathcal{V}(K)}{\mathcal{V}(K_2)} \frac{\ln(K/K_1) \ln(K_3/K)}{\ln(K_2/K_1) \ln(K_3/K_2)} \qquad (A.6)$$

$$x_3(K) = \frac{\mathcal{V}(K)}{\mathcal{V}(K_3)} \frac{\ln(K/K_1) \ln(K/K_2)}{\ln(K_3/K_1) \ln(K_3/K_2)}$$

In particular, if $K = K_j$, then $x_i(K) = 1$ for $i = j$ and zero otherwise.

Proof Writing the system (1.4) in the form

$$A \begin{pmatrix} x_1(t;K) \\ x_2(t;K) \\ x_3(t;K) \end{pmatrix} = B$$

straightforward algebra leads to

$$\det(A) = \frac{\mathcal{V}(t;K_1)\mathcal{V}(t;K_2)\mathcal{V}(t;K_3)}{S_0\sigma^2\sqrt{T}}$$

$$\times [d_2(t;K_3)d_1(t;K_2)d_2(t;K_2) + d_2(t;K_1)d_1(t;K_3)d_2(t;K_3)$$
$$- d_1(t;K_1)d_2(t;K_1)d_2(t;K_3) - d_1(t;K_3)d_2(t;K_3)d_2(t;K_2)$$
$$- d_2(t;K_1)d_1(t;K_2)d_2(t;K_2) + d_1(t;K_1)d_2(t;K_1)d_2(t;K_2)]$$

$$= \frac{\mathcal{V}(t;K_1)\mathcal{V}(t;K_2)\mathcal{V}(t;K_3)}{S_0\sigma^5 T^2} \ln\frac{K_2}{K_1} \ln\frac{K_3}{K_1} \ln\frac{K_3}{K_2}$$

(A.7)

which is strictly positive since $K_1 < K_2 < K_3$. Therefore, (1.4) admits a unique solution and (A.6) follows from Cramer's rule. □

The VV option price

We can now proceed to the definition of an option price that is consistent with the market prices of the basic options.

The above replication argument shows that a portfolio made of $x_i(K)$ units of the option with strike K_i (and Δ_0 units of the underlying asset) gives a local perfect hedge in a BS world. The hedging strategy, however, has to be implemented at prevailing market prices, which generates an extra cost with respect to the BS value of the options portfolio. Such a cost is to be added to the BS price (1.3), with $t = 0$, to produce an arbitrage-free price that is consistent with the quoted option prices $C^{MKT}(K_1)$, $C^{MKT}(K_2)$ and $C^{MKT}(K_3)$.

In fact, in the case of a short maturity, ie, for a small T, Equation (A.3) can be approximated as

$$(S_T - K)^+ - C^{BS}(K) - \Delta_0[S_T - S_0] - \Delta_0 \delta S_0 T$$
$$- \sum_{i=1}^{3} x_i[(S_T - K_i)^+ - C^{BS}(K_i)]$$
$$\approx r^d \left[C^{BS}(K) - \Delta_0 S_0 - \sum_{i=1}^{3} x_i C^{BS}(K_i) \right] T$$

so that setting

$$C(K) = C^{BS}(K) + \sum_{i=1}^{3} x_i(K)[C^{MKT}(K_i) - C^{BS}(K_i)] \quad (A.8)$$

we have

$$(S_T - K)^+ \approx C(K) + \Delta_0[S_T - S_0] + \Delta_0 \delta S_0 T$$
$$+ \sum_{i=1}^{3} x_i[(S_T - K_i)^+ - C^{MKT}(K_i)]$$
$$+ r^d \left[C(K) - \Delta_0 S_0 - \sum_{i=1}^{3} x_i C^{MKT}(K_i) \right] T$$

Therefore, when actual market prices are considered, the option payout $(S_T - K)^+$ can still be replicated by buying Δ_0 units of the underlying asset and x_i options with strike K_i (investing the resulting cash at rate r^d), provided one starts from the initial endowment $C(K)$.

The quantity $C(K)$ in (1.5) is thus defined as the VV option's premium, implicitly assuming that the replication error is also negligible for longer maturities (we analyse such replication error in the section below). Such a premium is equal to the BS price $C^{BS}(K)$ plus the cost difference of the hedging portfolio induced by the market implied volatilities with respect to the constant volatility σ. As we set $\sigma = \sigma_2$, the market volatility for strike K_2, (1.5) can be simplified to

$$C(K) = C^{BS}(K) + x_1(K)[C^{MKT}(K_1) - C^{BS}(K_1)]$$
$$+ x_3(K)[C^{MKT}(K_3) - C^{BS}(K_3)]$$

Remark A.2 Expressing the system (1.4) in the form $b = Ax$ and setting $c = (c_1, c_2, c_3)'$, where $c_i := C^{MKT}(K_i) - C^{BS}(K_i)$, and $y = (y_1, y_2, y_3)' := (A')^{-1} c$, we can also write

$$C(K) = C^{BS}(K) + y_1 \frac{\partial C^{BS}}{\partial \sigma}(K) + y_2 \frac{\partial^2 C^{BS}}{\partial \sigma^2}(K) + y_3 \frac{\partial^2 C^{BS}}{\partial \sigma \partial S_0}(K)$$

The difference between the VV and BS prices can thus be interpreted as the sum of the option's Vega, ∂Vega$/\partial$Vol and ∂Vega$/\partial$Spot, weighted by their respective hedging cost y.

47

In addition to being quite intuitive, this representation also has the advantage that the weights y are independent of the strike K and, as such, can be calculated once for all. However, we prefer to stick to the definition (1.5), because it allows an easier derivation of our approximations below.

Hedging error for longer expiries

The result shown above hinges on a perfect-hedged portfolio strategy, which grants a risk-free return on the initial investment needed to implement it only in the case of a short time to maturity. For longer expiries, the argument is no more valid and the ability to perform a self-financing strategy making the portfolio's return riskless cannot be proved. Anyway, we can try to gauge the hedging error that springs from carrying out the strategy for an arbitrary expiry, assuming a continuous rebalancing. To this end, we proceed as follows.

Assume that we run a book with a BS model and we continuously update the implied (ATM) volatility to the market level. Consider the time-t hedging portfolio made of $x_i(t)$ options $C_i(t)$, Δ_t shares and an amount β_t in the bank account, whose value is denoted by $\pi(t)$:

$$\pi(t) = \sum_{i=1}^{3} x_i(t; K) C^{\text{MKT}}(t; K_i) + \Delta_t S_t + \beta_t$$

where we set $\pi(0) = C^{\text{MKT}}(0; K)$. Assuming that the portfolio is self-financing, we have

$$d\pi(t) = \sum_{i=1}^{3} x_i(t; K) \, dC^{\text{MKT}}(t; K_i) + \Delta_t \, dS_t + \Delta_t \delta S_t \, dt + \beta_t r^d \, dt$$

$$= \sum_{i=1}^{3} x_i(t; K) \, dC^{\text{MKT}}(t; K_i) + \Delta_t \, dS_t + \Delta_t \delta S_t \, dt$$

$$+ \left[\pi(t) - \sum_{i=1}^{3} x_i(t; K) C^{\text{MKT}}(t; K_i) - \Delta_t S_t \right] r^d \, dt$$

Denote by ε_t the hedging error at time t:

$$\varepsilon_t = C(t; K) - \pi(t)$$

We have, remembering the definition (1.5) of $C(t;K)$,

$$d\varepsilon_t = dC^{BS}(t;K) + \sum_{i=1}^{3} x_i(t;K)[dC_i^{MKT}(t) - dC_i^{BS}(t)]$$

$$+ \sum_{i=1}^{3} dx_i(t;K)[C_i^{MKT}(t) - C_i^{BS}(t)]$$

$$+ \sum_{i=1}^{3} dx_i(t;K)[dC_i^{MKT}(t) - dC_i^{BS}(t)]$$

$$- \sum_{i=1}^{3} x_i(t;K)\, dC_i^{MKT}(t) - \Delta_t\, dS_t - \Delta_t \delta S_t\, dt$$

$$- \left[\pi(t) - \sum_{i=1}^{3} x_i(t;K)C_i^{MKT}(t) - \Delta_t S_t\right] r^d\, dt$$

Using again (1.5) and (A.3) and rearranging terms, we obtain

$$d\varepsilon_t = r^d \varepsilon_t\, dt + \sum_{i=1}^{3} dx_i(t;K)[C_i^{MKT}(t) + dC_i^{MKT}(t) - C_i^{BS}(t) - dC_i^{BS}(t)]$$

or, in shorthand notation,

$$d\varepsilon_t = r^d \varepsilon_t dt + \sum_{i=1}^{3} dx_i(t;K)[C_i^{MKT}(t+dt) - C_i^{BS}(t+dt)]$$

This immediately leads to the following.

Proposition A.2 *The total hedging error at maturity T is given by*

$$\varepsilon_T = \sum_{i=1}^{3} \int_0^T e^{r^d(T-t)}\, dx_i(t;K)[C_i^{MKT}(t+dt) - C_i^{BS}(t+dt)] \quad (A.9)$$

Equation (A.9) provides us with a useful insight into the accuracy of the replication strategy in the stochastic volatility world: the more volatile and net positive the difference between the market price and the flat-smile price of the three basic options, the higher the total hedging error ε_T. One can see the total hedging error as the sum (the integral in a continuous-time setting) of the differences in prices not taken into account by the flat-smile hypothesis (although with a floating ATM implied volatility), times the variations in their quantities in the portfolio. As only the differences between the true market and BS prices are relevant when re-balancing is needed, we can reasonably believe that the error is not considerably ample, and that it will be larger for very far out-of-the-money strikes, because more re-balancing is likely to be expected. Comparisons between the smiles generated by the VV method and by a stochastic volatility model (eg, the Heston or the SABR), calibrated to the same set of data, shows that this statement is well-grounded.

The implied risk-neutral density and smile asymptotics
The VV price (1.5) is defined without introducing specific assumptions on the distribution of the underlying asset. However, the knowledge of option prices for every possible strike identifies a (unique) risk-neutral density that is consistent with them. In fact, by the general result of Breeden and Litzenberger (1978), the risk-neutral density p_T of the asset S_T can be obtained by differentiating twice the option price (1.5):

$$p_T(K) = e^{r^d T} \frac{\partial^2 C}{\partial K^2}(K) = e^{r^d T} \frac{\partial^2 C^{BS}}{\partial K^2}(K)$$

$$+ e^{r^d T} \sum_{i \in \{1,3\}} \frac{\partial^2 x_i}{\partial K^2}(K)[C^{MKT}(K_i) - C^{BS}(K_i)] \quad \text{(A.10)}$$

The first term in the right-hand side is the lognormal density p_T^{BS} associated with the geometric Brownian motion with drift rate $r^d - \delta$ and volatility $\sigma = \sigma_2$. The second term, which is the deviation from lognormality induced by the VV smile, is more involved and can be calculated by differentiating twice the weights (A.6). We obtain

$$\frac{\partial^2 x_1}{\partial K^2}(K) = \frac{\mathcal{V}(K)}{K^2 \sigma^2 T \mathcal{V}(K_1) \ln(K_2/K_1) \ln(K_3/K_1)}$$

$$\times \left[(d_1(K)^2 - \sigma\sqrt{T} d_1(K) - 1) \ln \frac{K_2}{K} \ln \frac{K_3}{K} \right.$$

$$\left. - 2\sigma\sqrt{T} d_1(K) \ln \frac{K_2 K_3}{K^2} + \sigma^2 T \left(\ln \frac{K_2 K_3}{K^2} + 2 \right) \right]$$

$$\frac{\partial^2 x_3}{\partial K^2}(K) = \frac{\mathcal{V}(K)}{K^2 \sigma^2 T \mathcal{V}(K_3) \ln(K_3/K_1) \ln(K_3/K_2)}$$

$$\times \left[(d_1(K)^2 - \sigma\sqrt{T} d_1(K) - 1) \ln \frac{K_2}{K} \ln \frac{K_1}{K} \right.$$

$$\left. - 2\sigma\sqrt{T} d_1(K) \ln \frac{K_1 K_2}{K^2} + \sigma^2 T \left(\ln \frac{K_1 K_2}{K^2} + 2 \right) \right]$$

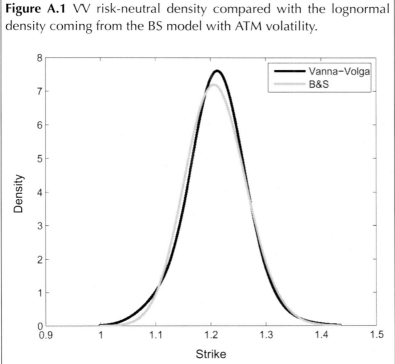

Figure A.1 VV risk-neutral density compared with the lognormal density coming from the BS model with ATM volatility.

A plot of the risk-neutral density associated to (1.5) is shown in Figure A.1, where it is compared with the corresponding lognormal density p_T^{BS}.[25]

The analytical expression (A.10) for the VV risk-neutral density allows us to characterise the asymptotic behaviour of the VV implied volatility ς by means of the results in Benaim and Friz (2006). In fact, it can easily be shown that the density q_T of $\ln S_T$, $q_T(k) = e^k p_T(e^k)$, is a regularly varying function at ∞ in that

$$\lim_{k \to \pm \infty} \frac{q_T(xk)}{q_T(k)} = x^\alpha$$

for some real number α. Moreover, $\ln[q_T(k)]/k$ goes to infinity for $k \to \infty$. Theorems 1 and 2 in Benaim and Friz (2006) then lead to the following.

Proposition A.3 The right and left asymptotic values of the VV implied volatility curve are both equal to $\sigma = \sigma_2$:

$$\lim_{k \to \pm\infty} \varsigma(e^k) = \sigma$$

Two consistency results

We now state two important consistency results that hold for the option price (1.5) and that give further support to the VV procedure.

The first result is as follows. One may wonder what happens if we apply the VV curve construction method when starting from three other strikes whose associated prices coincide with those coming from formula (1.5). Clearly, for the procedure to be robust, we would want the two curves to exactly coincide. This is indeed the case.

In fact, consider a new set of strikes $\mathcal{H} := \{H_1, H_2, H_3\}$, for which we set

$$C^{\mathcal{H}}(H_i) = C^{\mathcal{K}}(H_i) = C^{BS}(H_i) + \sum_{j=1}^{3} x_j(H_i)[C^{MKT}(K_j) - C^{BS}(K_j)] \tag{A.11}$$

where the superscripts $\mathcal{H}$ and $\mathcal{K}$ highlight the set of strikes the pricing procedure is based on, and weights x_j are obtained from $\mathcal{K}$ with formulae (A.6). For a generic strike K, denoting by $x_i(K; \mathcal{H})$ the weights for K that are derived starting from the set $\mathcal{H}$, the option price associated to $\mathcal{H}$ is defined, analogously to (1.5), by

$$C^{\mathcal{H}}(K) = C^{BS}(K) + \sum_{j=1}^{3} x_j(K; \mathcal{H})[C^{\mathcal{H}}(H_j) - C^{BS}(H_j)]$$

where the second term in the sum is now not necessarily zero, because H_2 is in general different than K_2. The following proposition states the desired consistency result.

Proposition A.4 The call prices based on $\mathcal{H}$ coincide with those based on $\mathcal{K}$, namely, for each strike K,

$$C^{\mathcal{H}}(K) = C^{\mathcal{K}}(K) \tag{A.12}$$

Proof The equality (A.12) holds if and only if

$$\sum_{j=1}^{3} x_j(K; \mathcal{H})[C^{\mathcal{H}}(H_j) - C^{BS}(H_j)] = \sum_{i=1}^{3} x_i(K; \mathcal{K})[C(K_i) - C^{BS}(K_i)]$$

Using (A.11) and rearranging terms, the left-hand side can be written as

$$\sum_{j=1}^{3} x_j(K; \mathcal{H})[C^{\mathcal{H}}(H_j) - C^{\mathrm{BS}}(H_j)]$$

$$= \sum_{j=1}^{3} x_j(K; \mathcal{H}) \sum_{i=1}^{3} x_i(H_j; \mathcal{K})[C(K_i) - C^{\mathrm{BS}}(K_i)]$$

$$= \sum_{i=1}^{3} \left[\sum_{j=1}^{3} x_j(K; \mathcal{H}) x_i(H_j; \mathcal{K}) \right] [C(K_i) - C^{\mathrm{BS}}(K_i)]$$

which is equal to the above equality because, for each strike K and $j = 1, 2, 3$,

$$x_i(K; \mathcal{K}) = \sum_{j=1}^{3} x_j(K; \mathcal{H}) x_i(H_j; \mathcal{K}) \qquad (A.13)$$

following from a tedious, but straightforward, application of the formula (A.6) for the weights. □

A second consistency result that can be proven for the option price (1.5) concerns the pricing of European-style derivatives and their static replication. To this end, assume that $h(x)$ is a real function that is defined for $x \in [0, \infty)$, is well behaved at infinity and is twice differentiable. Given the simple claim with payout $h(S_T)$ at time T, we denote by V its price at time 0, when taking into account the whole smile of the underlying at time T. By Carr and Madan (1998), we have

$$V = e^{-r^d T} h(0) + S_0 e^{-\delta T} h'(0) + \int_0^{+\infty} h''(K) C(K) \, dK$$

The same reasoning adopted in the section "The replication argument" on the local hedge of the call with strike K can also be applied to the general payout $h(S_T)$. We can thus construct a portfolio of European calls with maturity T and strikes K_1, K_2 and K_3, such that the portfolio has the same Vega, $\partial \mathrm{Vega}/\partial \mathrm{Vol}$ and $\partial \mathrm{Vega}/\partial \mathrm{Spot}$, as the given derivative. Denoting by V^{BS} the claim price under the BS model, this is achieved by finding the corresponding portfolio weights x_1^h, x_2^h and x_3^h, which always exist unique, see Proposition A.1. We can then define a new (smile-consistent) price for our derivative as

$$\overline{V} = V^{BS} + \sum_{i=1}^{3} x_i^h [C^{MKT}(K_i) - C^{BS}(K_i)] \qquad (A.14)$$

which is the obvious generalisation of (1.5). Our second consistency result is stated in the following.

Proposition A.5 The claim price that is consistent with the option prices (1.5) is equal to the claim price that is obtained by adjusting its BS price by the cost difference of the hedging portfolio when using market prices $C^{MKT}(K_i)$ instead of the constant-volatility prices $C^{BS}(K_i)$. In formulae

$$V = \overline{V}$$

Proof For each operator $\mathcal{L} \in \{\partial/\partial\sigma, \partial^2/\partial^2\sigma, \partial^2/\partial\sigma\partial S_0\}$ we have

$$\mathcal{L} V^{BS} = \mathcal{L}\left[e^{-r^d T} h(0) + S_0 e^{-\delta T} h'(0) + \int_0^{+\infty} h''(K) C^{BS}(K) \, dK \right]$$
$$= \int_0^{+\infty} h''(K) \mathcal{L} C^{BS}(K) \, dK$$

which, by definition of the weights $x_i(K)$, becomes

$$\mathcal{L} V^{BS} = \int_0^{+\infty} h''(K) \sum_{i=1}^{3} x_i(K) \, \mathcal{L} C^{BS}(K_i) \, dK$$
$$= \sum_{i=1}^{3} \int_0^{+\infty} h''(K) x_i(K) \mathcal{L} C^{BS}(K_i) \, dK$$
$$= \sum_{i=1}^{3} \left[\int_0^{+\infty} h''(K) x_i(K) \, dK \right] \mathcal{L} C^{BS}(K_i)$$

By the uniqueness of the weights x_i^h, we thus have

$$x_i^h = \int_0^{+\infty} h''(K) x_i(K) \, dK, \quad i = 1, 2, 3$$

Substituting into (A.14), we get

$$\overline{V} = V^{BS} + \sum_{i=1}^{3}\left[\int_{0}^{+\infty} h''(K)x_i(K)\,dK\right][C^{MKT}(K_i) - C^{BS}(K_i)]$$

$$= V^{BS} + \int_{0}^{+\infty} h''(K)\sum_{i=1}^{3} x_i(K)[C^{MKT}(K_i) - C^{BS}(K_i)]\,dK$$

$$= V^{BS} + \int_{0}^{+\infty} h''(K)[C(K) - C^{BS}(K)]\,dK$$

$$= V^{BS} + [V - V^{BS}] = V \qquad \square$$

Therefore, if we calculate the hedging portfolio for the claim under flat volatility and add to the BS claim price the cost difference of the hedging portfolio (market price minus constant-volatility price), obtaining $\overline{V}$, we exactly retrieve the claim price V as obtained through the risk-neutral density implied by the call option prices that are consistent with the market smile.

An example: smile consistent pricing of a variance swap

As an example, we apply the second consistency result above to a variance swap. This is a derivative paying out at maturity T the difference between the realised variance of the underlying asset and a fixed level, which is the swap variance making zero the value of the contract at inception. This contract can be (perfectly) statically replicated by a continuum of options, with strikes in the range running from zero to infinity. In the market, the swap variance level is conventionally expressed as volatility on an annual basis (the number of days can be 365 or a different number, say 255, to take into account business days only), and the realised variance is calculated by contractually specifying the fixing and the monitoring frequency (usually daily). Hence, the terminal payout (for one unit of notional) can be written as follows:

$$\mathbf{VS}(T) = \frac{365}{n}\sum_{i=1}^{n}\left(\ln\frac{S_i}{S_{i-1}}\right)^2 - \sigma_{VAR}^2$$

where 365 is the number of days used for annualising, n is the number of days until the expiry T of the contract, S_i is the underlying fixing price at time t_i and σ_{VAR} is the strike volatility. As commonly done in the financial literature for ease of calculation, we assume that we can replace the realised variance with its continuous-time limit:

$$\frac{365}{n}\sum_{i=1}^{n}\left(\ln\frac{S_i}{S_{i-1}}\right)^2 \approx \frac{1}{T}\int_0^T \sigma_t^2\,dt$$

The value at time 0 of the variance swap is the (risk-neutral) expected value of the terminal payout:

$$\mathbf{VS}(0) = e^{-r^d T} E\left[\frac{1}{T}\int_0^T \sigma_t^2\,dt - \sigma_{\mathrm{VAR}}^2\right]$$

By definition, at inception

$$\sigma_{\mathrm{VAR}}^2 = E\left[\frac{1}{T}\int_0^T \sigma_t^2\,dt\right]$$

Let us price the variance swap with the VV method. To this end, we need to calculate its BS (flat-smile) price and Vega, Vanna and Volga sensitivities. In a BS world, the expected variance is simply the square of the implied volatility common to all options expiring at time T. Assuming that this is the ATM volatility σ_{ATM}, we immediately have

$$\mathbf{VS}^{\mathrm{BS}}(0) = e^{-r^d T}[\sigma_{\mathrm{ATM}}^2 - \sigma_{\mathrm{VAR}}^2]$$

$$\frac{\partial \mathbf{VS}^{\mathrm{BS}}(0)}{\partial \sigma_{\mathrm{ATM}}} = 2e^{-r^d T}\sigma_{\mathrm{ATM}}$$

$$\frac{\partial^2 \mathbf{VS}^{\mathrm{BS}}(0)}{\partial \sigma_{\mathrm{ATM}} \partial S_0} = 0$$

$$\frac{\partial^2 \mathbf{VS}^{\mathrm{BS}}(0)}{\partial \sigma_{\mathrm{ATM}}^2} = 2e^{-r^d T}$$

Alternatively, the variance swap can be perfectly replicated by a continuum of options, when available, and it can be proved (see Carr and Madan (1998)) that the swap strike is given by

$$\sigma_{\mathrm{VAR}} = \sqrt{2\frac{e^{r^d T}}{T}\left(\int_0^F \frac{1}{K^2}P(K)\,dK + \int_F^\infty \frac{1}{K^2}C(K)\,dK\right)}$$

where F is the forward asset price and $P(K)$ denotes the put price with strike K.

The static replication and the VV method yield the same results, thanks to Proposition A.5. To confirm this, we calculate the strike

Table A.1 Variance swap strike volatilities.

Expiry	VV	Static replication
Three months	9.738%	9.738%
One year	9.914%	9.914%

volatility of two variance swaps on the euro/US dollar FX rate, with market data as of 1 July, 2005 (the spot rate is 1.2050, see also Tables 1.3 and 1.4): the first contract expires in three months (94 days) and the second in one year (367 days). The numerical integration is performed by a Gauss–Lobatto scheme, whereas the VV method has been described above. Table A.1 shows the results and makes it clear that the VV method produces outputs virtually indistinguishable from those implied by the static replication approach, with the main advantage that the former requires no numerical integration.

1 Although very likely superfluous, we just specify that Delta is the partial derivative of the option price with respect to the underlying asset's price.

2 In most cases, under this rule, the ATM strike is set equal to the forward price of the underlying asset.

3 It can be shown that the sticky strike, Delta and absolute rules all produce arbitrage opportunities, should the surface behave as predicted by them. This is the reason why they are mainly regarded as quoting mechanisms and not expressions of actual behaviours of volatility surfaces.

4 Three points for each expiry can be interpolated by a stochastic volatility model (eg, Heston's (1993) model), although they will typically not be sufficient to ensure a stable calibration. We address this issue in the next section, where we describe a robust, consistent and model-independent smile building method, requiring just the availability of the option prices for three strikes.

5 We drop the "%" sign after the level of the Δ, in accordance with the market jargon. Therefore, a 25Δ call is a call whose Delta is 0.25. Analogously, a 25Δ put is one whose Delta is -0.25.

6 The definition for Volga (and Vanna) will be provided below, when the VV method is illustrated.

7 Further remarks on the risk reversal and the butterfly, and their relationship with the three implied volatilities, are provided in the section devoted to the construction of a volatility surface in the FX market ("Building a volatility smile in practice").

8 The terms Vanna and Volga are commonly used by practitioners to denote the partial derivatives $\partial \text{Vega}/\partial \text{Spot}$ and $\partial \text{Vega}/\partial \text{Vol}$ of an option's Vega with respect to the underlying asset and its volatility, respectively. The reason for naming the procedure in this way will be made clear below.

9 For a description of the VV approach, with specific application to the FX market, see also Castagna and Mercurio (2007).

10 δ is the continuous dividend yield in the case of stocks, the foreign risk-free rate in the case of an exchange rate and it is set to r^d in the case where the underlying is an interest rate.

11 This explains the name assigned to the smile-construction procedure, given the meaning of the terms Vanna and Volga.

12 One can actually find cases where the inequality is violated for some strike K.

13 Extrapolation outside the available range of expiries is a minor issue, normally managed by traders by adding some spread over the last quoted option's maturity.

14 For a description of the FX option market and related issues, we also refer to Bisesti et al (2005).

15 For long maturities, it is market practice to consider the forward exchange rate as the ATM strike.

16 A positive σ_{RR} means that the call is favoured in that its implied volatility is higher than the implied volatility of the put; a negative number implies the opposite.

17 For precision's sake, on that date the three-month expiry counted 94 days.

18 We fix the SABR β parameter to 0.6. Other values of β also produce quite similar calibrated volatilities.

19 In the Eurostoxx50 options market, synthetic forwards are commonly traded for all of the available expiries, so that it easy to retrieve a reliable term structure of dividend yield.

20 For a description of the swaption and CMS markets, with related pricing issues, see also Mercurio and Pallavicini (2006).

21 The coefficient of $(dS_t)^2$ will be zeroed accordingly, owing to the relation linking an option's Gamma and Vega in the BS world.

22 In fact, given that partial derivatives are zeroed up to second order, the sensitivity to possible jumps is reduced considerably, although not completely eliminated.

23 "Continuously" typically means a daily or slightly more frequent update.

24 This explains the name assigned to the smile-construction procedure, given the meaning of the terms Vanna and Volga.

25 A different, although equivalent, expression for such a density can be found in Beneder and Baker (2005).

REFERENCES

Benaim, S. and P. Friz, 2006, "Regular variation and smile asymptotics", *Mathematical Finance*, to appear.

Beneder, R. and G. Baker, 2005, "Pricing multi-currency options with smile", Internal Report, ABN AMRO Bank.

Bisesti, L., A. Castagna and F. Mercurio, 2005, "Consistent pricing and hedging of an FX options book", *Kyoto Economic Review*, **74**(1), pp 65–83.

Black, F. and M. Scholes, 1973, "The pricing of options and corporate liabilities", *Journal of Political Economy*, **81**, pp 637–659.

Breeden, D. T. and R. H. Litzenberger, 1978, "Prices of state-contingent claims implicit in option prices", *Journal of Business*, **51**, pp 621–651.

Brigo, D. and F. Mercurio, 2006, *Interest Rate Models: Theory and Practice*, 2nd edn (Heidelberg: Springer Finance).

Carr, P. P. and D. B. Madan, 1998, "Towards a theory of volatility trading", in Jarrow, R. A. (ed), *Volatility* (London: Risk Books).

Castagna, A. and F. Mercurio, 2007, "The Vanna–Volga method for implied volatilities", *Risk*, January, pp 106–111.

Fengler, M. R., 2005, "Arbitrage-free smoothing of the implied volatility surface", SFB 649 Discussion Paper 2005-019, Humboldt University, Berlin.

Hagan, P., D. Kumar, A. S. Lesniewski and D. E. Woodward, 2002, "Managing smile risk", *Wilmott Magazine*, July, pp 84–108.

Heston, S. L., 1993, "A closed-form solution for options with stochastic volatility and applications to bond and currency options", *Review of Financial Studies*, **6**, pp 327–343.

Lee, R. W., 2004, "The moment formula for implied volatility at extreme strikes", *Mathematical Finance*, **14**(3), pp 469–480.

Malz, A., 1997, "Estimating the probability distribution of the future exchange rate from option prices", *Journal of Derivatives*, Winter, pp 18–36.

Mercurio, F. and A. Pallavicini, 2006, "Smiling at convexity", *Risk*, August, pp 64–69.

2

Shedding Light on Alternative Beta: A Volatility and Fixed Income Asset Class Comparison

David E. Kuenzi

Glenwood Capital Investments, LLC

Volatility is an alternative beta – a risk premium captured by hedge fund managers and investment bank proprietary traders – that is today moving closer to the mainstream and should be thought of as a veritable asset class.[1] For many investors, it is difficult to derive intuition as to why volatility should deserve an ongoing allocation within a larger portfolio. If volatility is an asset class, then to what accepted asset class can it be compared? Why is there a risk premium over the long term for investing in this asset class? Who is willing to pay this risk premium and why? In what environments might the risk premium be too narrow or negative and in what environments might it be substantial? These are critical questions for the institutional investors attempting to diversify various systematic exposures (or beta exposures) across a broader portfolio.

There is a strong case that a volatility investor can expect to earn positive returns over time just as a fixed income, credit or equity investor would. To best understand this, it is helpful to compare the volatility asset class to the fixed income asset class. As such, the purpose of this paper is to explore the likenesses between volatility and fixed income in order to establish more firmly the case for volatility as an asset class.

BROAD COMPARISON

We liken a short volatility exposure to a long bond exposure. Just as a bond issuer is willing to pay (and is in fact required to pay) a rate of interest in excess of the expected rate of inflation, a buyer of volatility is required to pay an implied volatility level in excess of the expected realised volatility.[2] In a general sense, the risk premium in the case of fixed income can be thought of as compensation for the uncertainty in the rate of inflation and for interest rate and duration-driven volatility. In the same way, the risk premium in the case of volatility can be thought of as compensation for uncertainty in the level of realised volatility and the volatility of implied volatility (which can lead to large mark to market moves in volatility instruments). In cases of severe and unexpected inflation, it is better to be short bonds, and in cases of severe and unexpected realised volatility, it is better to be long volatility. Market-required interest rates increase dramatically in the case of severe inflation, thus driving the value of the bond investment lower; in the same sense, market levels of implied volatility respond to increases in realised volatility, thus driving the value of a short volatility position lower.

Derman (2003) draws some comparisons between bonds and options as well, noting the equivalence between the way the instruments are quoted – interest rates as parameters for bonds and volatilities as parameters for volatility instruments. The quoted interest rate must be plugged into a present value formula in order to derive the price of the bond, while the quoted implied volatility must be plugged into a Black–Scholes (or related model) in order to get the price of the option. Derman (2003) and Derman, *et al* (1998) also note the similarities between the yield to maturity and implied volatility with reference to the instruments themselves. Both are essentially summary measures, indicating the average levels (of interest rates and volatility, respectively) that make the current price of the instruments fair.

Mean reversion is another commonality, as both interest rates and volatility are understood to be mean-reverting processes. Neither volatility nor interest rates can go beneath zero; negative volatility is not defined either mathematically or conceptually, and the occurrence of negative interest rates is virtually impossible.

Additionally, neither will grow perpetually through time as a stock price would.

Finally, both have instruments of varying maturities or expiries. As such, both have term structures that are related to a given level of interest rates or volatility. Given the mean-reverting quality noted above, this also means that the behaviours of their term structures have similar characteristics.

The similarities between fixed income and volatility are summarised in Table 2.1. We explore these commonalities – as well as some notable differences – in the sections below. We also explore the various methods that investors have at their disposal for capturing the volatility risk premium.

ESTABLISHING COMPARABLE DATA SERIES

In the ensuing sections, we make some very concrete comparisons between the fixed income and volatility asset classes. In doing so, we need to establish parallel instruments or metrics between the two markets. We note that the yield on a two-year Treasury bond can be thought of as the expected rate of inflation during the next 24 months plus a premium. Similarly, we note that the VIX Index, the most commonly quoted volatility index, measures one-month volatility of the S&P500 Index – or expected realised volatility over approximately 21 trading days – plus a premium.[3] The frequency of updated inflation information is monthly (the monthly CPI report), while the frequency of updated realised volatility information is daily (daily squared return of the S&P500 index). The monthly CPI number can be thought of as updated information on the extent to which the fixed income investor is capturing the intended risk premium. By the same token, the daily realised volatility number can be thought of as updated information on the extent to which the short volatility investor realised the intended risk premium on any particular trading day. Initial one-day implied minus one-day realised volatility can be thought of as a one-day accrual. If the annualised one-day realised is lower than the initial implied, the short volatility investor will generally have a positive profit and loss for that day, and *vice versa* if the realised is higher than the original implied. Therefore, in a very broad sense, these two time series (the two-year Treasury yield and the level of the VIX Index) present parallel items for comparison. We use monthly data for the

Table 2.1 Summary of comparison between fixed income and volatility as asset classes.

Comparison item	Fixed income	Volatility
Position	Long bonds	Short volatility: short options/short variance swaps/short volatility swaps
Driver of risk premium	Investors receive a risk premium for (a) providing governments and other entities with needed capital, (b) taking risk that inflation will exceed the interest received from the bond, and (c) taking interest rate risk (the term premium) associated with the volatility of market interest rates	Investors receive a risk premium for (a) selling insurance against a market crisis, (b) taking risk that realised volatility will exceed implied volatility, thus rendering the position unprofitable, and (c) taking ongoing mark-to-market risk associated with the volatility of implied volatility
Market quotes*	The standard for quoting prices for bonds is the interest rate (or yield to maturity), which is then used in a present value formula in order to compute the actual price paid for the security	The standard for quoting prices for volatility instruments is the instrument's implied volatility, which is then used in an options pricing model (eg, the Black–Scholes model) to compute the price paid for the instrument or the relevant swap rate
Summary nature of price quote*	The yield to maturity is the average interest rate that, if used to discount all cashflows, will make the bond price equal to the summed value of those discounted cashflows	The implied volatility is the average volatility over the life of an option that will make the expected present value of the option's replicating portfolio equal to the options current price
Mean-reverting property	It is widely accepted that interest rates are a mean-reverting process	It is widely accepted that implied volatility is a mean reverting process
Term structure	Bonds are offered at various maturities, thus forming what is typically an upward sloping term structure	Options and other volatility products are offered at various expiries/maturities, thus forming what is typically an upward sloping term structure

*These items were included in a similar table in a presentation written by Emanuel Derman (Derman, 2003).

two-year Treasury and daily data for the VIX, as these frequencies represent the respective frequencies for the updating of information regarding the capture of the intended risk premium.

THE RISK PREMIUM

Despite the existence of environments in which it is better to be short bonds, the literature suggests that over time there is a positive risk premium to owning bonds (see, for example, Ibbotson and Sinquefield, 1976; Cox, Ingersoll and Ross, 1981; Feinman, 2002).[4] By the same token, there are now some studies that suggest that there is a positive risk premium over time to being short volatility – or, conversely, that there is a negative risk premium to being long volatility. Bakshi and Kapadia (2003a) find that for a long delta-hedged call position on the S&P500 there is a negative risk premium (a positive risk premium to being short volatility). For at-the-money options, they find a risk premium of approximately −0.13% of the underlying index value and −8% of the value of the option.[5] In Bakshi and Kapadia (2003b, p. 51), they note that:

> Because of the negative correlation between market index returns and market index volatility, buyers of options may be willing to pay a premium because a long position in volatility helps hedge marketwide risk.

In a study focused more purely on variance swaps, Carr and Wu (2004) find that "the variance risk premiums are strongly negative" for the long variance investor (p. 37). Finally, in a study focusing on European equity index volatility, Hafner and Wallmeier (2006, p. 15) note that:

> ...results show that on average, investors are willing to accept a heavily negative risk premium for being long in realised variance. Equivalently, investors who are sellers of variance and are providing insurance to the market, require a significantly positive risk premium.

In short, buyers of options and volatility products are willing to pay sellers an insurance premium. As volatility tends to spike in a difficult environment for risky asset classes, and is therefore negatively correlated with the returns to equities and credit, investors are willing to pay a premium to hold this asset. It is this premium that short investors in the volatility asset class can capture over time.

The notion of a positive risk premium for bonds is straightforward: if the bond yield is higher than realised inflation, the investor has benefited from holding the security. Figure 2.1a shows the two-year constant maturity Treasury yield versus both prior realised inflation (average inflation during the preceding 24 months) and realised inflation (average inflation during the ensuing 24 months).[6] It is clear that, except in instances of sudden spikes in inflation, the risk premium has been positive for fixed income investors.

In Jackwerth and Rubinstein (1996), the authors note that "option-implied volatility is almost always biased upward from prior historical realisations" (p. 1613). This is in keeping with the notion of a positive risk premium for volatility sellers – who essentially capture this difference between initial implied volatility and trade *ex post* realised volatility. Figure 2.1(b) shows the VIX index versus both prior realised volatility during the preceding 21 trading days and realised volatility during the ensuing 21 trading days. As is the case of fixed income, investors are generally granted a positive risk premium except in cases of extreme spikes in volatility. The VIX is higher than both prior realised and realised volatility in most cases. In both Figure 2.1(a) and 2.1(b), it is somewhat clear that realised inflation and realised volatility exceed yields and implied volatilities, respectively, only when there has been a sudden and likely unforeseen spike in the respective series.

The information is Figure 2.1 is summarised in Tables 2.2(a) and 2.2(b). Table 2.2(a) shows that both over the entire period and over each sub-period, the risk premium for investors in the two-year Treasury bond was positive – based both on prior 24-month inflation as well as the inflation levels that were actually realised over the remaining life of the bond. Table 2.2(b) shows that the same held true for volatility investors. Implied volatility exceeded both prior realised volatility and actual realised volatility for both the entire period (from 2/1/1990 to 28/12/2006) and for both sub-periods. Together, Figure 2.1(b) and Table 2.2(b) suggest that there is a fairly steady risk premium offered to investors selling volatility.

Figure 2.1 Risk premiums offered by fixed income and volatility: (a): Two-year constant maturity Treasury compared with average prior inflation and average actual inflation; (b): VIX Implied volatility compared with prior realised volatility and actual realised volatility.

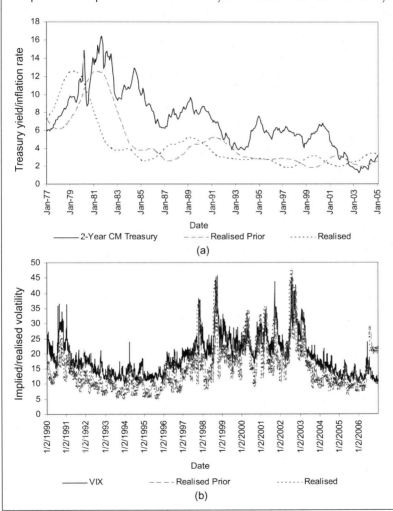

Table 2.2 Risk Premia offered by fixed income and volatility – summary of data: (a) Risk premium of two-year constant-maturity Treasury over prior 24-month average inflation and over actual 24-month average inflation; (b): VIX Volatility Index as compared with prior 21-day realised volatility and as compared with actual realised 21-day volatility.

(a)

	2-year treasury yield	Inflation: prior realised	Difference: 2-year Tsy-Prior	Inflation: actual realise	Difference: 2-year Tsy-Actual
All Data	7.16	4.54	2.62	4.30	2.86
1/31/1977 to 12/31/1990	9.59	6.24	3.35	5.98	3.61
1/31/1991 to 1/31/2005	4.74	2.85	1.89	2.63	2.12

(b)

	VIX level (implied vol)	Prior realised volatility	Difference: VIX-prior realised	Actual volatility	Difference: VIX-actual realised
All Data	19.06	14.35	4.71	14.31	4.75
1/2/1990 to 6/30/1998	17.11	11.76	5.35	11.75	5.36
7/1/1998 to 12/28/2006	21.02	16.95	4.07	14.31	6.71

MEAN-REVERTING PROPERTY AND THE NATURE OF THE TERM STRUCTURE

As noted previously, it is widely accepted that both interest rates and volatility are mean-reverting processes. Literature concerning the mean-reverting nature of interest rates is abundant and includes, among many other sources, Vasicek (1977) and Cox, Ingersoll, and Ross (1985). Literature concerning the mean-reverting nature of volatility includes, among other sources, Hull and White (1987) and Heston (1993).[7]

A shared mean-reversion characteristic leads to many similarities between the two asset classes. The most basic mean-reverting processes for each (corresponding to Vasicek (1977) and Hull and White (1987), respectively) can be written as:

$$dr_t = k_r(a_r - r_t)\, dt + \sigma_r\, dW_t^r \qquad (2.1)$$

$$dV_t = k_V(a_V - V_t)\, dt + \sigma_V\, dW_t^V \qquad (2.2)$$

where k is the mean-reversion parameter, a is the long-term mean, r_t is the instantaneous interest rate, V_t is the instantaneous level of implied volatility, σ is the volatility of rates and the volatility of implied volatility (for each equation, respectively), and dW_t is a standard Brownian motion. First, we note that the equations above are nearly identical; one can model the dynamics of each series using the same framework. Second, we estimate the mean-reversion parameter k using both sets of data (the two-year Treasury rate and the VIX). The results, shown in Tables 2.3(a) and 2.3(b), confirms that both are mean-reverting processes with a generally similar rate of mean reversion.[8]

The fact that both the fixed income and volatility markets involve mean-reverting processes and have instruments with various times to maturity provides for strikingly similar term structures. Figures 2.2(a) and 2.2(b) show simple term structures for both markets. Both are upward-sloping under normal circumstances. From a fixed income perspective, this reflects the increased inflation uncertainty over the long term as well as the increased instrument price volatility associated with a higher duration. From a volatility perspective, this reflects the increased uncertainty as to what realised volatility might be over the longer term as well as the increased instrument price volatility associated with higher vega.[9]

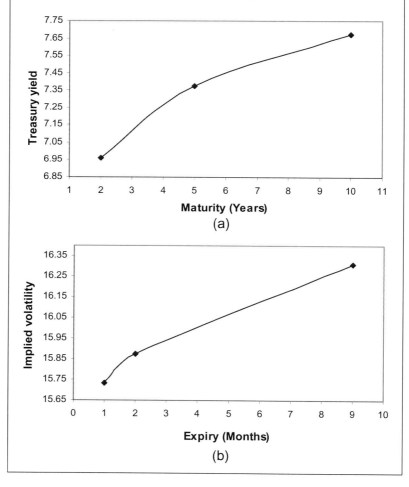

Figure 2.2 Fixed income and volatility term structures; (a): US Treasury term structure (monthly average 31/01/77 to 31/1/07); (b): Volatility term structure (daily average 03/06/02 to 31/01/07). The term structure data for interest rates consists of on-the-run Treasuries of the given maturity (Bloomberg series GT2 Govt, GT5 Govt, and GT10 Govt). The volatility data is the 50-delta-point data for S&P500 options (SPX) as provided by Bloomberg. The leap month is the first option with an expiry of nine months or longer. The same data is used in Table 2.4 and Figure 2.3.

Table 2.3 Mean-reversion parameters and related T-statistics: (a): Constant-maturity two-year Treasury rate – mean-reversion parameters and related T-statistics; (b): VIX Volatility Index – mean-reversion parameters and related T-statistics.

(a)

	Mean reversion parameter	T-statistic
All Data	0.0093	120.4
1/31/1977 to 12/31/1990	0.0364	49.4
1/31/1991 to 1/31/2005	0.0169	78.7

(b)

	Mean reversion parameter	T-statistic
All Data	0.0172	346.5
1/2/1990 to 6/30/1998	0.0244	205.3
7/1/1993 to 12/28/2006	0.0163	279.8

It is also informative to consider the term-structure behaviour of the two markets. Given that both markets have mean-reversion characteristics, one finds that the longer end of the curve is less volatile than the shorter end. This is driven by an expectation among market participants that some degree of mean reversion is likely to occur by the time the latter dates are reached. The near-term maturities/expiries, on the other hand, are much more likely to be affected by temporary shocks. Table 2.4 shows interest rate volatility and the volatility of implied volatility at different points of the term structure. Both the fixed income time series and the volatility time series have the same pattern – higher volatility for shorter maturities and lower volatility for latter maturities.

Another characteristic of these term structures is that both tend to invert when the absolute level of interest rates and volatility, respectively, is very high. This again is driven by the notion of mean reversion. If short-term interest rates increase to historically high levels, market participants are likely expect a reversion towards the long-term mean within a few years. As such, long-term interest rates are unlikely to rise as much. The same holds true for volatility. When short-dated volatility spikes, market participants are likely to take the view that markets (and therefore implied volatility) will

Table 2.4 Volatility of interest rates and volatilities across the term structure; (a): Volatility of interest rates at different points of the term structure (monthly 31/01/77 to 31/01/07); (b): Volatility of implied volatility at different points of the term structure (daily 03/06/02 to 31/01/07). These are the volatilities of the interest rate and 50 delta-point time series using data as described in Figures 2.2(a) and (b).

(a)

	2-year	5-year	10-year
Standard deviation of interest rates	3.20	2.95	2.76

(b)

	1-month	2-month	Leap-month
Standard deviation of implied volatility	7.12	6.15	5.82

settle down over the longer term. This will lead to a muted reaction of longer-term implied volatility to extreme events. This can best be seen in Figures 2.3(a) and 2.3(b), which show the relationship between the slope of the term structure and market level. As the level of both interest rates and implied volatility increases, the term structure of both interest rates and volatility is likely to invert.

Overall, the mean-reversion and term-structure related similarities between the two asset classes are dramatic. As such, many of the same types of analytics are pertinent in the analysis of these markets and in determining the ideal time to be long the related risk premium.

SOME DIFFERENCES

There are, however, some key differences between fixed income and volatility investing. The most critical of these is exposure to a market liquidity event or market sell-off. High-quality bonds such as US Treasuries will tend to perform well in a financial crisis, whereas a short volatility position will almost surely experience significant negative returns in a market crisis. The Treasury bond investor is short liquidity crisis risk; the short volatility investor will generally be long liquidity crisis risk. Treasuries are, however, highly exposed to any potential inflation scare. While volatility is

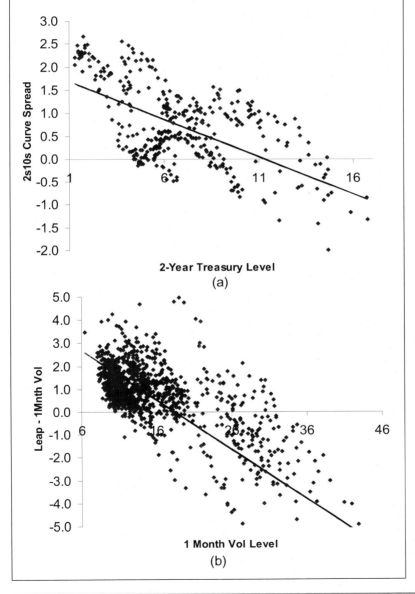

Figure 2.3 Relationship between level and curve spread; (a): Relationship between the level of the two-year Treasury yield and the 2s10s – curve spread (monthly 31/01/77 to 31/01/07); (b): Relationship between the level of the VIX Volatility Index and the 1-month/leap-month term spread (daily 03/06/02 to 31/01/07).

not directly exposed to such an event, short volatility positions would likely underperform in an inflation scare as well. Overall, short volatility positions are likely to underperform in any destabilising environment.

This has a number of implications for the means by which this alternative beta might be captured and the ways that such a volatility portfolio might be included as an element of a broader investment programme. Volatility exposures must be modelled with extreme events in mind, as this is what the short volatility investor is selling insurance against. The investor's volatility exposure should be such that the portfolio will remain in good health in the case that an extreme event were to occur. Ideally, it would be positioned such that the investor could sell yet more volatility at wider levels in such a situation. This also points to the skill brought to bear by the investment manager. Knowing how much volatility to sell and at which expiries is a complex undertaking.

The differences between the two markets compounds as one considers the minutiae. Options, for instance, have volatility smiles – an interaction between the moneyness of an option and the associated implied volatility. Bonds have coupons and an interaction between coupon level and yield to maturity. Bonds also have a sense of on-the-run (the most recently issued and most heavily traded) versus off-the-run. If we consider callable bonds, the credit quality of various issues and other characteristics of various types of bonds, the similarities and differences become extraordinarily complex.

CAPTURING THE RISK PREMIUM

In order to gain exposure to this alternative beta – to capture the risk premium associated with the volatility asset class – investors employ a variety of strategies. These include covered call writing, the sale of puts against short positions, the sale and delta-hedging of options, the sale of variance swaps and volatility swaps, and the sale of other more exotic variance swaps such as corridor variance swaps, conditional variance swaps, and gamma swaps. Table 2.5 provides an overview of the various methods that investors employ in order to obtain beta exposure to the volatility asset class.

The simplest of these is probably covered call writing – selling options on securities or futures for which the investor is long the underlying. This is a well-accepted strategy for which an index

Table 2.5 Summary of strategies for capturing the volatility risk premium.

Strategy	Implementation	Characteristics
Covered calls	Sell call options (typically at-the-money or slightly out-of-the-money) on an underlying already held as a long position in the investor's portfolio	Allows the investor to capture the volatility risk premium, but at the cost of an altered return distribution of the underlying portfolio – large gains will be truncated by the short call positions
Covered puts	Sell put options (typically at-the-money or slightly out-of-the-money) on an underlying already held as a short position in the investor's portfolio	Again, allows capture of the volatility risk premium, but provides for reduced downside protection in a sell-off, as the short put positions take out the short positions in the underlying
Delta-hedged options	Sell at-the-money options, hedge the delta exposure using the underlying; rebalance daily or more frequently depending on the size of the move	Provides for volatility exposure without direct market exposure. Generally gains if the implied volatility paid for the options is more than the actual realised volatility of the underlying. Requires ongoing attention to in order to rehedge
Short variance (volatility) swap	Receive fixed in a variance (volatility) swap (a rather simple process)	Receives the difference between the variance (volatility) strike and realised variance (volatility). From the client's perspective, it requires no rehedging
Short VIX futures	Sell VIX futures	One profits if future implied volatility is lower than current expectations for future implied volatility; this position does not capture a risk premium in the sense described in this chapter
Short corridor variance swaps, conditional variance swaps, or gamma swaps	Receive fixed in one of these contracts (again, a rather simple process)	These more exotic versions of variance swaps can be used (1) to reduce the variance strike level, (2) to express views on both volatility and the level of the underlying simultaneously, and (3) to express views on the shape of the volatility skew

and much information are available.[10] The sale of puts against short positions is the analogue to covered call writing for the short seller. Just as the covered call writer's gains are stymied in a stock-market rally, the gains of a seller of covered puts are reduced in a severe stock-market sell-off. In both cases, the seller of volatility should experience excess risk-adjusted returns over time due to the existence of the volatility risk premium combined with the diversification benefits of adding this alternative volatility beta to the exposures inherent in a traditional portfolio. The unattractive aspect of these strategies is that they alter the payout profile and return distribution of the underlying portfolio.

Delta-hedged option trading is the traditional method for obtaining volatility exposure without incurring directional exposures. This involves the sale of typically short-dated at-the-money options and the ongoing hedging of the directional exposure of the options. If, for instance, the investor sells eight 0.50-delta call options representing 800 index units, then the investor will buy futures or ETFs representing 400 index units. If the stock moves higher so that the delta increases to 0.75, then the investor will purchase an additional 200 index units. In this way, the investor remains neutral to all pure directional exposures but short volatility. One problem with this approach is that it is operationally and systems-intensive, requiring ongoing adjustments to the hedge.[11]

Variance swaps and volatility swaps require no such ongoing adjustments. The simplicity of these instruments from the client's perspective makes it quite easy to get access to volatility beta. The payout of a variance swap is:

$$\begin{aligned} Payout_{VarSwap} &= N\left(\frac{1}{T-t_0}\sum_{i=1}^{M}\left(\frac{S_i - S_{i-1}}{S_{i-1}}\right)^2 - K_{var}\right) \\ &= N\left(\frac{1}{T-t_0}\sum_{i=1}^{M}(R_i^2) - K_{var}\right) \end{aligned} \qquad (2.3)$$

where M is the total number of monitoring periods (usually business days) between swap inception at time t_0 to swap maturity at time T. S_i is the price of the underlying on day i, R_i is return of the underlying on day i, K_{var} is the initially agreed upon variance strike expressed in volatility points squared, and N is the notional amount. The investor has simply to enter into this contract and volatility exposure is locked in for the life of the swap, with no other hedging activity required.[12] (Volatility swaps are similar, except that the payout is to realised volatility minus a volatility strike. Variance swaps are easier for dealers to hedge and thus tend to be more liquid.) In this regard, variance and volatility swaps have opened up the volatility asset class to a whole new set of investors by providing the means for user-friendly exposure to volatility beta.

If a short variance swap can do the trick, why not also throw in some short VIX futures positions? VIX futures are ideal instruments for the purposes of expressing views on the direction of implied volatility, but they do not allow investors to capture the risk premium as described here. If held to expiry, VIX futures provide a payout roughly equal to the level of the futures contract at the time of sale (the VIX expected at expiry as of the date of the sale) minus the level of the VIX at expiry. This payout is independent of realised volatility except to the extent that realised has an impact on implied. In other words, VIX futures provide pure vega exposure (exposure to changes in implied volatility) with no gamma exposure (exposure to the difference between implied and realised).

For those wishing to express more complex views, however, there now exist a variety of more exotic variance swaps, such as corridor variance swaps, conditional variance swaps and gamma swaps. These instruments allow investors to express views on volatility and the level of the underlying simultaneously. They therefore also allow investors to express views on the shape of the volatility skew. The payouts of these instruments are as follows:

$Payout_{CorridorVarSwap}$

$$= N \left(\frac{1}{T - t_0} \sum_{i=1}^{M} (1_{\{S_{i-1} > L, S_{i-1} \leq U\}} R_i^2) - K_{Corridor} \right) \quad (2.4)$$

$Payout_{ConditionalVarSwap}$

$$= N \left(\frac{D}{M} \right) \left(\frac{1}{T - t_0} \frac{M}{D} \sum_{i=1}^{M} (1_{\{S_{i-1} > L, S_{i-1} \leq U\}} R_i^2) - K_{Conditional} \right)$$

$$(2.5)$$

$Payout_{GammaSwap}$

$$= N \left(\frac{1}{T - t_0} \sum_{i=1}^{M} \left(\frac{S_i}{S_0} R_i^2 \right) - K_{GammaSwap} \right) \quad (2.6)$$

where L is a lower bound on the underlying, U is an upper bound on the underlying and D is the number of days that the underlying has spent in the given range. D is defined as:

$$D = \sum_{i=1}^{M} 1_{\{S_{i-1} > L, \, S_{i-1} \leqslant U\}} \tag{2.7}$$

Each of these instruments can play a different role for investors. The corridor variance swap allows investors to obtain access to the volatility risk premium subject to the underlying being within a range. (It is important to remember that, if L is set to zero and U is set to infinity, the corridor variance swap collapses to a standard variance swap.[13]) If an investor wanted to take advantage of the volatility risk premium but also believed that the underlying was heading straight up, the investor might sell a corridor variance swap with L equal to 95% of the current underlying price and U equal to infinity (no upper bound). In this case, realised variance will accrue so long as the underlying is above 95% of its level at swap inception.

Conditional variance swaps are quite similar to corridor variance swaps. As noted by JP Morgan (2006), "The difference between a corridor and a conditional is that in a corridor variance realized outside the range is counted as zero, whereas in a conditional variance swap all variance realized outside the range is simply ignored" (p. 6). As such, the short corridor swap investor would prefer that the underlying immediately go outside the range and stay there for the life of the swap, while the short conditional swap investor would prefer that volatility remain very low within the range.

Gamma swaps simply scale realised variance by the level of the underlying. These can be useful in trading the volatility skew (long variance swaps and short gamma swaps if the skew is steep and vice versa if the skew is flat; see Mougeot, 2006, for details). Overall, the instruments available to investors provide for an ability to invest quite easily in this risk premium and to express any number of nuanced views in the process.

Given the variety of methods for accessing volatility risk premiums noted above, it is clear that volatility portfolio management processes can run the gamut from relatively simple to highly complex. In any case, the central decision for the volatility investor wishing to receive this risk premium is to determine the extent to which the premium is sufficient at any given time – whether the level of implied is large enough to offset potential spikes is realised. (Again, this is not too different from the fixed income investor who must decide whether the risk premium on bonds is sufficient to offset potential increases in inflation.) Variance and volatility swaps – along with the related exotics – allow investors to focus on these critical decisions rather than being overwhelmed with the analytical, trading and operational issues associated with running delta-hedged options portfolios. Banks are offering these instruments on a variety of underlyings, and especially on those underlyings with liquid options markets. This includes a variety of equity indexes, individual equities and currencies. This gives volatility investors a rich set of instruments to choose from. The investor is therefore left to build investment processes focused on an evaluation of the volatility risk premium associated with each of these underlyings and the best way to structure a portfolio of volatility products without a tremendous amount of operational overhead.

CONCLUSION

In coming to terms with volatility as an asset class, it is intuitively helpful to build a comparison between volatility and fixed income. These two asset classes share a wide variety of characteristics and from many perspectives can be approached through a similar lens. The drivers of their respective risk premiums, the way they are quoted and priced and their mean-reverting and term structure properties share many parallels. While these similarities have existed as long as options have been traded, until recently it has been difficult for investors to access these risk premiums efficiently due to the analytical, trading and operational issues involved with delta-hedging. With the advent of variance swaps (along with their more exotic cousins), it is now just as straightforward for investors to add this alternative beta to their portfolios as it is to buy government bonds. Given that the evidence shows that there is indeed a positive risk premium associated with selling volatility and that the related return stream is not 100% correlated with the returns of traditional assets, it is clear that the addition of volatility investments to a traditional portfolio is likely to increase risk-adjusted returns over the long term.

1   For evidence of hedge fund exposure to volatility, see Kuenzi and Shi (2007).

2   If held to expiration or maturity, a short volatility portfolio (such as a delta-hedged short straddle, a short-variance swap, or a short volatility swap) generally has a payout equal to (or approximately equal to) the implied volatility at the time of initial trade execution minus the actual realised volatility of the underlying over the period the portfolio was held. As such, if implied is consistently larger than actual realised, the volatility seller will make money.

3   The VIX index, calculated by the Chicago Board of Trade, is an index measuring the one-month implied volatility of S&P500 options contracts. For the VIX calculation methodology, see CBOE (2003).

4   Morningstar provides an ongoing annual update of the returns and risk premiums associated with various asset classes in a publication called *Stocks, Bonds, Bills, and Inflation Yearbook 2007* (2007).

5   In Bakshi and Kapadia (2003b), the authors come to a similar result for options on individual stocks, except that the risk premium is lower in absolute value. The reason they give for this (in keeping with their evidence) is that the systematic component of volatility is priced but the stock-specific, or idiosyncratic, component is not.

6   In Figure 1 and Table 2, we use the Constant Maturity two-year Treasury rate (Bloomberg item H15T2Y Index), as this rate will be directly comparable to the 24-month simple average of the monthly inflation rate. For volatility, we use the VIX index (Bloomberg item VIX Index). This can be thought of as a "constant maturity" one-month implied volatility level, which makes it directly comparable to the 21-day realised volatility.

7   For additional analysis and sources concerning the mean-reverting nature of interest rates, see Brigo and Mercurio (2001), and for additional analysis and sources concerning the mean-reverting nature of volatility see Psychoyios, Skiadopoulos, and Alexakis (2003).

8   We estimate the mean reversion parameter k using time series regression. We note that such a regression has the form $V_{t+dt} = \alpha + \phi V_t + \varepsilon$. We subtract V_t from both sides, set $k = -(\phi - 1)$, $a = \alpha/k$ and $\varepsilon_t \approx \sigma dW_t$, and we get Equation (2.2). A similar process reproduces equation (2.1). As such, we estimate the mean reversion parameter k from the time series regression and report the related t-statistic for ϕ.

9   An option's vega is defined as $\partial P/\partial V_t$, or the change in the option's price for a change in the level of implied volatility. Vega is increasing in time to expiry.

10 This has been one of the more popular strategies during the last few years. So much so that the CBOE has launched a covered call index (see Whaley, 2002; Feldman and Roy, 2005).

11 Derman, *et al* (1998) make the same observation. They also note the simplicity of obtaining volatility exposure through the use of "realised volatility contracts" and juxtapose this very simple approach with the more complex delta-hedging approach. (This brief piece was clearly well ahead of its time.)

12 Investors should be wary of the varying levels of vega exposure ($\partial P/\partial V_t$), of the change in position value for a change in implied volatility, that the variance swaps are subject to over the course of their existence and the associated mark-to-market implications. See Kuenzi (2005) for details.

13 See Carr and Lewis (2004) for a more precise treatment of this topic.

REFERENCES

Allen, Peter, *et al*, 2006, "Conditional Variance Swaps: Product Note", JPMorgan European Equity Derivatives Strategy, 3 April.

Bakshi, Gurdip and Nikunj Kapadia, 2003a, "Delta-Hedged Gains and the Negative Market Volatility Risk Premium", *Review of Financial Studies* **16**(2), Summer, pp 527–566.

Bakshi, Gurdip and Nikunj Kapadia, 2003b, "Volatility Risk Premiums Embedded in Individual Equity Options: Some New Insights", *Journal of Derivatives*, Fall, pp 45–54.

Brigo, Damiano and Fabio Mercurio, 2001, *Interest Rate Models: Theory and Practice* (Berlin: Springer-Verlag).

Carr, Peter and Keith Lewis, 2004, "Corridor Variance Swaps", *Risk*, February, pp 67–72.

Carr, Peter and Liuren Wu, 2004, "Variance Risk Premia", Working Paper, available at: http://papers.ssrn.com/sol3/papers.cfm?abstract_id=577222.

CBOE, 2003, "VIX CBOE Volatility Index", available at: http://www.cboe.com/micro/vix/vixwhite.pdf.

Cox, John C., Jonathan E. Ingersoll Jr and Stephen A. Ross, 1981, "A Re-Examination of Traditional Hypotheses About the Term Structure of Interest Rates", *Journal of Finance*, **36**(4), September, pp 769–99.

Cox, John C., Jonathan E. Ingersoll Jr and Stephen A. Ross, 1985, "A Theory of the Term Structure of Interest Rates", *Econometrica* **53**(2), March, pp 385–407.

Derman, Emanuel, 2003, "Trading Volatility as an Asset Class", presentation, available at: http://www.ederman.com/new/docs/gaim-trading_volatility.pdf.

Derman, Emanuel, *et al*, 1998, "Investing in Volatility." *Futures and Options World*, available at: http://www.ederman.com/new/docs/fow-investing_in_volatility.pdf.

Feinman, Joshua N., 2002, "Asset Returns in the Long Run", *Journal of Investing*, Fall, pp 66–76.

Feldman, Barry and Dhruv Roy, 2005, "Passive Options-Based Investment Strategies: The Case of the CBOE S&P500 BuyWrite Index", *Journal of Investing*, Summer, pp 66–83.

Hafner, Reinhold and Martin Wallmeier, 2006, "Volatility as An Asset Class: European Evidence", Working Paper, Fribourg Switzerland.

Heston, Steven L., 1993, "A Closed Form Solution for Options with Stochastic Volatility with Applications to Bond and Currency Options", *Review of Financial Studies*, **6**(2), pp 327–343.

Hull, John and Alan White, 1987, "The Pricing of Options with Stochastic Volatilities", *Journal of Finance*, **42**(2), June, pp 281–300.

Ibbotson, Roger G., and Rex A. Sinquefield, 1976, "Stocks, Bonds, Bills, and Inflation: Year-by-Year Historical Returns (1926-1974)", *Journal of Business*, **49**(1), pp 11–47.

Jackwerth, Jens Carsten and Mark Rubinstein, 1996, "Recovering Probability Distributions from Option Prices", *Journal of Finance*, Vol LI, No 6, pp 1611–1631.

Kuenzi, David E., 2005, "Variance Swaps and Non-Constant Vega", *Risk*, October, pp 79–84.

Kuenzi, David E., and Xu Shi, 2007, "Asset Based Style Analysis for Equity Strategies: The Role of the Volatility Factor", *Journal of Alternative Investments*, Summer 2007, pp 10–23.

Mougeot, Nicolas, 2006, "Smile Trading", BNP Paribas Equities and Derivatives Research, 28 February 2006.

Psychoyios, Dimitris, George Skiadopoulos and Panayotis Alexakis, 2003, "A Review of Stochastic Volatility Processes: Properties and Implications", *Journal of Risk Finance*, Spring, pp 43–59.

Stocks, Bonds, Bills, and Inflation Yearbook 2007, 2007 (Chicago: Morningstar).

Vasicek, Oldrich, 1977, "An Equilibrium Characterization of the Term Structure", *Journal of Financial Economics*, 5, pp 177–88.

Whaley, Robert E., 2002, "Return and Risk of CBOE Buy Write Monthly Index", *Journal of Derivatives*, Winter, pp 35–42.

3

Trend Following as a Long Volatility Strategy

Patrick Kremer; Hari P. Krishnan; Marc Malek[1]

Conquest Capital Group LLC; Heptagon Capital; Conquest Capital Group LLC

There is a widespread belief among investors that trend following futures funds are "long volatility". As equity market volatility (either realised or implied) increases, these managers are thought to do better than usual and provide some protection against global equity market declines. This assumption has often been the primary reason for adding trend followers to an investor's portfolio. In this chapter, we caution the reader against using trend following funds as reliable portfolio insurance. However, we do provide some evidence that returns are positively correlated to large moves in the VIX (the S&P500 implied volatility index). We also explore the connection between the signal horizon of a trend following breakout system and protection against spikes in the VIX over a specific time interval. Finally, we examine whether trend followers can still provide protection if interest rates are stable or rising.

The graph in Figure 3.1 shows how upward movements in the VIX typically correspond to large negative returns for the S&P500 (also known as the SPX). Here we show the average SPX return for all changes in the VIX larger than a given percentile. This is sometimes thought of as a conditional expected return. For example, the 75th percentile return is an equally weighted average of SPX returns during the largest 25% of VIX moves. While it may seem strange to think of the VIX as an independent variable, the graph does show that any strategy that is long volatility tends to provide protection

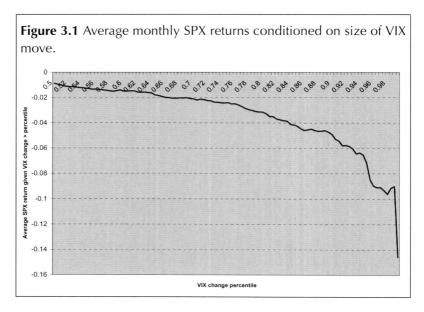

Figure 3.1 Average monthly SPX returns conditioned on size of VIX move.

against large downward moves in the SPX. In this chapter, we want to look at the dependence of trend following returns on changes in the VIX rather than the SPX, since a manager can switch between long and short positions in SPX futures depending on the direction of the trend. Thus, a fund's correlation with the SPX will tend to be unstable. In this chapter we establish cases where a trend following system has relatively stable dependence on changes in the VIX.

Since average SPX returns tend to decline as the VIX moves sharply up, the question now is whether managed futures funds are long volatility. There is some empirical evidence that managed futures have performed well during times of crisis. The time series in Figure 3.2 shows the evolution of the Barclays CTA index from January 1990 to September 2006, assuming a base value of 100.

The index returned 5.92%, 1.79% and 9.56% respectively in August 1998 (the Russian default crisis and LTCM), September 2001 (the terrorist attack in New York) and June–July 2002 (the collapse of Enron, Tyco and others).

The academic literature has largely been influenced by Fung and Hsieh's paper (2001), which adapts Merton's model for a perfect market timer to managed futures funds. The idea is that a perfect timer who can go long or short and trade dynamically has a return profile resembling a lookback straddle. Note that a long straddle

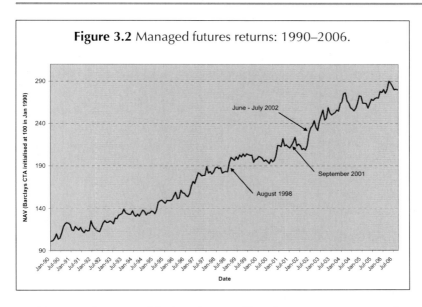

Figure 3.2 Managed futures returns: 1990–2006.

position can be created by buying a call and put on an asset at the same strike, and the lookback feature entitles the option holder to the largest payout of the call and put over the life of the option. While trend followers are not perfect market timers (for example, they enter many losing trades and generally do not participate in the beginning of a trend), Fung and Hsieh argue that the analogy roughly applies. They estimate the returns generated by a rolling lookback straddle position in five broad categories (short rates, bonds, commodities, equity indexes and currencies), then perform a multifactor regression against an equally weighted index of more than 400 funds. As it turns out, their regression gives significant results, with an R-squared close to 50% over a roughly 10 year horizon.

It is tempting to conclude from Fung and Hsieh that trend followers are very likely to profit from rising equity volatility, based on the following line of argument.

- A dynamically traded position in each market is qualitatively and to some degree statistically similar to a long straddle in the market.
- By definition, the buyer of a straddle is long volatility.
- The collection of a large number of long volatility positions in different markets is likely to be long equity market volatility,

as there may be some correlation between changes in volatility across different markets.

However, some investors would contend that these results do not imply that managed futures is a long volatility strategy. Trend followers generally had sizable long bond futures positions during the secular US interest rate decline from 1982 to 2004. This was perhaps the most persistent trend available in the market, based on the policy of central banks. Since bonds tend to rally during flights to quality, it may be somewhat accidental that trend followers were properly positioned against extreme event risk. In a rising or non-trending interest rate environment, they might even be short volatility, that is, negatively correlated to changes in the VIX.

Dobrovolsky and Malek (2006) provide a more detailed argument against the widely held idea that trend following is a long volatility strategy. They make the following intuitive points.

- Managers tend to increase long or short exposure as a trend builds, which corresponds to a long gamma position but really does not have a direct connection to vega.
- As market returns become increasingly choppy, realised volatility can go up without the formation of a trend; this can be the worst scenario for a trend follower as many false signals are generated.
- Movements in the VIX are not necessarily connected with implied volatility changes in other markets, such as commodities.

Their empirical results are based on returns for the Conquest Managed Futures Select (MFS) fund. Conquest MFS is an investable strategy designed to replicate the returns of major trend following indexes using breakout systems across a variety of markets and trading horizons. In the next section, we describe the methodology behind MFS in more detail. For now, we simply summarise the conclusions in Dobrovolsky and Malek. Dobrovolsky and Malek choose five representative markets and calculate the correlation between realised volatility and the performance of different breakout systems in each market. The correlation between the performance of different breakout systems and changes in realised volatility for a given market turns out to be fairly small. More generally, they find that the correlation between changes in the VIX and composite MFS returns is also quite low (roughly 25% from 1990 to 2006, using a daily time step).

However, there is some interesting structure in the data. The correlation between VIX changes and MFS returns is highly dependent on move size. If either VIX changes or MFS returns are more than two standard deviations away from average, the correlation increases from under 10% to over 40% (based on several hundred daily realisations above two standard deviations). This suggests that the VIX–MFS correlation conditioned on large moves of the VIX may also be quite large. An investor who wants to protect against spiking VIX levels, which tend to correspond to extreme market events, may then want to include managed futures in a diversified portfolio. The analysis suggests that sharp moves in the VIX usually coincide with global market trends, while smaller changes may simply imply that equity markets have become choppier. The reader might wonder why it is not more efficient simply to buy a put on the SPX to protect against sharp equity declines. We would argue that, while allocating to a fund that has been statistically long volatility is far less accurate, an investor is not paying a premium for protection and may in fact be positively compensated in the long term.

THE CONQUEST MFS STRATEGY

Since returns from the Conquest MFS programme have been used in the analysis, it is worth describing why these returns are relevant. The MFS programme is designed to replicate the returns of most trend following indexes with complete transparency and minimal backfitting. Positions are initiated based on a simple n-day breakout system that is always in the market, according to the following trading rules.

- If today's high price is higher than the high over the past n days, a buy signal is initiated.
- Conversely, if today's low price is lower than the low over the past n days, a sell signal is initiated.
- The US dollar amount invested in a breakout system is inversely proportional to the volatility of the underlying contract.

- For example, if a 200-day breakout is triggered in markets A and B and A's historical volatility is twice as large as B's, half as much is invested in A as in B.
- Multiple breakout system triggers in a single market are aggregated.
- For example, if a contract is at its five- and seven-day high, twice as much is bought as would be if the contract were only at its five-day high.
- If no new signals are generated, the current long or short position is maintained.

MFS applies these trading rules to roughly 50 markets over 20 time frequencies ranging from five to 200 days. For example, the decision to go long or short corn futures will depend on whether the sum of the breakout signals across different horizons is positive or negative. The sector allocations to stock indexes, bonds, currencies and commodities are then chosen to match roughly some of the larger managed futures funds in the industry.

While no explicit attempt is made to optimise the signal-generation process or the allocation to different markets, the returns of MFS have a high (>80% using simulated returns from 1990 to 2004 and realised returns thereafter) correlation to the major managed futures indexes. Thus, MFS appears to be a statistically robust and intuitive proxy for trend followers. The advantage of using MFS over a peer group index is that breakout systems can be tested over different horizons against changes in volatility. This will then demonstrate which systems have tended to provide the most protection in the past and choose specific managed futures funds accordingly.

EMPIRICAL RESULTS

Here, we show that there is a reasonably strong correlation between large moves in the VIX and MFS returns. We identify large VIX changes over an n-day horizon using a simple two-step process.

- First, we calculate changes in the VIX over an n-day moving window from 1990 to 2006.
- Next, we select all changes that are more than 1 standard deviation in magnitude.

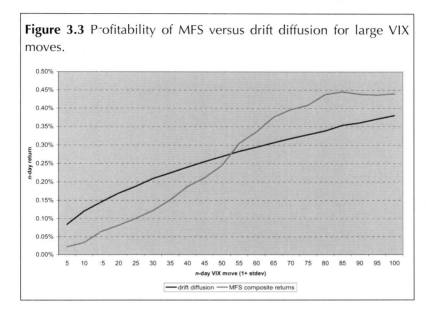

Figure 3.3 Profitability of MFS versus drift diffusion for large VIX moves.

Although we have eliminated large blocks of data, we are still left with a rich sample set of roughly 500 realisations for each n-day horizon. Note that large moves are not symmetrical: a jump in the VIX is more likely to be up than down. More precisely, the skewness of monthly VIX changes from January 1990 to August 2006 was roughly +0.75, compared with 0 for a theoretical normal distribution. Figure 3.3 shows performance of various n-day breakout systems for VIX moves of 1 standard deviation or larger. We specify the length (in trading days, ranging from five to 100) of large changes in the VIX along the x-axis and average performance over the same horizon along the y-axis.

The drift diffusion is generated from a simulated discrete diffusion process over different n-day horizons. We include only returns greater than 1 standard deviation above the mean and take the average over any given horizon. Meanwhile, the MFS composite returns line gives average MFS returns for VIX moves greater than 1 standard deviation. It can be seen that the conditional distribution of returns scales very differently from a normal distribution and that average returns improve most sharply in the 45–55 trading day range. Note that returns are net of estimated trading costs from 1990 to 2004 and realised costs thereafter. Assuming that MFS is a

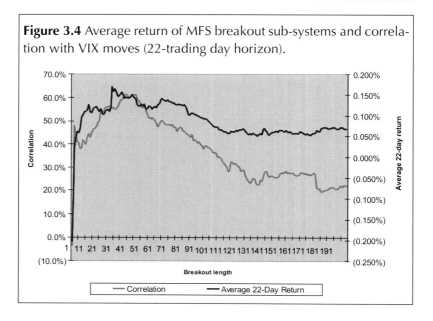

Figure 3.4 Average return of MFS breakout sub-systems and correlation with VIX moves (22-trading day horizon).

reasonable proxy, this implies that a typical trend follower is more likely to provide protection over a quarterly than monthly window.

In Figure 3.3, we looked at how MFS composite returns vary as a function of large VIX changes over different horizons. We now fix the horizon and examine the performance of breakout systems over different frequencies. Figure 3.4 details performance over a 22-day trading horizon, which covers nearly all calendar months. We have chosen a period of roughly one month because fund of funds managers generally provide monthly NAVs and try to minimise variation around a target return over monthly horizons.

While the top line gives the average 22-day MFS return of each breakout system, the bottom line shows the correlation of each system to large VIX changes. The average return rises rapidly, then is reasonably stable for all systems larger than 10 days. However, there is a mild decay as the breakout horizon goes beyond 85 days. This means that an investor's conditional expected return given large changes in the VIX is not very sensitive to the breakout horizon, though short to medium term systems tend to give the best results. The correlation line shows much more sensitivity to the horizon. For breakout horizons beyond 50 days, there is a sustained decline in correlation, from 60% to 20%. For very large

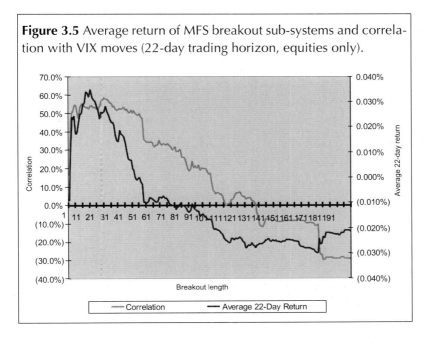

Figure 3.5 Average return of MFS breakout sub-systems and correlation with VIX moves (22-day trading horizon, equities only).

VIX changes, 40–50 day breakout systems tend to provide the best monthly protection.

If we restrict our attention to equity indexes, the decay in returns is much more pronounced. It appears as though the longer-term systems do not have much time to get into a trending market within the 22-day horizon. The correlation of long-term breakout systems to large VIX changes is negative, implying that longer-term equity index trends often reverse when the VIX moves much more than usual. The average holding period across markets for an n-day MFS breakout system from 1990 to 2006 was roughly equal to $1.7 \times n$. This means that, at any point in time, an n-day system had maintained a long or short position for an average of $0.85 \times n$ trading days. On average, a 100-day breakout system would have been triggered 85 days ago, based on trend formation from the previous 100 days.

In Figure 3.6, we analyse conditional performance and correlation for equity and fixed income markets. While the average 22-day return is higher for nearly all breakout systems, the maximum (large VIX change, breakout system return) correlation does not increase. This allows us to reach the following tentative conclusions.

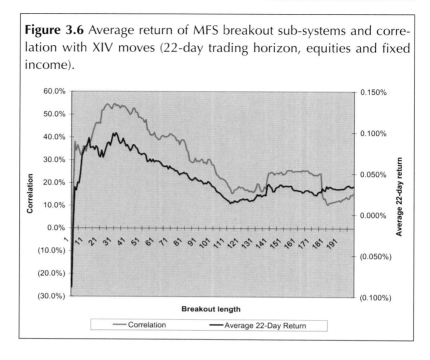

Figure 3.6 Average return of MFS breakout sub-systems and correlation with XIV moves (22-day trading horizon, equities and fixed income).

- Trend following in bond markets clearly boosted realised returns when the VIX moved a lot, but did not necessarily improve diversification around a short volatility portfolio.
- In the absence of rising bond prices, an investor needs to focus on shorter-term breakout systems to protect against a sharp rise in the VIX.

PRACTICAL CONCLUSIONS

An investor should not take the idea of trend following as a put on the equity market too literally. There are times when the instantaneous correlation between global equities and trend followers will be large and positive. This was apparent in 2005 and 2006, as many managers established long positions in equity index futures and commodities. At the same time, commodities have become increasingly equity sensitive based on demand from India and China.

However, there are ways to improve the odds that managed futures will provide protection when it is needed most.

- An active fund of funds manager can try to estimate short-term correlation to the market using position-level data or a consolidated risk report. If the correlation is thought to be high, it may be worth shifting capital from managed futures into short-biased hedge funds or index puts.
- A buy-and-hold investor may want to identify funds that trade over short to medium-term horizons, without too much exposure to bonds. Note that a short-term contrarian fund generally has a very different return profile from a short-term trend follower and may be vulnerable to large changes in the VIX.
- A more sophisticated client can invest in a separate account where the fund manager explicitly avoids trading bull market signals – for example, buying stock index futures. This fund may have a lower risk-adjusted return, as only a subset of signals are traded. However, the constrained portfolio is more likely to provide protection if the VIX rises.

Trend following is one of the few strategies in the investment universe that have low to negative correlations with equities, yet positive expected returns over the risk-free rate. Accordingly, we believe it plays a valuable role in an investor's overall portfolio. However, an investor should be careful to distinguish between statistical protection and insurance, which is much more precise but almost invariably has a negative expected return.

1   Marc Malek and Patrick Kremer are principals and employees of Conquest Capital Group LLC. No fund or investment programme is offered hereby and this article is not intended to and does not constitute investment advice. Hari P. Krishnan wrote this while an executive director at Morgan Stanley. This article was written in his personal capacity and not in his capacity as an employee of Morgan Stanley. Morgan Stanley has not sponsored this article and does not endorse its views. This does not constitute investment, legal, tax or accounting advice of Morgan Stanley.

REFERENCES

Fung, W. and D. A. Hsieh, 2001, "The Risk in Hedge Fund Strategies: Theory and Evidence from Trend Followers", *Review of Financial Studies* **14**, pp 313–341.

Dobrovolsky, S. and M. Malek, 2006, "Volatility Exposure of CTA Programs and Other Hedge Fund Strategies", preprint, August.

4

Basket Volatility and Correlation

Matthias R. Fengler, Kay F. Pilz, Peter Schwendner[1]

Sal. Oppenheim

The simplest equity correlation products are equity index options. In most situations, index options are also the most liquid options on each market. In markets where there are also liquidly traded single stock options, there should be an equilibrium between index options and the corresponding basket of single stock options that is ensured by dispersion traders. This is because prices of index options are determined by the volatility of the underlying basket. The benefit of index options compared with single stock options is the relative cheapness of volatility that is a result of the portfolio effect. Therefore, index options are also a component of many structured products.

Since the early 1990s, the first best-of and worst-of structures emerged on the markets. The high correlation sensitivity of worst-of options made them attractive to investors who were looking for cheap equity exposure and did not believe in a large dispersion among stocks. Besides that, worst-of puts were a popular component of reverse convertibles. Best-of options, in contrast, did not get the same attention due to their high prices.

After the "new economy" bubble had burst in 2001, investors lost confidence in equity stories for individual stocks and were looking for structures that on the one hand provided capital protection and on the other hand offered some participation on a selection of

---

1 This work reflects the views of the authors only and not those of Sal. Oppenheim.

stocks without too much single stock exposure. The development of "Mountain Range" products satisfied this demand with long-term and highly path-dependent structures that, for example, resembled a call on the average performance of a basket from which at certain dates the best or worst performing stocks were removed (see Overhaus 2002; Quessette 2002). Banks usually modelled these structures by local volatility models or Black–Scholes models with skew adjustments.

Since 2004, these structures were combined with Cliquet-like features such as a "momentum bond" paying the worst absolute return of 25 stocks in a basket for each year. These structures bear significant forward volatility risk and thus require a different modelling approach. At this time, a liquid over-the-counter (OTC) market for standard baskets emerged, especially for the so-called "world basket", which consists of Eurostoxx50, Nikkei225 and S&P500, all quantoed into euros. High-dividend yields and the quanto feature make this basket an attractive investment to a euro-based investor. This liquidity gives us later the chance directly to compare implied and historical correlation measures.

As a result of this growing product business, large short correlation exposures in the trading books of the issuing banks were built up, since most products are long correlation. To achieve low option values, widespread baskets with low average correlation were chosen. This led to decreasing margins and increasing demand for a better understanding and hedging of the correlation exposures.

The questions we wish to answer in this chapter concern, first, which pricing models are available and adequate; second, how to estimate the correlation parameters that are put into the models; third, how to account for their estimation risk; and, finally, how to hedge correlation risk.

PRICING MODELS
The Black–Scholes model
We start by reviewing the most popular models for equity correlation products. The models we are discussing in this section are the Black–Scholes, the local volatility, the weighted Monte Carlo and the multivariate-variance gamma model.

The Black–Scholes framework for $i = 1, \ldots, n$ correlated underlyings with constant volatilities is given by

$$dS_i = (r - q_i) S_i(t)\, dt + \sigma_i S_i(t)\, dW_i(t)$$
$$\rho_{ij}\, dt = dW_i(t)\, dW_j(t)$$

where S denotes the stock price, r the interest rate, q the dividend yield, σ the constant volatility parameter, ρ a correlation coefficient and W a Brownian motion. The correlation matrix that can be identified via

$$\rho_{ij} \sigma_i \sigma_j t = \mathrm{cov}\left(\ln\left(\frac{S_i(t)}{S_i(0)}\right), \ln\left(\frac{S_j(t)}{S_j(0)}\right) \right)$$

This means that, in the Black–Scholes framework, the instantaneous correlation matrix can be directly related to the covariance matrix of the realised return paths.

For the pricing of path-dependent options, Monte Carlo methods are usually employed. For options on baskets, a dynamic model for the basket $B_t = \sum_{i=1}^n w_i S_i(t)$ can be constructed by summing up the weighted constituent processes:

$$\frac{dB_t}{B_t} = (r - q_B)\, dt + \frac{\sum_{i=1}^n w_i S_i(t) \sigma_i\, dW_i(t)}{\sum_{i=1}^n w_i S_i(t)} = (r - q_B)\, dt + dZ(t)$$

Here q_B is the basket dividend yield, and w_i denotes the weights of the ith constituent in the basket. We point out that, in this SDE, the stochastic process $Z(t)$ is not a Brownian motion, since it has "stochastic volatility": the sum of the lognormally distributed spot-price processes does not result in a lognormally distributed process, even under the assumption of constant volatilities of the individual processes. Therefore, even a small basket skew will be generated in this model.

In the Black–Scholes framework, since the early 1980s there has been a stream of literature with analytical approximations. For minimum and maximum options, analytical solutions such as Stulz (1982) and Johnson (1987) exist, but the implementation costs are prohibitive for dimensions greater than two. So, for dimensions greater than three, techniques such as quasi-random sequences or FFT are employed. Basket options can be priced with approximation techniques for the basket process. Gentle (1993) approximates the arithmetic payout by the geometric payout, and Huynh (1994) proposes an Edgeworth expansion of the lognormal distributions. Brigo *et al* (2003) suggest moment matching to the lognormal distributions, while Milevsky and Posner (1998) propose moment matching to a reciprocal gamma process. Ju (2002) presents a Taylor expansion of the ratio of the characteristic function of the arithmetic average to that of the lognormal around zero volatility. In a comprehensive study, Krekel *et al* (2004) compare the pricing properties of these approximation techniques. According to them Ju (2002) does the best job. The drawbacks of these Black–Scholes approximation techniques are that they do not work for path-dependent options and account for only a weakly skewed basket volatility surface.

The local volatility model

The natural step from Black–Scholes with constant volatilities would be time-dependent volatilities. For equity options, this does not provide a large improvement, because the term structure of volatilities is much less important than the skew along the strike axis. Therefore, the next step we discuss is local volatility.

The local volatility framework as proposed by Derman and Kani (1994) and Dupire (1994) for n correlated underlyings is given by

$$dS_i/S_i(t) = (r - q_i)\, dt + \sigma_i(S_i(t), t)\, dW_i(t)$$
$$\rho_{ij}\, dt = dW_i(t)\, dW_j(t)$$

where the single-underlying local volatility surfaces $\sigma_i(S_i(t), t)$ are calibrated independently. The most popular method for calibration include Andersen and Brotherton-Ratcliffe (1997) and Lagnado and Osher (1997).

An issue for this model and for all models that mix processes with non-constant volatility is the decorrelation effect that makes the terminal correlation lower than the instantaneous correlation. A consequence is that it is not suitable to put time-series correlation directly into the model. The relationship between terminal and instantaneous correlation reads

$$\rho_{ij}^{terminal}(T)$$
$$= \frac{\int_0^T S_i(u)S_j(u)\sigma_i(S_i(u),u)\sigma_j(S_j(u),u)\rho_{ij}^{instantaneous}\,du}{\sqrt{\int_0^T \{S_i(u)\sigma_i(S_i(u),u)\}^2\,du \int_0^T \{S_j(u)\sigma_j(S_j(u),u)\}^2\,du}}$$
$$< \rho_{ij}^{instantaneous}$$

A reference for this effect with many examples can be found in Rebonato (2004).

For the pricing of high-dimensional path-dependent products with local volatility, Monte Carlo is usually used. For Asian options or discrete barriers, this is not a problem. But there are convergence issues, especially for continuous barriers, so, near the barrier, very small time steps would be needed. One possibility would be to employ Brownian bridge techniques to reduce the time step needed.

We propose a different method for products for which the path dependency of the payout can be separated from the correlated multi-underlying dynamics. An example for this situation is a barrier option on a basket, where the barrier is triggered by a certain value of the basket. The solution is a two-step approach. In the first step, a basket volatility surface is computed via an n-dimensional local volatility model for vanilla options on the basket. This model can easily be evaluated with a Monte Carlo algorithm that uses relatively large time steps. In a second step, the basket volatility surface is plugged into a one-dimensional barrier model for the basket. A further speed-up for computing the basket volatility surface is delivered by control variates. A basket of vanillas is an excellent control for vanillas on baskets. The basket of vanillas can be computed analytically, so the desired basket option price can be computed via the regression

$$V_C = V_{MC} - b(C_{MC} - C_{analytical}), \quad b = \frac{\text{cov}(V_{MC}^i, C_{MC}^i)}{\text{var}(C_{MC}^i)}$$

Figure 4.1 explains this regression equation: as the errors of the Monte Carlo prices C_{MC}^i for the control basket are correlated with the errors of the Monte Carlo prices V_{MC}^i for the basket option, the Monte Carlo error of the basket option price V_C can be reduced by

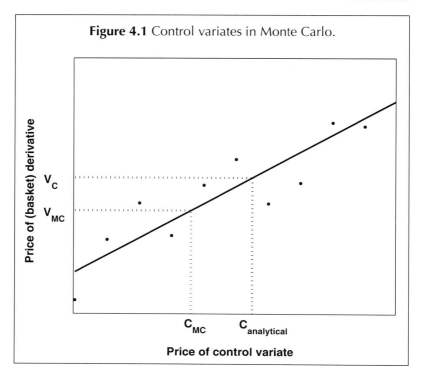

Figure 4.1 Control variates in Monte Carlo.

subtracting the correlated part of the error from the Monte Carlo price V_{MC}.

A standard reference for this general technique is Glasserman (2003).

Computation of greeks in the local volatility model

So far we have discussed how to price path-dependent options on a basket with a local volatility for each constituent in a two-step Monte Carlo approach. The next natural question concerns how to compute greeks for these products, especially the most important of them, the delta.

The first question is a trading decision: which dynamic assumptions do we put on the volatility surface when the spot moves? Should it remain fixed over the strike axis ("sticky strike")? Or should it float with the moneyness, which means that an option with a fixed moneyness is priced on the same volatility, even when the spot moves ("sticky moneyness")? The third possibility would be that we do not make an *ex ante* assumption and that we leave it to the model to decide about the implied volatility dynamics ("sticky implied tree"). The three concepts were outlined by Derman (1999). The recent literature discusses these concepts in detail with hedging simulations (Crépey, 2004; Engelmann et al, 2006) and comes to mixed results depending on the specific simulation setup.

The second question is a numerical one: given a certain stickiness assumption, should we "bump" the whole model to compute the delta as a difference between two prices that were the result of a full-model recalibration, or should we use the chain rule?

The "recalibration" procedure can be described as follows:

$$\text{Basket: } B = \sum_i a_i S_i \quad \text{Basket Option: } C = C(B(S_i))$$

Recalibration Constituent Delta :

$$\Delta_1 = \frac{dC}{dS_1}$$
$$= \frac{C(B(S_1 + dS, S_2, \ldots, S_n), \sigma_B(S_1 + dS, S_2, \ldots, S_n)) - C(B, \sigma_B)}{dS}$$

The chain rule procedure would be first to compute the delta for the basket option and to apply the chain rule to derive the constituent delta. In the same notation, the formulas are:

Chain Rule Constituent Delta:

$$\Delta_1 = \frac{dC}{dS_1} = \frac{\partial C}{\partial S_1} + \frac{\partial C}{\partial \sigma_B} \frac{\partial \sigma_B}{\partial S_1} = a_1 \frac{\partial C}{\partial B} + \frac{\partial C}{\partial \sigma_B} \frac{\partial \sigma_B}{\partial S_1}$$

The recalibration procedure is more exact from an economic standpoint, but the chain rule variant has the benefit of being numerically cheaper, since no second Monte Carlo run is needed.

A different approach from local volatility is weighted Monte Carlo (WMC), (Avellaneda et al, 2001). While standard Monte Carlo attaches the same $1/N$ probability to each path, WMC uses different path probabilities to account for the volatility skew. To determine the probabilities, market prices for a vector of instruments have to be available as a calibration set. Since there are much less observable market instruments than Monte Carlo paths, the calibration problem is underdetermined. Therefore, additional constraints such as the Kullback–Leibler distance of the probability vector to a prior – for example, the uniform probability $1/N$ – have to be employed to receive a stable calibration.

Other pricing approaches

The benefits of WMC are that variance reduction techniques can easily be incorporated and that the method does not suffer from the decorrelation effect we discussed in the section about local volatility. Recent work improves WMC by including synthetic options in the calibration set that prevent arbitrage in the resulting paths (Elices and Giménez, 2006).

Other approaches are copula methods (for instance, Qu, 2005), where, instead of sampling the multidimensional path of the spot vector, the terminal distribution of the correlated constituents is computed by fitting a copula from the marginal distributions that are drawn from the prices of call spreads. Of course, this does not work for path-dependent payouts.

The last approach in our survey is the multivariate variance gamma model suggested by Luciano and Schoutens (2005). This approach differs from the others in that the dependence between the constituents is not achieved by correlating their returns directly, but by imposing a common stochastic time change from a gamma process G_t on them:

$$S_i(t) = S_i(0) \exp((r - q_i)t + \theta_i G_t + \sigma_i W_i(G_t) + \omega_i t)$$

where ω_i is a compensator such that $S(t)$ is a martingale.

G_t has an appealing economic interpretation as a common business time for all underlyings. The size of the jumps for each underlying are independent.

The calibration to market data is possible by Fourier techniques, as the characteristic function of the process can be used to price vanillas efficiently. This model matches single expiries, ie a string of vanilla options along the strike axis with the same maturity, quite well. For an entire volatility surface, extensions like stochastic volatility via stochastic time changes for each underlying are natural extensions.

Figure 4.2 shows three variance gamma processes that are driven by a common time change. This can easily be identified in the graph, as the three paths jump all at the same time, but with different amplitude and possibly in different directions.

HEDGING CORRELATION RISK AND CROSS GAMMAS

In a world where single assets follow a geometric Brownian motion $dS_i = \mu_i S_i\, dt + \sigma_i S_i\, dW_i$ with $dW_i\, dW_j = \rho_{ij}\, dt$ (for $i, j = 1, \ldots, n$)

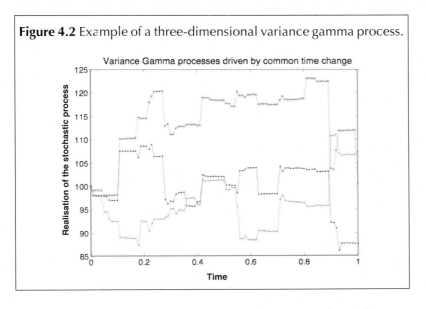

Figure 4.2 Example of a three-dimensional variance gamma process.

the value process V of a multi-asset instrument depending on $S_1, \ldots, S_n$ is determined by

$$dV = \left(\frac{\partial V}{\partial t} + \frac{1}{2}\sum_{i,j=1}^{n} \Gamma_{ij}\sigma_i\sigma_j\rho_{ij}S_iS_j\right)dt + \sum_{i=1}^{n} \Delta_i\, dS_i$$

which follows immediately from Itô's formula. Here the deltas are denoted by $\Delta_i \equiv \partial V/\partial S_i$ and the (cross) gammas by $\Gamma_{ij} \equiv \partial^2 V/\partial S_i \partial S_j$. The relationship indicates that from an infinitesimal point of view the effects of Γ_{ij} can be hedged by a riskless asset, but as soon as the hedge portfolio is adjusted only at discrete times – which is presumably the case for most practical purposes – the gamma exposure has to be covered by appropriate positions in instruments, which depend on the same correlation vehicle as the considered multi-asset instrument. The change of the multi-asset instrument is then given by

$$\delta V \approx \frac{\partial V}{\partial t}\delta t + \sum_{i=1}^{n} \Delta_i \cdot \delta S_i + \frac{1}{2}\sum_{i,j=1}^{n} \Gamma_{ij} \cdot \delta S_i \cdot \delta S_j$$

where the random variable δS_i describes the change in the Spot S_i from time t to $t + \delta t$. Unfortunately, for nearly all multi-asset structures, no liquid hedging instruments exist for all correlations ρ_{ij}.

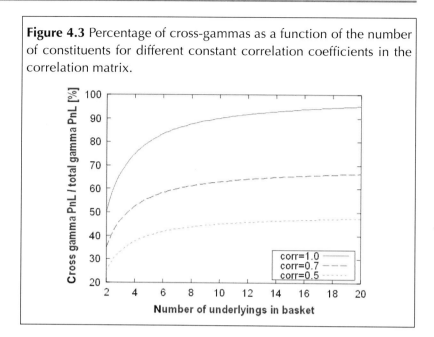

Figure 4.3 Percentage of cross-gammas as a function of the number of constituents for different constant correlation coefficients in the correlation matrix.

For example, an option written on a basket with three stocks S_1, S_2 and S_3 requires for a complete hedge of its gamma exposure instruments with a non-zero gamma (eg, options again), but not written only on the single underlyings S_1, S_2 and S_3, but also on the pairs S_1, S_2 and S_1, S_3 and S_2, S_3. The latter instruments are usually not traded liquidly and therefore the cross-gamma exposure has to be neglected or it has to be reallocated from the cross entries to the diagonal of the matrix $(\Gamma_{ij})_{1 \leq i,j \leq n}$.

Since the number of cross-gamma terms grows quadratically in the number of underlyings in the basket, the idea of neglecting the cross-gamma exposure is definitely not appropriate. Figure 4.3 illustrates the proportion of cross-gamma exposure to the whole gamma exposure for different numbers of underlyings and different levels of correlation (the entries in the gamma matrix are assumed to be constant for all pairs). Especially for highly correlated assets, the cross-gamma PnL dominates the gamma PnL already for fewer than 10 constituents. This leads to the conclusion that cross-gammas cannot be ignored.

This brings us back to the second idea of reallocating the cross-gammas to the diagonal. From the relation above for δV we get

$$\text{Gamma} - PnL(\delta S_1, \ldots, \delta S_n)$$

$$= \frac{1}{2}(\delta S_1 \cdots \delta S_n) \begin{pmatrix} \Gamma_{11} & \cdots & \Gamma_{1n} \\ \vdots & & \vdots \\ \Gamma_{1n} & \cdots & \Gamma_{nn} \end{pmatrix} \begin{pmatrix} \delta S_1 \\ \vdots \\ \delta S_n \end{pmatrix}$$

$$= \frac{1}{2} \sum_{i,j=1}^{n} \Gamma_{ij} \cdot \delta S_i \cdot \delta S_j$$

Writing $\delta S \equiv (\delta S_1, \ldots, \delta S_n)^T$ for the spot vector and $\Gamma \equiv (\Gamma_{ij})_{1 \leq i,j \leq n}$ for the gamma matrix, the aim is to find a matrix

$$\Gamma^* \equiv \begin{pmatrix} \Gamma_{11}^* & 0 & 0 \\ 0 & \ddots & 0 \\ 0 & 0 & \Gamma_{nn}^* \end{pmatrix}$$

such that the gamma PnL will be approximately the same when substituting Γ by Γ^*, ie,

$$\text{Gamma} - PnL(\delta S_1, \ldots, \delta S_n) = \tfrac{1}{2}\delta S^T \cdot \Gamma \cdot \delta S \approx \tfrac{1}{2}\delta S^T \cdot \Gamma^* \cdot \delta S$$

In other words the diagonal gamma exposure will be overhedged by a value that ideally coincides with the cross-gamma exposure. It is clear that a linear combination of random variables $\delta S_i \cdot \delta S_j$ (for $1 \leq i, j \leq n$) cannot be expressed by the subset $\delta S_i \cdot \delta S_i$ (for $1 \leq i \leq n$) and therefore the cross-hedge cannot be perfect for all realisations of spot changes. In the sequel the usual measures, mean and variance, will be used to benchmark different approaches to reallocating the cross-gamma exposure.

The first approach will be motivated heuristically by using the infinitesimal relationship $dS_i \, dS_j = \rho_{ij}\sigma_i\sigma_j S_i S_j \, dt$ to verify that

$$\frac{1}{2} dS^T \cdot \Gamma \cdot dS = \frac{1}{2} \sum_{i=1}^{n} \sum_{l=1}^{n} \Gamma_{il} S_i S_l \sigma_i \sigma_l \rho_{il} \, dt$$

$$= \frac{1}{2} \left\{ \sum_{i=1}^{n} \Gamma_{ii}(dS_i)^2 + \sum_{i=1}^{n} \frac{(dS_i)^2}{S_i \sigma_i} \sum_{\substack{l=1 \\ l \neq i}}^{n} \sigma_l S_l \rho_{il} \Gamma_{il} \right\}$$

which leads to the reallocated diagonal gammas

$$\Gamma_{ii}^* = \Gamma_{ii} + \sum_{\substack{l=1 \\ l \neq i}}^{n} \frac{S_l \sigma_l}{S_i \sigma_i} \rho_{il} \Gamma_{il}$$

Let $D \equiv \delta S^T \cdot (\Gamma - \Gamma^*) \cdot \delta S/2$ denote the error coming from the exercised gamma hedge instead of the perfect gamma hedge. A tedious but straightforward calculation shows that $E[D] = O(\delta t^2)$ and the variance depends on the variances of the products of the random increments $\delta W_i \delta W_j$. The choice of the Γ^* as proposed in the equation above leads – neglecting $O(\delta t^2)$ – to an unbiased hedge error, but smaller variances of D can be achieved by accepting a bias in the cross-gamma hedge. In this case one has to keep in mind that the difference between the basket option value and the hedge increases as time goes by.

Ashraff, Tarczon and Wu (1995) propose a different approach of hedging the cross-gamma position of a basket option by considering a combined hedge of all risk exposures, consisting of a risk-free investment, the underlying stocks and options on these stocks. The procedure described above minimises the variance of the hedge error when requiring the reallocation procedure to be unbiased.

Notice that the mentioned cross-gamma hedges are stable only while all other market parameters are constant over time. Figure 4.4 shows in the top panel a simulated basket price consisting of two equally weighted stocks both starting at 100 at time 0. The bottom panel shows the evolution of the hedge error when only the diagonal gammas are considered (light grey line) and for the cross-gamma hedge proposed above (black line), respectively.

The discussion above shows that cross-gamma hedging in the equity market is neither trivial nor straightforward. It is much easier for liquid FX markets. Main currencies are traded for each other, consider for example

$$S_1 = EUR/USD, \quad S_2 = USD/JPY, \quad S_3 = EUR/JPY = S_1 \cdot S_2$$

Computing the variances of $\log(S_1 \cdot S_2) = \log(S_3)$ leads to $\rho_{12} = (\sigma_3^2 - \sigma_1^2 - \sigma_2^2)/2\sigma_1\sigma_2$, which has a nice geometrical interpretation (Wystup, 2002). The cosine of the USD angle α in Figure 4.5 is the correlation between EUR/USD and USD/JPY, $\cos(\alpha) =$

Figure 4.4 Simulation of a cross gamma hedge. Top: Simulated spot price of a basket with two constituents. Bottom: Evolution of the hedge error when the cross gammas are reallocated to the diagonal gammas (black line) and when only the diagonal gammas are hedged (light grey line), respectively.

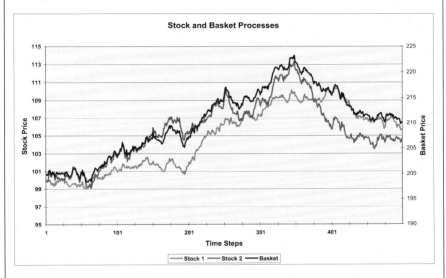

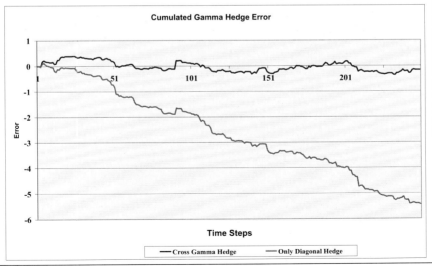

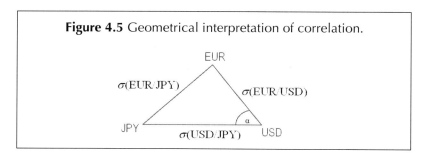

Figure 4.5 Geometrical interpretation of correlation.

$\rho_{EUR/USD,USD/JPY}$. This demonstrates that hedging FX correlation can be replaced by FX vega hedging.

We conclude the discussion of cross-gamma hedges by mentioning the following relationships betweens cross-gammas and vega and correlation risk, respectively, in the Black–Scholes context (Reiß et al, 2002). For a European option C holds

$$\frac{\partial C}{\partial \sigma_i} = S_i T \sum_{j=1}^{n} \rho_{ij} \Gamma_{ij} S_j \sigma_j$$

$$\frac{\partial C}{\partial \rho_{ij}} = \Gamma_{ij} S_i S_j \sigma_i \sigma_j T$$

The next section discusses how to calculate the correlations that then could be used in the cross-gamma hedges of this section.

TIME-SERIES CORRELATION AND IMPLIED CORRELATION

The simplest way to calculate correlation coefficients is to estimate them from time series of log-returns. The main drawback of this procedure is that the log-returns $\{X_i, Y_i\}_{1 \leqslant i \leqslant n}$ need to be independently and identically distributed to apply these estimators. Especially, the condition "identical" is hardly satisfied in practice and a violation leads to a valuation that is biased, when simple statistical estimators are used. Nevertheless the most important correlation estimators will be discussed in the following, because there are no alternative procedures that can be applied in a comparable universal way like these estimators.

Historical estimation of the correlation

Correlations are calculated for a specific time t by using the time-series values of time t and T many preceding times before. In this sense $\bar{X}_t$ denotes the arithmetic mean calculated at time t using the time-series values $\{X_t, X_{t-1}, \ldots, X_{t-T}\}$.

The most popular method is the classical Pearson estimator,

$$\rho_{X,Y}^{Pearson}(t) = \frac{\sum_{i=0}^{T}(X_{t-i} - \bar{X}_t) \cdot (Y_{t-i} - \bar{Y}_t)}{\sqrt{\sum_{i=0}^{T}(X_{t-i} - \bar{X}_t)^2 \sum_{i=0}^{T}(Y_{t-i} - \bar{Y}_t)^2}}$$

A different version of Pearson's estimator weights the particular summands in Pearson's formula exponentially, where smaller weights are assigned to time-series values the more they lie back in time,

$$\rho_{X,Y}^{ExpPearson}(t) = \frac{\sum_{i=0}^{T_0} \lambda^i (X_{t-i} - \bar{X}_t) \cdot (Y_{t-i} - \bar{Y}_t)}{\sqrt{\sum_{i=0}^{T_0} \lambda^i (X_{t-i} - \bar{X}_t)^2 \sum_{i=0}^{T_0} \lambda^i (Y_{t-i} - \bar{Y}_t)^2}}$$

T_0 denotes the start time of the time series and the nicety parameter λ has to be between 0 and 1, where a λ close to 1 generates a slow decay of the weights and a λ close to 0 a fast decay. This method is also used by RiskMetrics.

Instead of the real valued differences of the log-returns to their mean value, ranks can be used to make more robust the correlation estimate. If $R(X_{t-i})$ (for some $0 \leqslant i \leqslant T$) denotes the rank of the log-return X_{t-i} within the set $\{X_t, \ldots, X_{t-T}\}$, the rank correlation due to Spearman is given by

$$\rho_{X,Y}^{Spearman}(t) = \frac{\sum_{i=0}^{T}(R(X_{t-i}) - \overline{R(X)}) \cdot (R(Y_{t-i}) - \overline{R(Y)})}{\sqrt{\sum_{i=0}^{T}(R(X_{t-i}) - \overline{R(X)})^2 \cdot \sum_{i=0}^{T}(R(Y_{t-i}) - \overline{R(Y)})^2}}$$

Note that the mean of the ranks depends only on T, but not on the particular log-returns and not on the time t. In case two log-returns X_{t-i}, X_{t-j} have exactly the same values, the ranks $R(X_{t-i})$ and $R(X_{t-i}) + 1$ of these values will be averaged and this average is then assigned to each log-return as the corresponding rank. Cases with more than two equal log-returns are treated similarly.

A correlation coefficient that incorporates only the signs of the log-returns is Kendall's Tau (Kendall and Gibbons, 1990). For the log-returns $\{X_{t-i}\}_{0\leqslant i\leqslant T}$ and $\{Y_{t-i}\}_{0\leqslant i\leqslant T}$ every combination $((X_{t-i}, Y_{t-i}), (X_{t-j}, Y_{t-j}))$ is considered regarding the sign of this product. More precisely, for all $0 \leqslant i < j \leqslant T$ let

- c denote the number of concordant cases, ie, $(X_{t-i} - X_{t-j}) \cdot (Y_{t-i} - Y_{t-j}) > 0$,
- d denote the number of discordant cases, ie, $(X_{t-i} - X_{t-j}) \cdot (Y_{t-i} - Y_{t-j}) < 0$,
- b_X denote the number of X ties, ie, $X_{t-i} = X_{t-j}$ and
- b_Y denote the number of Y ties, ie, $Y_{t-i} = Y_{t-j}$

(points with double ties should be excluded before). A sampled version of Kendall's Tau is defined by

$$\tau = \frac{c - d}{\sqrt{c + d + b_X} \cdot \sqrt{c + d + b_Y}}$$

and it estimates the difference between the probability of concordance and the probability of discordance. Lindskog (2000) proposes the linearisation

$$\rho_{X,Y}^{Kendall} = \sin\left(\frac{\pi}{2}\tau\right)$$

if the random variables (X, Y) are drawn from a bivariate elliptical distribution.

The plots in Figure 4.6 show the four discussed correlation coefficients for log-returns of "Deutsche Bank" and "Commerzbank". In the top figure the parameters $T = 50$ and $\lambda = 0.96$ are used, in the bottom figure $T = 100$ and $\lambda = 0.98$.

Implied estimation of the correlation

As indicated above, it is more appropriate to use implied correlations from market prices. The log-returns of a basket $B(t) = \sum_{i=1}^{n} a_i S_i(t)$ with constituents driven by the Black–Scholes SDE as given in the previous section have the variance

$$\sigma_{Basket}^2 \equiv \text{Var}\left(\frac{dB}{B}\right) = \sum_{i=1}^{n} w_i^2 \sigma_i^2 + 2 \sum_{j=1, i<j}^{n} w_i w_j \sigma_i \sigma_j \rho_{ij}$$

where w_i is the relative weight of the ith stock and is given by

$$w_i = \frac{a_i S_i(t)}{\sum_{j=1}^{n} a_j S_j(t)}$$

Note that the relative weights w_i are stochastic processes themselves, while the absolute weights a_i are constant over time. Obviously, one cannot solve the variance equation above for all ρ_{ij}.

Figure 4.6 Estimated correlations of the log-returns of Deutsche Bank and Commerzbank (the methods of Pearson, Pearson with exponential weights, Spearman and Kendall are used with different time horizons).

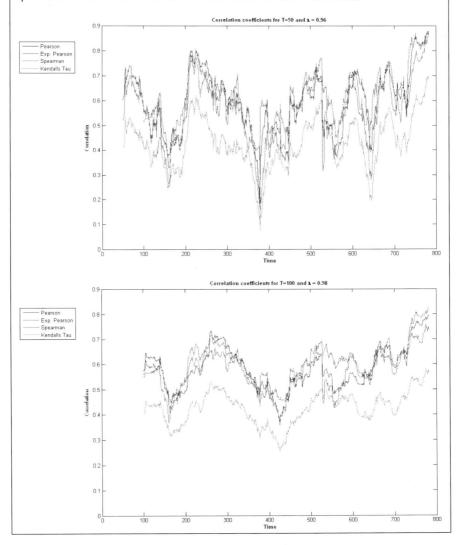

One possibility to overcome this problem is to compute an average correlation ρ, which replaces the pairs correlation coefficients in the correlation matrix. This means the full correlation matrix

$$\begin{bmatrix} 1 & \rho_{12} & \cdots & \rho_{1n} \\ \rho_{12} & 1 & \cdots & \rho_{2n} \\ \vdots & \vdots & \ddots & \vdots \\ \rho_{1n} & \rho_{2n} & \cdots & 1 \end{bmatrix} \text{ is replaced by } \begin{bmatrix} 1 & \rho & \cdots & \rho \\ \rho & 1 & \cdots & \rho \\ \vdots & \vdots & \ddots & \vdots \\ \rho & \rho & \cdots & 1 \end{bmatrix}$$

such that the basket variance σ_{Basket}^2 does not change. The value for ρ is calculated by setting ρ_{ij} constant in the variance equation above,

$$\rho = \frac{\sigma_{Basket}^2 - \sum_{i=1}^n w_i^2 \sigma_i^2}{2 \sum_{j=1, i<j}^n w_i w_j \sigma_i \sigma_j} = \frac{\sum_{j=1, i<j}^n w_i w_j \sigma_i \sigma_j \rho_{ij}}{\sum_{j=1, i<j}^n w_i w_j \sigma_i \sigma_j}$$

There are two main advantages of using the implied average correlation matrix instead of the historical-pairs correlation matrix estimated from time series. First, the equicorrelation matrix leads to the same basket variance as does the unknown full-correlation matrix. Second, it is much easier to establish positive definiteness, because the equicorrelation matrix is positive definite if $-(1/(n-1)) < \rho < 1$ (see for example Mardia *et al*, 1979), whereas for large-correlation matrixes the initial estimate is not positive-definite and it is usually hard to find a legitimate method of adaptation.

A skew structure $\rho(K, T)$ for the implied correlation can be mapped from the implied volatility surface by using strike and time-dependent volatilities $\sigma_i(K, T)$ in the formula for ρ above. Figure 4.7 shows the implied-correlation surface of the DAX index calculated from liquid Eurex options.

Vehicles for trading equity correlation

The following list summarises the most important instruments for trading equity correlation.

- *Index options versus single stock options*: As demonstrated above, a long basket option induces a correlation long position.
- *Index variance swaps versus stock variance swaps*: If the payout of a variance swap is given by

$$\text{Notional}_{Variance} \times (\sigma_{realised}^2 - K^2)$$
$$= \text{Notional}_{Vega} \times \left(\frac{\sigma_{realised}^2 - K^2}{2K} \right)$$

Figure 4.7 Implied correlation surface for the DAX Basket calculated from implied volatility of DAX Options and the implied volatilities from the DAX constituent options.

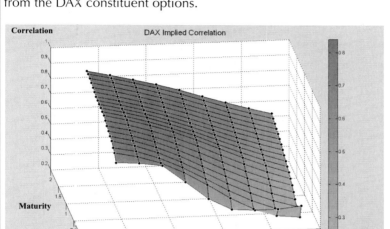

the weights for the portfolio of single-variance swaps are $a_i = \rho w_i K_i / K$.

- *Correlation swaps*: Payout is the realised average pair correlation Notional $\times (\rho_{realised} - K)$ with

$$\rho_{realised} = \frac{2}{n(n-1)} \sum_{j=1, i<j}^{n} \rho_{ij}$$

Interestingly, from the OTC market one can observe that correlation swaps trade below implied correlation extracted from options or variance swaps, which is consistent with the "toy model" in Bossu (2007). There, for the variances, the driving processes

$$d\,\text{var}_{Index} = r \cdot \text{var}_{Index}\,dt + 2\omega_{Index}\frac{T-t}{T}\,\text{var}_{Index}\,dW_{Index}$$
$$d\,\text{var}_i = r \cdot \text{var}_i\,dt + 2\omega_i\frac{T-t}{T}\,\text{var}_i\,dW_i \quad (1 \leqslant i \leqslant n)$$

are assumed, which yield for the fair value of the correlation swap at time $t = 0$ the approximation $V_0 \approx \exp(-rT)\rho$.

MEASURING CORRELATION UNCERTAINTY: BOOTSTRAPPING CORRELATION MATRIXES

An important input factor to multi-asset pricing models is the correlation matrix measuring the dependence between the constituents of the basket. Given the lack of data, correlation matrixes are often estimated from historical price observations. This entails two important issues. First, in a strict sense, what we seek is correlation valid over the future rather than a historical one. Second, even if we are happy to live with a historical estimate, we must be aware that this estimate contains an estimation error. A natural question, therefore, is how good the estimate of the correlation matrix actually is and how this error translates into the basket option prices that are to be computed. In this section we outline a procedure that is based on bootstrap techniques, and it aims to answer that question. The idea is to generate distributions of the correlation matrix that are mapped into a price distribution of the multi-asset option prices. It is developed by Fengler and Schwendner (2004) and sketched in this section.

The bootstrap: idea and methodology

The bootstrap is a technique for estimating the sampling distribution of an estimator or a test statistic by resampling from the sample. It can be employed when the distribution is known to exist but is difficult to compute. The bootstrap was first devised by Efron (1979). Comprehensive treatments can be found in the monographs by Hall (1992) and Mammen (1992). Simply stated, the key theorem of the bootstrap says that the distribution of a consistent estimator for some (unknown) population value can be approximated by the sampling distribution of the estimate. Therefore an approximate confidence interval with significance level of $(1-\alpha)$ can be based on the $(1-\alpha)$-quantiles of a resampling distribution of the estimator.

The technique works for identically and independently distributed random variables as follows. Suppose we have a sample of n return vectors of n underlying assets which we denote by χ. We like to estimate the correlation matrix ρ_{ij}.

Step 1. Generate a resample χ^* from χ as an unordered collection of n elements drawn randomly and with replacement from χ such that the probability that the drawn element is equal to any of

Figure 4.8 Illustration of the bootstrap procedure. The top line shows the original sample with blocks of three subsequent returns. The lower line is the bootstrap sample, which consists of blocks randomly drawn from the original sample. By drawing with replacement, the bootstrap sample contains iterations or does not include some of the original blocks at all.

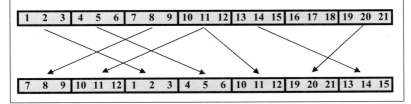

the elements in the sample is n^{-1}. The resample χ^* will have repeats or may not include some elements at all.

Step 2. Compute ρ^* from χ^*.

Step 3. Repeat Steps 1 and 2 for many times M.

Step 4. Approximate the sampling distribution by the empirical distribution of the pseudo-random variables ρ^* based on the M runs of Steps 1 and 2.

For dependent data, the bootstrap should be carried out in a way that preserves the dependence structure present in the data. This can be achieved by dividing the data into non-overlapping blocks with equal block length (also called *block bootstrap*; an up-to-date review on the bootstrap with dependent data is found in Härdle, Horowitz, and Kreiss, 2003). Instead of drawing single values from χ, one draws the blocks with replacement, and computes the correlation from this pseudo-time series. This procedure is illustrated in Figure 4.8. It should be noted that, in general, there is also a bootstrap theory based on drawing without replacement. In case of correlation, however, we must draw with replacement, as otherwise the bootstrap distribution is singular: we would always obtain the same correlation matrix. The choice of the block length is delicate, as it intimately depends on the underlying data-generating process. In the literature optimal block lengths vary between $n^{1/5}$ to $n^{1/3}$, depending on the particulars of the data-generating process.

From the block bootstrap one obtains a sampling distribution of correlation matrixes, from which we compute multi-asset option prices. This yields a distribution of option prices. From this option price distribution we can deduce the impact of uncertainty in the correlation estimate.

Case study: basket, min and max options
Fengler and Schwendner (2004) apply the block bootstrap to equity-correlation matrixes and price calls on the basket, and calls on the maximum and the minimum of the basket. The pricing model is a Black–Scholes framework with a constant correlation matrix as described in the section 'Time-series correlations and implied correlation', above. The block length is chosen to be three days; the number of simulation is $M = 20,000$. The analysis uses time series of six blue-chip companies from the German DAX index: Allianz (ALV), BMW, Commerzbank (CBK), Deutsche Bank (DBK), DaimlerChrysler (DCX) and Deutsche Telekom (DTE). The data is taken from 1999 and 2002, which is to say from two fundamentally different market regimes.

These market regimes are reflected in the accuracy of the estimated correlation matrixes. In the 1999 market, the bullish market, correlations are moderate; however, their sampling distribution is relatively large (see Figure 4.9). This will lead to large pricing errors. In 2002, the bearish market, correlations are very high, in particular within sectors such as banking, but correlations can be estimated at a much better accuracy (see Figure 4.10).

In Figure 4.11 the resulting price distributions are displayed. The vertical lines denote the 5% and the 95% quantiles of the distributions, which correspond to a 90% confidence interval around the fair price from a trader's point of view. This is because a trader faces only a one-tailed risk for the bid and ask price. The top panel shows the call on the basket comprising all six assets. Since diversification is smaller in a low-correlation environment, the 1999 basket option is cheaper. As expected, the price distribution of the 1999 data is wider than for the 2002 case. Note, however, that compared with the fair price, the bid–ask spread covering the risk from correlation uncertainty must be up to 3%.

The middle panel of Figure 4.11 shows the maximum options on the six assets. In the maximum option the long position is short in correlation, hence the prices in 1999 are higher than those in 2002. Bid–ask spreads are approximately the same size in both scenarios.

BASKET VOLATILITY AND CORRELATION

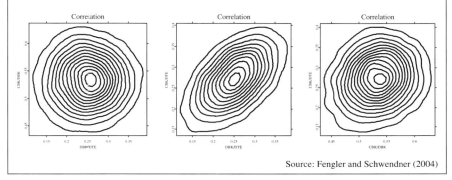

Figure 4.9 1999 data: contour plots. Bivariate contour plots of the (marginal) bootstrap distributions of estimated correlations in the three-asset case obtained via a kernel-smoothing procedure are shown. We thank Institutional Investor, Inc. Journals Group, for the permission for reproduction.

Source: Fengler and Schwendner (2004)

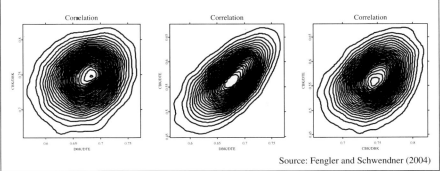

Figure 4.10 2002 data: contour plots. Bivariate contour plots of the (marginal) bootstrap distributions of estimated correlations in the three-asset case obtained via a kernel-smoothing procedure are shown. We thank Institutional Investor, Inc. Journals Group, for the permission for reproduction.

Source: Fengler and Schwendner (2004)

Figure 4.11 Price densities. Price densities obtained from a kernel smoothing procedure. Fair price denoted by the black dot. Bid–ask spreads, quoted as the 5% and the 95% interval, indicated by vertical lines. Prices obtained by 50,000 Monte Carlo simulations. Figure reproduced by courtesy of Institutional Investor, Inc. Journals Group.

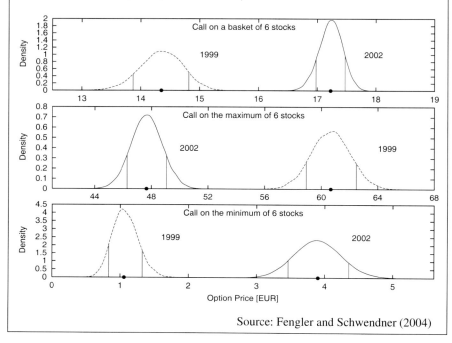

Source: Fengler and Schwendner (2004)

This can be explained by observing that the higher precision of the estimated correlations, which diminishes the spread, is dominated by the fact that the correlation vega increases as correlations rise. The lower panel displays the minimum option. The high correlation in 2002 reduces dispersion and volatility of the basket and results in higher prices for 2002 than for 1999. The higher precision of the correlation estimates leads to smaller bid–ask spreads relative to the 2002 low-correlation scenario. Note, however, that the bid–ask spreads required are extremely large, up to 30%.

ESTIMATION OF LARGE COVARIANCE MATRIXES – RANDOM MATRIX THEORY

The bootstrap approach shows that correlation estimates can contain noise. But the case study is on a six-asset case only. How does the situation alter if we look at even larger correlation or covariance matrixes? As the number of constituents of a basket increases, the noise is likely to increase too. How does this affect the estimation of correlation matrixes? A field of research developed in statistical physics, the random matrix theory (RMT), gives deeper theoretical insights on these issues.

Marcenko–Pastur law

By the classical law of large numbers, the covariance estimator tends to the population value, as the number of observations T tends to infinity, while the number of assets n is fixed, provided the structure in the covariance matrix is not time-dependent or stochastic. However, if the number of the constituents in a basket is large or the number of observations is small this result does no longer hold. An important result of RMT states that the covariance estimator may even diverge!

Consider the sample covariance matrix of stock returns of n assets: each return is observed over T days. Suppose that the returns are iid standard normally distributed. In this case the population covariance matrix is the unit matrix, ie, its eigenvalues are known to be equal to one. However, with T and n tending to infinity, the eigenvalues of the sample covariance matrix behave stochastically in the limit. More precisely, as $T \to \infty$, $n \to \infty$, and $Q = T/n > 1$, the probability density function $f(\lambda)$ of the eigenvalues λ of the covariance matrix is given by

$$f(\lambda) = \frac{Q}{2\pi} \frac{\sqrt{(\lambda_+ - \lambda)(\lambda - \lambda_-)}}{\lambda}$$

where $\lambda_\pm = 1 + 1/Q \pm 2\sqrt{1/Q}$ are the maximum and the minimum eigenvalues. This distribution is known as the Marcenko–Pastur law (Bai, 1999). In Figure 4.12 we display the density function for some Q.

Although asymptotic by nature, the Marcenko–Pastur law is a valuable result, since it allows us to gauge the noise that is inherent to large covariance matrixes. The smaller Q, ie, the smaller the ratio of time observations to the cross-section, the bigger the variance of this distribution. In finance, one typically has small Qs: for instance, for a basket with 100 constituents and two years of data, Q would be around five. This implies that, under the assumptions of the

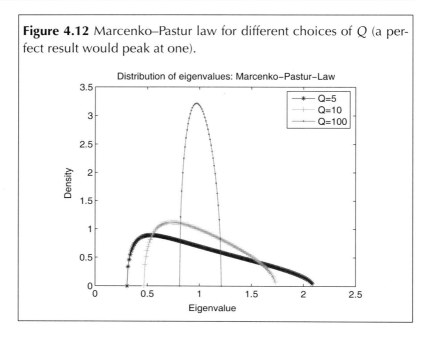

Figure 4.12 Marcenko–Pastur law for different choices of Q (a perfect result would peak at one).

RMT, the eigenvalues will be spread somewhere in the interval $[\lambda_-, \lambda_+] = [0.306; 2.094]$. This implies significant distortions of the estimated entries in the covariance matrix.

To turn to a more practical example, we study the case of estimating the covariance matrix of a large index, the DAX, which comprises 30 German blue-chips. We suppose the availability of two years' data, ie, $T = 500$ and $Q = 16.7$, which implies $[\lambda_-, \lambda_+] = [0.57; 1.55]$ under the assumption of the RMT. In Figure 4.13, we present simulation results for this case. In a single draw, we generate 500 iid standard normal random variables, and compute the covariance matrix and its eigenvalues. As predicted by the RMT, the histogram in Figure 4.13 shows that the 30 eigenvalues assume any value in the interval $[0.57; 1.55]$, instead of being concentrated at one. We compare this figure with a histogram computed in exactly the same way but from the correlation matrix of the 30 DAX constituents. In Figure 4.14 the histogram of all the 30 eigenvalues is given. They are concentrated in the neighbourhood of one, with one but significant exception visible in the neighbourhood of 12. In portfolio optimisation this value is usually identified with the "market", that is to say a common factor driving all constituents of

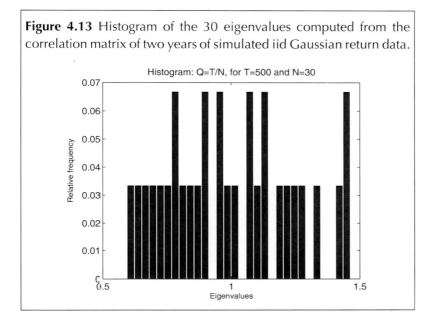

Figure 4.13 Histogram of the 30 eigenvalues computed from the correlation matrix of two years of simulated iid Gaussian return data.

the market. However, zooming into the remaining 29 eigenvalues (Figure 4.15), we see that this plot resembles very much the earlier plot (Figure 4.13), which comes from pure white noise. Studies of this type were suggested by Laloux *et al* (2000). They conclude that large correlation matrixes estimated from equity return data contain a large degree of randomness, which implies that many applications in finance such as portfolio optimisation, VaR computations, and option pricing might fail (see also Plerou *et al*, 2002).

This view has been challenged by Pafka and Kondor (2003). They demonstrate that a portfolio optimisation in the spirit of Markowitz might generate irrational weights. However, once the weights are fixed, the noise appears to cancel out. Thus, there is only a need to stabilise the determination of the weights, rather than to question the results of portfolio optimisation as such. Therefore, one possible way of responding to this problem is the build structured covariance matrixes – for example, built out of submatrixes belonging to industry sectors (see Plerou *et al*, 2002). Another choice, typically pursued in option pricing, is to construct the equicorrelation matrixes that are built out of one single entry ρ only (see the section 'Time-series correlation and implied correlation' above), ie, they

Figure 4.14 Histogram of the 30 eigenvalues computed from the correlation matrix of two years of DAX return data.

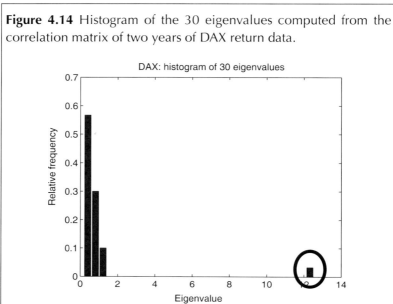

Figure 4.15 Histogram of the 29 smallest eigenvalues computed from the correlation matrix of two years of DAX return data (this plot zooms into the left corner of Figure 4.13).

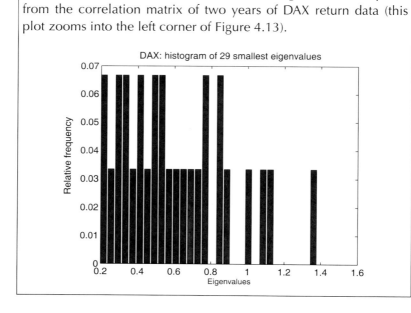

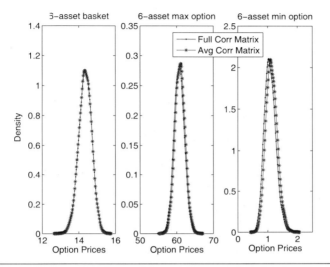

Figure 4.16 Price distributions of the 1999 data obtained for the three option type cases using the equicorrelation approach and the full correlation matrix.

have the structure

$$\bar{\rho} = \begin{pmatrix} 1 & \rho & \rho \\ \rho & 1 & \rho \\ \rho & \rho & 1 \end{pmatrix}$$

A convenient side effect of this approach is that the matrix is positive-definite, if $-(1/(n-1)) < \rho < 1$. Finally, as a compromise between these two orthogonal approaches, Ledoit and Wolf (2003) suggest generating a covariance or correlation matrix as a result of shrinking between both limiting cases: they obtain a new correlation matrix via

$$\bar{\rho}_{shrink} = \delta\bar{\rho} + (1-\delta)\bar{\rho}_{full}$$

where $0 < \delta < 1$ is a suitably chosen shrinkage constant.

A natural question is whether this equicorrelation approach can do any better in option pricing. To study this problem we reiterate the bootstrap analysis on the three different option types using the full correlation matrix and the equicorrelation matrix with the average correlation as a single entry (see the section 'Time-series correlation and implied correlation' above for the construction).

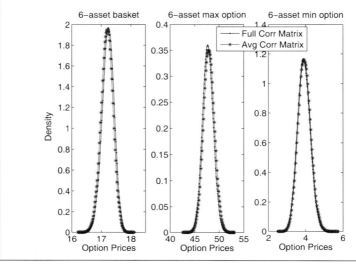

Figure 4.17 Price distributions of the 2002 data obtained for the three option type cases using the equicorrelation approach and the full correlation matrix.

The resulting price distributions are displayed in Figures 4.16 and 4.17. As we can see, the two price distributions almost coincide. There are only small but rather negligible shifts in location. We therefore conclude that noise in option pricing cannot be reduced by using the equicorrelation approach. Since option pricing is about computing averages, the noise cancels out. This corresponds to the results of Pafka and Kondor (2003). However, future research must explore, whether this result holds for much larger baskets, and, more importantly, whether it extends to more sophisticated pricing problems, such as barrier options on best-off and worst-off baskets.

Case study: options on the world basket

We conclude this chapter with a case study of the world basket, which consists of the three indexes, EuroStoxx50, Nikkei225 and S&P500, equally weighted and quantoed to the euro. This basket is ideal for an analysis of implied versus historical correlation, because there is a liquid OTC market for vanilla options on the quanto basket, a liquid OTC market for call swaps quanto euro (that is, the difference between a quanto call on a basket of two

Figure 4.18 Bootstrapped distributions for different fixings of the euro–yen exchange rate.

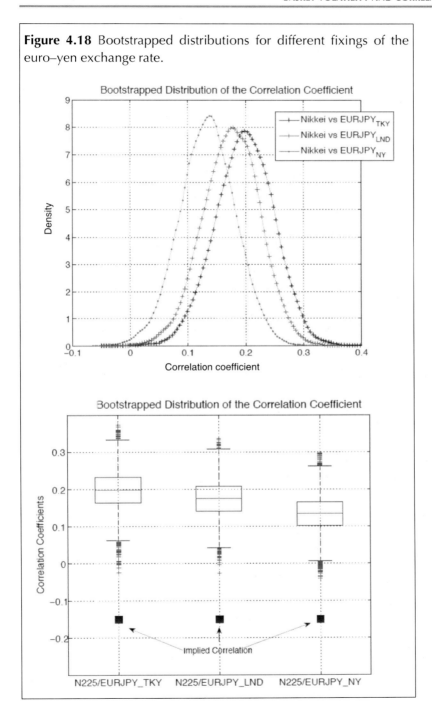

Table 4.1

Implied correlation	Euro Stoxx50	S&P500	Nikkei225
EuroStoxx50	1	84%	75%
S&P500	84%	1	58%
Nikkei225	75%	58%	1

indexes and one quanto call on each index respectively) and also a liquid OTC market for all quanto forwards. Now we can compute all implied FX–index correlations from the quanto forwards and all index–index correlations from the call swaps.

First we compute the implied quanto correlation euro–yen versus Nikkei225 from the Nikkei225 quanto euro forwards. Because of $F = S \exp((r_f - q - \sigma_S \sigma_{FX} \rho_{S,FX}) \cdot T)$, these forwards imply a short position in correlation. Figure 4.18 demonstrates the relevance of the fixing (Tokyo, London or New York) used for calculation. The top part of the figure shows the bootstrapped distributions of the correlation coefficient from historical time series and the bottom part shows box plots for these distributions in relation to the implied correlations. The implied correlation is in all three cases far below the 25% quantile of historical correlation. One reason for this difference may be the negative interest rate difference between yen and euro yield curves. This leads to an attractive pricing of those structured products, which contain a short position of the Nikkei225 quanto euro. Hedging activities by banks then induce a high demand for Nikkei225 quanto euro forwards, which pushes the implied correlation to a low value.

Next, the implied index–index correlations calculated from OTC market quotes are compared to various time-series correlations. The implied correlations given in Table 4.1 were computed on 25 October, 2005.

The time series correlations in Table 4.2 were calculated for a moving window of 250 and 500 days and decay parameters $\lambda = 0.97$, $\lambda = 0.99$ respectively.

Figure 4.19 shows again the bootstrapped distributions of the time series correlation coefficients in the top part and a box plot of these values compared with the implied correlation in the bottom part.

Table 4.2

Pairs	Implied correlation	Pearson		Exponential Pearson		Spearman Rank	
		250 days	500 days	$\lambda = 0.97$	$\lambda = 0.99$	250 days	500 days
S&P/EuroStoxx	84%	38%	42%	37%	31%	40%	42%
Nikkei/EuroStoxx	75%	37%	40%	40%	39%	35%	39%
S&P/Nikkei	58%	4%	13%	0%	−14%	8%	13%

Figure 4.19 Bootstrapped distributions for different stock indexes.

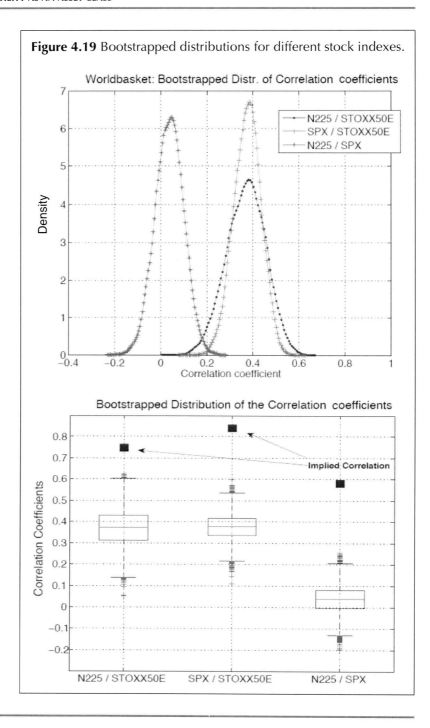

Again, we can see a mismatch between implied and historical correlations, more precisely:

- Time-series estimators give a broad range of results, depending on the method used and the number of days incorporated in the calculation or the choice of the decay parameter λ.
- All time-series estimators yield results that are far below the implied correlation.
- Even the upper tails of the bootstrap distribution are below the implied correlation.

One explanation for this difference between implied and historical correlation could be a high demand for structured products written on the world basket. Since most of these products are delta long, vega long and correlation long, the issuing institutions hedge their short-correlation exposure on the OTC market and increase thereby the implied correlations. Another plausible explanation would be the inadequacy of the model used to compute implied correlations, because this model does not account for a correlation skew: a correlation that depends on the time and spot level. This means that further research has to be performed to find a suitable model that eliminates this deficiency.

REFERENCES

Andersen, L. B. G. and R. Brotherton-Ratcliffe, 1997, "The Equity Option Volatility Smile: An Implicit Finite-difference Approach", *Journal of Computational Finance*, **1**(2), pp 5–37.

Ashraff, J., J. Tarczon and W. Q. Wu, 1995, "Safe Crossing", *Risk*, **8**(7), pp 56–57.

Avellaneda, M., *et al*, 2001, "Weighted Monte Carlo: A New Technique for Calibrating Asset-pricing Models", *International Journal of Theoretical and Applied Finance*, **4**(1), pp 91–119.

Bai, Z. D., 1999, "Methodologies in Spectral Analysis of Large Dimensional Random Matrices, A Review", *Statistica Sinica*, **9**, pp 611–677.

Bossu, S., 2007, "A New Approach for Modelling and Pricing Correlation Swaps", Working Paper, Dresdner Kleinwort.

Brigo, D., *et al*, 2003, "Approximated Moment-matching Dynamics for Basket-options Pricing", *Quantitative Finance*, **4**(1), pp 1–16.

Crépey, S., 2004, "Delta-hedging Vega Risk?", *Quantitative Finance*, **4**(5), pp 559–579.

Derman, E., 1999. "Regimes of Volatility", *Risk*, **12**(4), pp 55–59.

Derman, E. and I. Kani, 1994, "Riding on a Smile", *Risk*, **7**(2), pp 32–39.

Dupire, B., 1994, "Pricing with a Smile", *Risk*, **7**(1), pp 18–20.

Efron, B., 1979, "Bootstrap Methods: Another Look at the Jackknife", *Annals of Statistics*, **7**, pp 1–26.

Elices, A. and E. Giménez, 2006, "Weighted Monte Carlo", *Risk*, **19**(5), pp 78–83.

Engelmann, B., M. R. Fengler and P. Schwendner, 2006, "Better than its Reputation: An Empirical Hedging Analysis of the Local Volatility Model for Barrier Options", Working Paper.

Engelmann, B. and P. Schwendner, 1998, "The pricing of multi-asset options using a Fourier grid method", *Journal of Computational Finance*, **1**(4), pp 63–72.

Fengler, M. R., 2005, "Semiparametric Modeling of Implied Volatility", in *Lecture Notes in Finance* (Berlin, Heidelberg: Springer).

Fengler, M. R. and P. Schwendner, 2004, "Quoting multiasset equity options in the presence of errors from estimating correlations", *Journal of Derivatives* **11**(4), pp 43–54.

Gentle, D., 1993, "Basket Weaving", *Risk*, **6**(6), p 15.

Glasserman, P., 2003, *Monte Carlo Methods in Financial Engineering* (New York: Springer).

Hall, P., 1992, *"The Bootstrap and the Edgeworth Expansion"* (Berlin, Heidelberg: Springer).

Härdle, W., J. Horowitz and J.-P. Kreiss, 2003, "Bootstrap Methods for Time Series", *International Statistical Review*, **71**(2), pp 435–459.

Huynh, C. B., 1994, "Back to Baskets", *Risk*, **7**(5), pp 59–61.

Johnson, H., 1987, "Options on the Maximum or the Minimum of Several Assets", *Journal of Financial and Quantitative Analysis*, **22**(3), pp 277–283.

Ju, E., 2002, "Pricing Asian and Basket Options via Taylor Expansion", *Journal of Computational Finance*, **5**(3), pp 79–103.

Kendall, M. and J. D. Gibbons, 1990, *"Rank Correlation Methods"* (London: Edward Arnold).

Krekel, M., *et al*, 2004, "An Analysis of Pricing Methods for Basket Options", *Wilmott Magazine* (May).

Lagnado, R. and S. Osher, 1997, "A Technique for Calibrating Derivative Security Pricing Models: Numerical Solution of an Inverse Problem", *Journal of Computational Finance*, **1**(1), pp 13–25.

Laloux, L., *et al.* 2000, "Random Matrix Theory and Financial Correlations", *International Journal of Theoretical and Applied Finance*, **3**(3), pp 391–397.

Ledoit, O., and M. Wolf, 2003, "Improved Estimation of the Covariance Matrix of Stock Returns with an Application to Portfolio Selection", *Journal of Empirical Finance*, **10**(5), pp 603–621.

Lindskog, F., 2000, "Linear correlation estimation", Preprint, ETH Zürich.

Luciano, E., and W. Schoutens, 2005, "A Multivariate Jump-driven Financial Asset Model", ICER Working Paper, June.

Mammen, E., 1992, "When Does Bootstrap Work? Asymptotic Results and Simulations, Number 77", in *Lecture Notes in Statistics* (Berlin, Heidelberg: Springer).

Mardia, K. V., J. T. Kent and J. M. Bibby, 1979, *"Multivariate Analysis"* (London, New York, Toronto: Academic Press).

Milevsky, M. A. and S. E. Posner, 1998, "A closed-form approximation for valuing basket options", *Journal of Derivatives*, **4**(5), pp 54–61.

Overhaus, M., 2002, "Himalaya Options", *Risk*, **15**(3), pp 101–104.

Pafka, S. and I. Kondor, 2003, "Noisy Covariance Matrices and Portfolio Optimization II", *Physica A*, **319**, pp 487–494.

Plerou, V., *et al.* 2002, "Random Matrix Approach to Cross Correlations in Financial Data", *Physical Review E*, **65**, pp 1–18.

Qu, D., 2005, "Pricing Basket Options with Skew", *Wilmott Magazine*, July, pp 58–64.

Quessette, R., 2002, "New Products, New Risks", *Risk*, **15**(3), pp 97–100.

Rebonato, R., 2004, *Volatility and Correlation*, Second Edition (Chichester: John Wiley & Son).

Reiß, O. and U. Wystup, 2002, "Efficient Computation of Option Price Sensitivities using Homogeneity and Other Tricks", in J. Hakala and U. Wystup (eds), *Foreign Exchange Risk* (London: Risk Books), pp 127–142.

Stulz, R., 1982, "Options on the Minimum or the Maximum of Two Risky Assets", *Journal of Financial Economics*, **10**, pp 161–181.

Wystup, U., 2002, "How the Greeks would have Hedged Correlation Risk of Foreign Exchange Options", in J. Hakala and U. Wystup (eds), *Foreign Exchange Risk* (London: Risk Books), pp 143–146.

5

Rethinking Volatility in the Era of Markov Processes, Fractal Geometry and Guided Random Walks

Peter Krause

Krause Financial Systems

In my experience, the best options traders are "smart, but not too smart" – they operate at a level that accepts the concrete reality of abstractions that more intelligent people reject as overly insubstantial. Consequently, overly analysing volatility is a dangerous and destructive activity, because it might push successful traders into doubting their tools. While I might raise a few theoretical objections to some of the modelling approaches that underpin the options world, I make every effort to end on a happy note.

I have found that resistance to the concept of volatility can be deeply cosmological. As a teleological matter, the idea of a random universe and the idea of an ordered universe are equally non-falsifiable: bizarre coincidences could be pure flukes, and the manipulations of a divine hand might also be responsible for seemingly unrelated events. It is no coincidence that great traders are frequently superstitious, since the psychological mindset that connects unrelated events will also see the subtle connections between loosely related events that elude conventional statistical analysis.

While faith in the efficiency of markets is becoming a national religion, the firms whose profitability is predicated on the inefficiency of financial markets have been amassing greater wealth than that accumulated by the priests of any previous religion in history. The essential disconnection between the popular and academic understanding of financial markets and the fundamental social reality of trading communities has created the opportunity in which trading firms have thrived. The simple fact is that the statistical tools that are used to model markets and manage risk are insufficient to predict levels of profitability, because of unique characteristics of financial time series that elude traditional statistical analysis.

"Volatility" imposes the concept of statistical randomness on processes that almost certainly have a hidden and structural order. Statistical randomness is an idea from math and science, while, as George Soros has pointed out, social processes reinforce and subvert themselves in ways that are alien to traditional probability theory. Markets are people, and people get excited and depressed, frequently falling under the invisible power of group delusions.

At the most basic level, even neophytic options traders know that histograms of market data (particularly when adjusted for takeovers and bankruptcies) show fat tails, which is to say that, if human height were distributed in the same way as market movements, there would be a lot more rabbit-sized people and a lot more people taller than giraffes. At a portfolio level, concepts such as "Sharpe Ratio" and "value at risk", with normal distributions embedded in their DNA, are inadequate to evaluate strategies that presume non-normal distributions, but, as long as the whole machine makes money, nobody is very concerned with improving the theoretical apparatus for understanding the sources of profitability or devising better means of capital allocation to diversify and profit from the various skews of different strategies.

But dealing with abnormal distributions is a trifle compared with creating a function that accurately mimics the social processes that create financial time series. Modelling financial data with a histogram is like trying to appreciate Shakespeare by doing word counts. There is an astonishing context to specific items of financial data, and price movements lose much of their meaning when examined in isolation.

Traders will tell you that there are only two ways to make money in underlying markets: either betting on mean reversion or betting on momentum, and the folk wisdom helps explain the statistics: going back to the tedious histograms referred to in the previous paragraph (and you can find them in any number of finance books), mean reversion beefs up the centre of the distribution while momentum fattens the tails. If you are holding an option until expiration, the existence of momentum and mean reversion are not very relevant to your option valuation; but, if you are hedging that option, understanding the nature of the process that governs the underlying movement can be the difference between a winning and losing position.

Mean reversion and momentum are essential aspects of the human experience. Momentum is as real as human enthusiasm and panic, and mean reversion is as real as reality (that is to say the thing that is ignored in moments of enthusiasm and panic). The greatest investors in history have put it in different ways: George Soros talks about boom–bust cycles, Benjamin Graham talks about learning to take advantage of one's unmedicated manic-depressive business partner; and Meyer Rothschild talks about "buying when there is blood in the streets".

If we accept Fisher Black's other famous formula, namely that

$$\text{Stock Price} = \text{Stock Value} \pm \text{noise} \pm \text{information}$$

it is intuitively clear that Black's "noise" can push prices away from values and "information" can pull prices back.

Mean reversion is also easily demonstrable in financial time series by looking at the relationship between the high–low volatility and the close–close volatility. If the market were a perfect fractal, the period used for calculating volatility to be irrelevant, but, since markets exhibit different behaviours on the hourly versus the daily scale, there are, of course, other forces at work.

There are clear causes for the differences between day trades and close-to-close trades. People who trade on an hour-to-hour horizon often do not hold positions overnight (to avoid margins and reduce risk), and corporations increasingly withhold market-moving information until after the markets close. So, respecting my readers' intelligence enough that they do not need me to repeat numbers that can be found elsewhere, it is pretty clear, from an intuitive-social perspective, that the belief in a fractal structure in the market is contradicted by data, common sense and market knowledge.

Until the next generation of behavioural finance experiments will replicate the phenomena of momentum and mean reversion in a laboratory, we have to settle for watching them in the financial markets every single day.

Fixing the intellectual problem of volatility is not a simple matter of adjusting the distribution to accommodate a different set of probabilities, because the forces of momentum and mean reversion move the anticipated price path outside of a statistical distribution and into a randomly distributed set of bounded Markov processes. Once we enter a world of mean reversion and momentum, there are an infinite number of "solutions" for each set of option prices; and a volatility curve, or a density function with skew and kurtosis, gives people a common language for discussing a subtle reality: in many ways, a clunky model that knows its own dishonesty is better than an elegant lie with skew and kurtosis.

So how would these preliminary comments help us make money from options?

One of the central axioms for opportunity in financial markets is that complexity begets inefficiency. Another axiom of statistics asserts that, at a certain point, randomness is an excellent proxy for complexity. A multilayered process can have distinct threads that combine to create something that approximates a random process. As it stands, the concept of volatility is an uneasy average between momentum and mean reversion, so, rather than having a model that combines those two higher order factors of the statistical process, "volatility" assumes that the two factors will balance each other out, and ignores them both.

The tools being used to understand financial markets are fundamentally inadequate, but those tools allow people with a specific cast of mind to locate opportunities. The fact that the statistical models used by risk managers and academics do not sufficiently capture the sources of traders' alpha creates an opportunity for firms that are willing to back insufficiently understood yet profitable strategies. The strategies exist because the theoretical justification for the strategies does not exist. If the strategies were completely understood, the market would abolish them.

Over the past 20 years, firms that have all used the same basic "options tricks" have demonstrated impressive earnings patterns over time, and even become attractive targets for acquisition. Time and again, these large option firms (for example, O'Connor & Associates, Chicago Research and Trading, Hull Trading Company) are acquired by large financial firms who eventually shutter the option firm's trading wing in a panic because they are unable to quantify mathematically the sources of profitability. This only allows the cycle to continue as the next trading firms – often founded by refugees from the previous trader firms – generate profits and are acquired.

This has all been much too theoretical, so I will close with a practical example.

It is one of the paradoxes of the options markets that, on some days, both long and short-premium market participants make money. Each participant thinks the other participant is a little nuts, and possibly a little stupid, but the secret of their simultaneous profitability is that they hedge on different time horizons, so a long-gamma trader is able get his hedges in every hour, and take advantage of interday swings, which a short-gamma trader hedges near the close, and quietly banks the premium decay. In a very simplistic way, the long-gamma trader is able to monetise the fractal dimension of the stock underlying, since mean reversion increases the fractal dimension.

But, wait! If long-premium traders and short-premium traders both make money, should a no-premium trader not make even more money? Well, if the long and short-premium traders are market makers, and can monetise the bid–ask spread, then they will outperform a no-premium trader. But what would it look like if one simultaneously ran the long and short-premium books, and crossed the options premium? The stock-trading pattern of this book would be almost indistinguishable for a statistical arbitrage book. And, thus, gentle reader, we can see how the exploitation of distributional oddities helps us move from the puddle of the options market to the great ocean of statistical arbitrage.

Their profits have to come from somewhere, of course, and the answer is that a long-gamma trader, with hedging orders waiting at specific prices, extracts the long-gamma trader's profits from the general volume-weighted average price (VWAP). Since the gamma hedger's buy price is lower and his sell price is higher, so the net buying VWAP of all other market participants is slightly higher and the net selling VWAP of all other market participants is slightly lower. Thus, with enough gamma hedgers in a stock, it becomes theoretically impossible for an open-market participant to get the VWAP in their stock execution.

But the first rule of markets is that nothing is forever, so heading into summer 2007, institutional VWAPs were migrating to dark liquidity pools, while an oversaturation of gamma hedging orders and statistical arbitrage algorithms were reducing the mean reverting volatility that they were hoping to monetise. And the spectacular collapse of statistical arbitrage algorithms in the volatility explosion of August 2007 was partially caused because statistical arbitrage algorithms and gamma hedging orders placed by purchasers of institutional covered calls had reduced the statistically measured volatility of underlying stock prices to the point where the stock's historic volatility was no longer a viable proxy for the volatility of the underling businesses.

Part II

The VIX

6

Construction and Interpretation of Model-free Implied Volatility

Torben G. Andersen[1]; Oleg Bondarenko

Kellogg School of Management, Northwestern University, IL;
University of Illinois at Chicago, IL

Both market and academic interest in equity-index volatility measures has grown rapidly in recent years. The best known example is the publication of the so-called volatility index, or VIX, by the Chicago Board of Options Exchange (CBOE). Practitioners and academics alike have established that this index correlates significantly, not only with future equity market volatility, but also with global risk factors embedded in credit spreads or sovereign debt spreads. This explains the moniker of "global fear index" which has been attached to the VIX measure in the public press. Given the evident asset market implications, this is an area of growing interest for financial and macro economists. Moreover, public and over-the-counter markets have emerged to enable direct trading of volatility as measured by realised return volatility indicators over a prescribed future horizon for a host of different financial assets.

These developments have been facilitated by the development of a "model-free" implied volatility (MFIV) measure which, at least in principle, can be derived directly from a comprehensive cross-section of European put and call option prices with strikes spanning the full range of possible values for the underlying asset

---

[1] The work of Andersen is supported by a grant from the NSF to NBER and by CREATES funded via the Danish National Research Foundation. The paper was initiated while Bondarenko was visiting Kellogg. Any errors remain our responsibility.

at option expiry. Recent research has confirmed that this pricing relationship is robust and remains approximately valid for a broad class of relevant return generating processes, including jump-diffusive semimartingales models. This is in sharp contrast with the traditional Black–Scholes implied volatility (BSIV) measure which relies on a specific, and counterfactual, assumption on the return dynamics. The latter induces the well-documented smile and smirk patterns in implied volatility across the strikes so the BSIV is a direct function of the particular option used for the computation. The VIX replaces the multitude of BSIV measures with a unique value obtained as a weighted average across all observed option prices with appropriate time to maturity and, as mentioned above, it remains valid under general assumptions regarding the return dynamics.

Nonetheless, the requirements of theory for deriving the MFIV measure are not met by existing data, so some approximations are inevitable. There are, in particular, practical limitations in terms of the existence of liquid options with strike prices covering the entire support of the return distribution. As such, robust computational procedures are crucial. On this dimension, the VIX has come in for criticism. For example, Jiang and Tian (2005b) found that the CBOE implementation introduces random noise as well as systematic errors into the index.

In order to assess the implications of this criticism and explore some conceptual issues concerning the construction of the volatility index, it is useful to reflect on the notion that it is intended to capture. The theoretical foundation for the MFIV, and thus the VIX, makes this transparent: the index aims to measure the expected integrated variance, or more generally return variation, over the coming month, evaluated under the so-called risk-neutral, or pricing (Q), measure. As volatility is stochastic, the MFIV measure will typically differ from the expected return variation under the actual, or objective (P), measure. As such, the MFIV is not a pure volatility forecast for the underlying asset, but rather bundles this forecast with market pricing of the uncertainty surrounding the forecast. This implies that, in general, implied volatilities will include premiums compensating for the systematic risk associated with the exposure to equity-index volatility. Even so, all else being equal, the volatility index will rise in response to a perceived increase in future (objective P-measure) volatility and *vice versa*. Consequently, the MFIV index should be strongly correlated with future realised volatility (RV). In fact, because derivatives markets aggregate the views of many agents who make trading decisions based on current information stemming from diverse sources, including but vastly exceeding the information contained in historical returns, many scholars deem implied volatility forecasts as superior to other predictors generated by alternate methods, eg, univariate time series models, on purely *a priori* grounds. Of course, this issue has been explored from different angles in the literature, but it has proven difficult to reach a firm conclusion owing to the relatively short time span of reliable option prices, the large degree of noise present in standard measures of *ex-post* realised return volatility and, most importantly, the unobserved nature of the risk premiums embedded in implied volatilities.

It is impossible to decisively establish the superiority of a given implied volatility index relative to others because any observed implied volatility level may be rationalised by appeal to an embedded unobserved premium. Nonetheless, there are a number of dimensions on which such indices may be assessed. First, consistent pricing of options of a given maturity across all possible strikes induces a risk-neutral density which must satisfy certain regularity conditions to exclude arbitrage opportunities. A primary requirement is that the risk-neutral density is strictly positive for all possible future values of the underlying asset. From this perspective, a striking feature of the computation of the VIX is that the CBOE truncates the tails of the return distribution at the point where no reliable option prices with corresponding strikes can be inferred. Moreover, the extent to which reliable option prices are available in these tail regions differs across trading days, so that the severity of the truncation varies stochastically over time. One sensible alternative is to apply a more theoretically coherent technique of extending the risk-neutral density into the tails, and we do so later in this chapter. However, any such procedure must rely on partially unverifiable assumptions, given the inherent data limitations. This will inevitably introduce a degree of random noise into the measure. Hence, it is intuitively appealing to focus on measures computed only over regions of the risk-neutral density where it may be inferred in a reliable fashion. Of course, such a truncated implied volatility measure should not be seen as representing the full MFIV, but rather as a deliberately down-scaled version. In fact, this interpretation can be formalised rigorously as the construction may be viewed as a variant of the so-called model-free "corridor implied volatility" (CIV) measure, briefly discussed by Carr and Madan (1998). Hence, it may be appropriate to view the VIX as an (imperfect) CIV index rather than a MFIV measure. As the notion of CIV is not widely known and has never, as far as we know, been explored in practice, we provide a detailed exposition of the concept, linking it theoretically and empirically to the corresponding MFIV, VIX and BSIV measures.

Second, we compare the forecast performance of alternative implied volatility measures. Although there is no requirement that a superior implied volatility measure is also a superior predictor of future volatility, inconsistently constructed or excessively noisy measures will tend to display poor coherence with the underlying market volatility movements and perhaps even contain predictable forecast errors which may be eliminated through alternative constructions of the measures. Hence, relative predictive ability can serve as an indirect indicator of the quality of the measures. Of course, it is also of independent interest to establish which implied volatility measures correlate most strongly with the underlying asset volatility and thus provide useful guidance for volatility prediction. We facilitate efficient inference regarding predictive performance by obtaining accurate measurements of the underlying *ex-post* RV. We rely on recently developed techniques for constructing RV measures from high-frequency intraday return series on the underlying asset for this purpose.

Third, we investigate the statistical properties of each candidate implied volatility series relative to relevant historical RV measures. This sheds additional light on issues concerning the presence of risk premiums, systematic forecast biases and the presence of noise in the series.

We study the above issues in an empirical setting where we can obtain relatively precise measures of the underlying return variation and we have access to high-quality options data so that we may construct alternative implied volatility measures, both of the model-free and the Black–Scholes variety, with good accuracy. The market setting associated with the published VIX measure is not convenient in this regard owing to the underlying being a cash equity index. The index has 500 underlying stocks whose prices are never observed simultaneously so that the resulting index is plagued by well-established lead-lag or non-synchronicity biases at high frequencies. This has implications for our ability to measure the underlying RV with precision from the intraday index returns. Moreover, the corresponding options data is not readily available. Such issues are alleviated greatly by instead using the S&P500 futures market and the associated options which are traded on the Chicago Mercantile Exchange (CME). At the same time, the cash and futures return volatility are intimately linked so that a volatility measure for one market should serve as a good proxy for the volatility of the other.

In summary, in this chapter we argue that the VIX index is closely related to the concept of CIV. We then relate different CIV measures, distinguished by corridor width, to the ideal MFIV, the BSIV and a couple of historical RV measures. In this first empirical study of CIV, we establish that broad corridor CIV measures are good substitutes for sensible empirical measures of MFIV while some narrower corridor width CIV measures tend to mimic the BSIV measure. We systematically document the volatility forecast properties of these measures and find, in contrast to some existing evidence, that the narrow corridor or BSIV measures are more useful predictors of future volatility than the broad corridor MFIV or VIX measures. The statistical properties of the various measures are consistent with the interpretation that the broad CIV measures embed large and time-varying risk premiums which encroach on their usefulness as direct indicators of future volatility. Importantly, these findings should not be taken as a criticism of the MFIV concept. Instead, they point to practical empirical implications of the dual features of market-based measures, namely as vehicles that simultaneously provide forecasts of future volatility and price the risk associated with this expected future (stochastic) return variation.

The chapter unfolds as follows. 'Theoretical background' provides the basic theoretical exposition of the model-free, barrier and CIV measures and their relationship with the Black–Scholes measure. In that context, we also provide an explicit comparison of the Black–Scholes prices for certain variance contracts with those prevailing in the marketplace. This serves to highlight the inadequacy of the Black–Scholes setting for understanding the market pricing of these newly developed variance products. In addition, we review the concept of realised return volatility which is used both as the *ex-post* measure of actual RV and as an *ex-ante* volatility forecast indicator. 'Data' describes the origin of our data and some details of the data cleaning and construction. 'Empirical results' reports on the empirical results. We first provide some descriptive statistics to convey the basic behaviour of the new corridor volatility measures relative to the more traditional volatility series. We then explore both the in-sample and out-of-sample performance of the various volatility measures as predictors of future volatility. Finally, 'Conclusion' provides concluding remarks.

THEORETICAL BACKGROUND

This section provides the theoretical foundation for the volatility concepts and measurements explored in our analysis. We begin with a formal introduction of the concept of barrier and corridor variance contracts. We next review the basic features of the so-called RV measures which are used to obtain relatively accurate measures of the actual (*ex-post*) return variation of the underlying asset. Finally, we review the implementation procedures we adopt in order to convert the various alternative volatility concepts into practical measures amenable for empirical analysis.

Barrier variance and corridor variance contracts

Throughout this section we fix the current time at $t = 0$ and we consider only contracts which payout at a future fixed date T. For $0 \leq t \leq T$, F_t denotes the time t value of the S&P500 futures contract expiring at date T' where $T \leq T'$. Moreover, the prices of European put and call options with strike K and expiration date T are given by $P_t(K)$ and $C_t(K)$. To simplify the exposition, the risk-free rate is assumed to be zero.[2] In the following, $k = K/F_t$ indicates the strike-to-underlying ratio or moneyness of an options contract. Although moneyness, k, varies with the underlying price F_t, we suppress this time dependence for notational convenience. Thus, a put (call) is out-of-the-money (OTM) if $k < 1$ ($k > 1$), is at-the-money (ATM) if $k = 1$ and is in-the-money (ITM) if $k > 1$ ($k < 1$). We also use $\tau = T - t$ to denote time to maturity.

The option prices may be computed using the risk-neutral density (RND), denoted by $h_t(F_T)$:

$$P_t(K) = E_t^Q[(K - F_T)^+] = \int_0^\infty (K - F_T)^+ h_t(F_T) \, dF_T$$

$$C_t(K) = E_t^Q[(F_T - K)^+] = \int_0^\infty (F_T - K)^+ h_t(F_T) \, dF_T$$

The RND satisfies the relationship first exposed by Ross (1976), Breeden and Litzenberger (1978) and Banz and Miller (1978),

$$h_t(F_T) = \left.\frac{\partial^2 P_t(K)}{\partial K^2}\right|_{K=F_T} = \left.\frac{\partial^2 C_t(K)}{\partial K^2}\right|_{K=F_T} \tag{6.1}$$

Let $g(F_T)$ denote a general payout at time T. The function $g(F_T)$ is assumed to have a finite second derivative which is continuous almost everywhere. Following Carr and Madan (1998) and Bakshi and Madan (2000), for any $x \geq 0$, $g(F_T)$ can be represented as

$$g(F_T) = g(x) + g'(x)(F_T - x) + \int_0^x g''(K)(K - F_T)^+ \, dK$$
$$+ \int_x^\infty g''(K)(F_T - K)^+ \, dK \tag{6.2}$$

By setting $x = F_0$ and taking expectations in Equation (6.2), one obtains

$$E_0^Q[g(F_T)] = g(F_0) + \int_0^{F_0} g''(K) P_0(K) \, dK + \int_{F_0}^\infty g''(K) C_0(K) \, dK$$
$$= g(F_0) + \int_0^\infty g''(K) M_0(K) \, dK \tag{6.3}$$

where $M_t(K)$ denotes the minimum of the put and call,

$$M_t(K) = \min(P_t(K), C_t(K))$$

In other words, of the two plain vanilla options with strike K, $M_t(K)$ equals the price of that which is currently OTM.

In the current setting, the futures price process F_t is a martingale under the risk-neutral measure. Suppose that it follows the general diffusion:

$$\frac{dF_t}{F_t} = \sigma_t \, dW_t \tag{6.4}$$

where W_t is a standard Brownian motion and σ_t is a strictly positive, cadlag (stochastic) volatility process. Note that we allow the volatility process to feature jump discontinuities. By Itô's lemma,

$$g(F_T) = g(F_0) + \int_0^T g'(F_t)\,dF_t + \frac{1}{2}\int_0^T g''(F_t)F_t^2\sigma_t^2\,dt \qquad (6.5)$$

which implies that

$$E_0^Q[g(F_T)] = g(F_0) + \frac{1}{2}E_t^Q\left[\int_0^T g''(F_t)F_t^2\sigma_t^2\,dt\right] \qquad (6.6)$$

Combining Equations (6.3) and (6.6), one finds that

$$E_0^Q\left[\int_0^T g''(F_t)F_t^2\sigma_t^2\,dt\right] = 2\int_0^\infty g''(K)M_0(K)\,dK \qquad (6.7)$$

It is convenient to define the down-barrier indicator function as follows,

$$I_t = I_t(B) = 1[F_t \leq B]$$

with B denoting the barrier. We now consider the contract with time T payout equal to the (down-)*barrier integrated variance*,

$$\text{BIVAR}_B(0, T) = \int_0^T \sigma_t^2 I_t(B)\,dt$$

In other words, the contractual payment is given by the realised variance calculated only when the futures price lies below the barrier B. As B diverges to ∞, the payout approaches the standard integrated variance:

$$\text{IVAR}(0, T) = \int_0^T \sigma_t^2\,dt$$

Carr and Madan (1998) show how to synthesize the continuously monitored barrier variance when the underlying process is continuous. The no-arbitrage value of the down-barrier variance contract can be derived from the relationship in (6.7). Suppose that the function $g(F_T)$ is chosen as

$$g(F_T) = g(F_T; B) = \left(-\ln\frac{F_T}{B} + \frac{F_T}{B} - 1\right)I_T$$

In the following we exploit the following properties of this $g(F_T)$ function:

(a) it is equal to zero for all values of $F_T \geq B$;
(b) its first derivative is continuous for all F_T,

$$g'(F_T) = \left(-\frac{1}{F_T} + \frac{1}{B}\right) I_T$$

(c) its second derivative is continuous for all $F_T \neq B$,

$$g''(F_T) = \frac{1}{F_T^2} I_T$$

The relationship in (6.7) then implies that the value of the barrier variance contract is

$$\text{BVAR}_0(B) = E_0^Q\left[\int_0^T \sigma_t^2 I_t\, dt\right] = 2\int_0^B \frac{M_0(K)}{K^2}\, dK \qquad (6.8)$$

The square root of the above expression can be interpreted as the option-implied barrier volatility:

$$\text{BIV}_0(B) = \sqrt{2\int_0^B \frac{M_0(K)}{K^2}\, dK} \qquad (6.9)$$

In the limiting case of $B = \infty$, the barrier implied volatility coincides with the so-called model-free implied volatility MFIV_0. The concept of the MFIV was developed in original work of Dupire (1993) and Neuberger (1994).[3] The concept is referred to as "model-free" because it does not rely on any particular parametric model, unlike the BSIV. CBOE uses this concept as the basis for its recently redesigned volatility index VIX.

The contract which pays the corridor variance can be constructed from two barrier variance with different barriers. Let B_1 and B_2 denote the lower and the upper barriers and consider the contract with time T payout,

$$\text{CIVAR}_{B_1,B_2}(0,T) = \int_0^T \sigma_t^2 I_t(B_1, B_2)\, dt$$

where the indicator function $I_t(B_1, B_2)$ is defined as

$$I_t(B_1, B_2) = I_t = 1[B_1 \leq F_t \leq B_2]$$

In other words, this contract pays the corridor variance, or the variance calculated only when the futures price is between the barriers B_1 and B_2. The value of the corridor variance contract is

$$\text{CVAR}_0(B_1, B_2) = E_0^Q\left[\int_0^T \sigma_t^2 I_t \, dt\right] = 2\int_{B_1}^{B_2} \frac{M_0(K)}{K^2} \, dK \quad (6.10)$$

Carr and Madan (1998) also introduce the contract which pays future variance along a strike. This contract can be obtained as the limiting case of the corridor variance contract when the distance between the upper and lower barriers shrinks to zero and when the payout is properly rescaled to have a non-negligible value:

$$\text{SVAR}_0(B) = \lim_{\Delta B \to 0} \frac{B}{\Delta B} \text{CVAR}_0(B, B + \Delta B) = 2\frac{M_0(B)}{B} \quad (6.11)$$

Note that we rescale the payout by $B/\Delta B$ as opposed to just $1/\Delta B$ as in Carr and Madan (1998). This minor modification has the effect that, for Black–Scholes and most other canonical option models, the value of the along-strike variance contract depends only on the moneyness B/F_0 and not on the level of the underlying, F_0, itself.

Barrier variance contracts under the Black–Scholes model
In the Black–Scholes (1973) model, the instantaneous volatility is constant, $\sigma_t = \sigma$, and the value of the barrier variance can be computed in closed form as

$$\begin{aligned}
&\text{BVAR}_0(B) \\
&= 2\left(N(y)(\sigma\sqrt{\tau}y - 1) + \frac{F_0}{B}N(y - \sigma\sqrt{\tau}) + \sigma\sqrt{\tau}n(y) - g(F_0)\right) \\
&= 2\left(N(y)\left(-1 - \ln\frac{F_0}{B} + \frac{1}{2}\sigma^2\tau\right)\right. \\
&\quad + \left.\frac{F_0}{B}N(y - \sigma\sqrt{\tau}) - \sigma\sqrt{\tau}n(y) + \left(1 - \frac{F_0}{B} + \ln\frac{F_0}{B}\right)I_0(B)\right)
\end{aligned}$$
$$(6.12)$$

where

$$y = -\frac{\ln(F_0/B)}{\sigma\sqrt{\tau}} + \frac{1}{2}\sigma\sqrt{\tau}$$

and $n(\cdot)$ and $N(\cdot)$ denote the standard normal probability and cumulative density functions (pdf and cdf) respectively.

When $\sigma\sqrt{\tau}$ is small, the above expression can be approximately written as

$$\text{BVAR}_0(B) \approx \sigma^2 \tau I_0(B)$$

Intuitively, if the current futures price is below the barrier ($F_0 < B$), then for small $\sigma\sqrt{\tau}$ it will remain there almost surely and the down-barrier variance is identical to the integrated variance. On the other hand, if the current futures price is above the barrier, the futures will remain above until maturity, almost surely, and the down-barrier variance is zero.

To provide some initial intuition, the top panel of Figure 6.1 plots the function

$$U_0(p) = \frac{\text{BVAR}_0(H_0^{-1}(p))}{\text{BVAR}_0(\infty)}$$

which is equal to the normalised barrier variance expressed in terms of the cumulative risk-neutral probability $p = H_0(B)$. By construction, the function $U_0(p)$ is monotonically increasing on $[0, 1]$ with $U_0(0) = 0$ and $U_0(1) = 1$. The figure assumes that $\tau = 21$ trading days and that σ is set to the average ATM implied volatility over the studied period.

For comparison, the bottom panel of Figure 6.1 plots the same function $U_0(p)$ computed from S&P500 options, for a representative day in our dataset 19 April, 2000, when $\tau = 21$ trading days. The shape of the function $U_0(p)$ now differs dramatically from the Black–Scholes case, mainly reflecting the very fat left tail of the empirical RND. It is evident that the same features that induce systematic patterns in the Black–Scholes implied volatilities will also prevent the Black–Scholes model assumptions from delivering realistic market pricing of barrier variance contracts across the support of the RND.

Realised volatility measures

Given the futures price dynamics under the Q-measure specified in Equation (6.4), the logarithmic futures price process under the actual P-measure will follow a semimartingale with the identical spot volatility process, σ_t. For short-term (log-)price increments, the semimartingale property implies that the size of the innovation term is an order of magnitude larger than the size of the expected mean term. Hence, for high-frequency returns, the drift may be

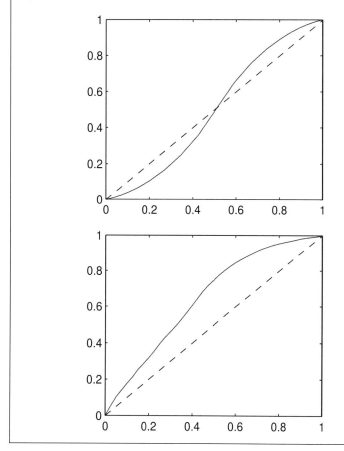

Figure 6.1 The top panel plots the normalised barrier variance $U_0(p)$ for the Black–Scholes model, when $\sigma = 0.165$ and $\tau = 21$ trading days. The bottom panel plots the normalised barrier variance $U_0(p)$ for S&P500 on 19 April, 2000, when $\tau = 21$ trading days. On that day, S&P500 = 1427.47, VIX = 27.02.

neglected. This line of reasoning is entirely general and provides a formal basis for the use of RV as an *ex-post* measure of return variation. Assuming that we have $n+1$ log-price observations available over the relevant measurement horizon, obtained at times $0 = t(0) < t(1) < \cdots < t(n-1) < t(n) = T$, we may define RV as the cumulative sum of squared returns,

$$\mathrm{RV}_n(0, T) = \sum_{i=1}^{n} [\ln F_{t(i)} - \ln F_{t(i-1)}]^2$$

Conditional on the observed price path over $[0, T]$, RV provides an unbiased estimator of the underlying quadratic return variation, which is simply the integrated variance, $\mathrm{IVAR}(0, T)$ in the current setting. Consequently, the conditional expectation at time $t = 0$ of the future quadratic return variation, denoted by V_0, will also equal the conditional expectation of future RV, ie,

$$V_0 = E_0^P \left[\int_0^T \sigma_t^2 \, dt \right] = E_0^P [\mathrm{RV}_n(0, T)] \qquad (6.13)$$

This relationship is critical as we cannot directly observe realisations of the integrated variance, while we can construct empirical measures of realised return volatility. Hence, the latter will serve as our empirical proxy for the former. Theory stipulates that we exploit as many returns in the computation as possible: the precision of the RV measure improves as the sampling frequency increases and, eventually, in the limit of continuous sampling, converges to the underlying integrated variance.[4] In practice, the semimartingale property is violated at the highest sampling frequencies owing to the presence of market microstructure noise in the recorded prices which may induce sizeable biases. Consequently, we follow the common procedure of aggregating five-minute squared futures returns over the course of the trading day to obtain a reasonably precise and unbiased empirical measure of the underlying return variation.[5]

We also need to measure the return variation during the overnight period when the futures market is closed. In accordance with the general properties for RV, the measure will remain unbiased if we add the squared overnight return, obtained as the squared close-to-open logarithmic price change, to the measure obtained over the trading period. We denote (the square root of) this RV measure, constructed from high-frequency data and the overnight return as indicated, by RVH. Obviously, the absence of detailed information on the price evolution overnight has a detrimental impact on the overall precision of the measure but the effect is limited owing to the comparatively low volatility associated with non-trading periods.

Even though the use of high-frequency return-based RV measures has become widespread in recent years, the reliance on daily squared returns for computation of realised monthly return volatility remains common. In order to facilitate comparison across studies and obtain a direct indication of the practical advantage of using the high-frequency-based measure, we also include a RV measure computed as (the square root of) the cumulated daily squared returns, and denoted by RVD, in the subsequent empirical analysis.

Construction of the volatility measures

In the empirical study, we compare and contrast properties of the interrelated volatility measures introduced above. These measures are constructed daily and assume a fixed horizon or time to maturity of $\tau = 1$ month (21 trading days).

We consider four CIVs, denoted by CIV1–CIV4, with barriers defined as fixed percentiles of the RND. Specifically, we compute the CIV as

$$\text{CIV}_0(B_1, B_2) = \sqrt{2 \int_{B_1}^{B_2} \frac{M_0(K)}{K^2} dK} \qquad (6.14)$$

with the barriers chosen so that $B_1 = H_0^{-1}(p)$ and $B_2 = H_0^{-1}(1-p)$ for $p = 0.25$, 0.10, 0.05 and 0.025 for CIV1–CIV4, respectively. In other words, CIV1–CIV4 correspond to increasingly wider corridors, where the corridor for CIV1 covers the range from the 25th and 75th percentiles of the RND, the corridor for CIV2 covers the range from the 10th and 90th percentiles and so on. The MFIV corresponds to the limiting case of $p = 0$. The two broad corridor CIV measures, CIV3 and CIV4, were chosen with an eye towards the largest width of the RND which may be estimated with precision for almost all trading days. They serve as potential proxies for the MFIV in that they capture the expected variation over very wide ranges of the RND, but can be measured with better accuracy. The narrower corridor measures, CIV1 and CIV2, are included to highlight the different properties that arise from focusing on ranges of the RND which display a lower sensitivity to the variance risk premium.

To construct the CIVs, we first estimate the RND by means of the positive convolution approximation (PCA) method developed by Bondarenko (2003). The procedure exploits the relationship in Equation (6.1) to infer the conditional RND $h_0(F_T)$ and directly addresses some important limitations of actual option data, namely that: (a) options are only traded for a discrete set of strikes, as opposed to a continuum; (b) very low and very high strikes are not usually available; and (c) option prices contain substantial measurement errors stemming from non-synchronous trading, price discreteness and bid–ask bounce. The PCA method is fully non-parametric, guarantees arbitrage-free density estimates, controls against overfitting in a small sample setting and has been shown to be accurate in simulations. In addition to the estimate for RND, the method also provides the input into computing the put pricing function $P_0(K)$, the risk-neutral cdf $H_0(K)$ and the barrier variance function $BVAR_0(K)$ for arbitrary strikes. The latter allows us to compute the full set of corridor variance measures.

Other option-implied measures that we consider include the ATM BSIV and the CBOE's VIX. In theory, VIX should be very close to MFIV. However, as Jiang and Tian (2005b) point out, the specific procedure adopted by the CBOE to compute the VIX index introduces several potential biases. They identify three types of approximation errors, namely: (i) truncation errors owing to the fact that very low and very high strikes are not available in practice; (ii) discretisation errors induced owing to the numerical integration being implemented using a relatively coarse grid of available strikes; and (iii) errors arising from a Taylor series expansion approximation. In practice, the errors (ii) and (iii) are small and, in principle, can be rendered negligible through improved implementation. On the other hand, the errors stemming from (i) can be considerable and there is no simple solution.

Intuitively, the published VIX can be interpreted as a CIV measure with barriers set to the lowest and highest strikes that CBOE uses on a given day to compute the index. The fact that the barriers change stochastically from day to day, depending on the liquidity in certain segments of the options market, may induce systematic biases in the VIX.

Finally, in addition to option-implied measures, we also rely on RVs, computed using either daily or high-frequency returns.

The realised variance measure, RVD, is computed as the sum of 21 trading day close-to-close squared log-returns. The realised high-frequency data-based variance measure, RVH, also covers 21 trading days, but now all of the five-minute intra-trading day and the overnight close-to-open squared log-returns within the month are cumulated.

DATA

The full sample period is from January 1990 to December 2006. Our data stems from several sources. From the CME we obtain daily prices of options on the S&P500 futures and transactions data for the S&P500 futures themselves. From the CBOE, we obtain daily levels of the newly redesigned VIX index. Although the CBOE changed the methodology for calculating the VIX in September 2003, they have backdated the new index to 1990 using historical option prices. Finally, from the US Federal Reserve, we obtain Treasury bill rates, which are used to proxy for the risk-free interest rate.

The S&P500 futures have four different maturity months from the March quarterly cycle. The contract size is US$250 times S&P500 futures price (before November 1997, the contract size was US$ 500 times S&P500 futures price). On any trading day, the CME futures options are available for six maturity months: four months from the March quarterly cycle and two additional nearby months ("serial" options). The CME options expire on a third Friday of a contract month. However, the quarterly options expire at the market open, while the serial options expire at the market close. For the serial options, we measure time to maturity as the number of calendar days between the trade date and the expiration date. For the quarterly options, we use the number of calendar days remaining less one.

The option contract size is one S&P500 future. The minimum price movement is 0.05. The strikes are multiples of five for near-term months and multiples of 25 for far months. If at any time the S&P500 futures contract trades through the highest or lowest strike available, additional strikes are usually introduced.

The CME options on the S&P500 futures and options on the S&P500 Index itself, traded on the CBOE, have been the focus of many empirical studies. For short maturities, CME and CBOE option prices are virtually indistinguishable. Nevertheless, there are a number of practical advantages to using the CME options. First, as is well known, there is a 15-minute difference between the close of the CBOE markets and the NYSE, AMEX and NASDAQ markets, where the S&P500 components are traded. This difference leads to non-synchronicity biases between the recorded closing prices of the options and the level of the Index. In contrast, the CME options and futures close at the same time (3:15 PM CST). Second, it is easier to hedge options using highly liquid futures as opposed to trading in the 500 individual stocks. On the CME, futures and futures options are traded in pits side by side. This arrangement facilitates hedging, arbitrage and speculation. It also makes the market more efficient. In fact, even traders of the CBOE options usually hedge their positions with the CME futures. Third, an additional complication is that the S&P500 index pays dividends. Owing to this, to estimate the risk-neutral densities from CBOE options, one must make some assumptions about the index dividend stream. No such assumptions are needed for the CME futures options. A disadvantage of the CME options is their American-style feature. However, we conduct our empirical analysis in such a way that the effect of the early exercise feature is minimal.

For each trading day, we estimate the implied volatility measures CIV1–CIV4, MFIV and ATM BSIV. To obtain these values, we follow several steps, which are described in more detail in Appendix 6. Briefly, the steps include: (1) filtering out unreliable option data; (2) checking that the option prices satisfy the theoretical no-arbitrage restrictions; (3) inferring forward prices for European puts and calls; (4) estimating the RND for a continuum of strikes; and (5) estimating the implied volatilities. For illustration, Figure 6.2 depicts the BSIV, normalised option prices and the risk-neutral pdf and cdf for a representative trading day in the sample.

The RV measure RVD is computed from official daily closing prices on the S&P500 futures, while the RVH measure is obtained from the last recorded transaction price within each five-minute interval over the trading period combined with the overnight change from the official closing price to the opening price the subsequent trading day.

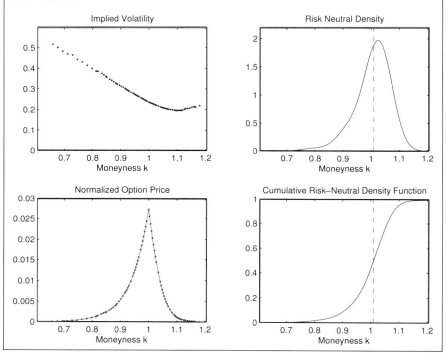

Figure 6.2 S&P500 option data for 19 April, 2000 when $\tau = 21$ trading days. The left panels show the Black–Scholes implied volatility $IV_t(k)$ and the normalised OTM option price $M_t(k)/F_t = \min(P_t(k), C_t(k))/F_t$ for different values of moneyness $k = K/F_t$. The solid curve indicates option prices corresponding to the estimated RND. The right panels show the estimated RND $h_t(k)$ and the cumulative RND function $H_t(k)$. The dashed line indicates the median of the RND. On that day, S&P500 = 1427.47, VIX = 27.02.

EMPIRICAL RESULTS

This section presents our empirical findings. We first review the basic statistical properties of the various volatility measures and then investigate their relative performance as predictors of the subsequent volatility of the underlying S&P500 futures.

Related recent work with a focus on the properties of MFIV and its relation to general asset market dynamics includes Andersen et al (2006b), Ang et al (2006), Bakshi and Kapadia (2003), Bakshi and Madan (2006), Bliss and Panigirtzoglou (2004), Bollerslev et al

(2007), Bollerslev and Zhou (2007), Bondarenko (2007), Carr and Wu (2004), Duan and Yeh (2007), Todorov (2007) and Wu (2004).

Basic features of the volatility measures

The top two panels of Figure 6.3 depict the level and daily returns for the S&P500 futures over our full sample period. The bottom panel plots the associated realised one-month return volatility series, RVH, along with the CBOE VIX index measure. As explained in the previous section, the VIX may be viewed as an indicator of future monthly volatility while RVH provides a measure of the actual RV over that month. A couple of points are evident from the graph. First, there is good coherence between the VIX index and the ensuing market volatility. However, because RVH is recorded daily but represents monthly (future) volatility, there is a great deal of induced serial correlation in this series.[6] Hence, this feature must be interpreted with some care. Second, it is evident that the VIX series almost uniformly exceeds the subsequent RV. This is consistent with earlier work establishing the presence of a substantial negative variance risk premium in the VIX index. In other words, investors are on average willing to pay a sizeable premium to acquire a positive exposure to future equity-index volatility. Of course, the CBOE VIX is computed on the basis of options written on the S&P500 cash index while we compute the RV from S&P500 futures. This may involve a mismatch which could explain the large and persistent gap between the two volatility measures. In order to control for such effects we turn to an analysis of various MFIV measures computed directly from options on S&P500 futures contracts which are compatible with the RVH series. We also include the VIX measure in the analysis to facilitate comparison with existing work.

Table 6.1 reports various summary statistics for nine volatility measures, RVD, RVH, VIX, BSIV, CIV1, CIV2, CIV3, CIV4 and MFIV, over the full sample and two sub-samples. Focusing on the full sample, we first note that the mean of the VIX is compatible with the level of the MFIV extracted from the CME futures options, and they both exceed the level of actual RV of the underlying asset, whether measured by RVD or RVH, by a margin of more than 23% (0.185 versus 0.150). Second, VIX is highly correlated with both the MFIV and the broadest corridor variance measure, CIV4, even if the VIX is slightly higher and a bit more persistent than the corresponding

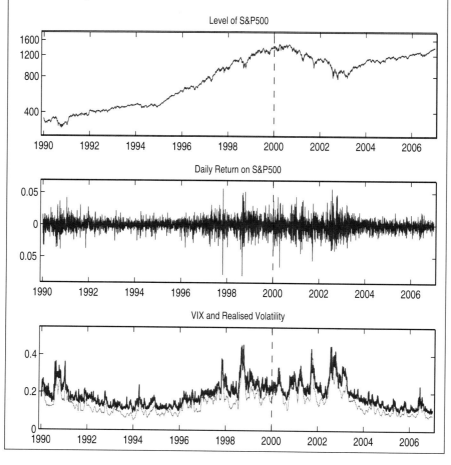

Figure 6.3 The top panel plots the level of S&P500 index (log scale). The second panel plots daily returns on S&P500 index. The bottom panel plots VIX (the thick curve) and RVH (the thin curve). RVH is computed using high-frequency returns over 21 trading days. VIX and RVH are annualised and given in decimal form. The vertical dashed line separates the estimation and forecast periods.

Table 6.1 Summary statistics for volatility measures RVD, RVH, VIX, BSIV, CIV1, CIV2, CIV3, CIV4 and MFIV. Statistics are reported for the full sample and two sub-samples and include mean, standard deviation, skewness, kurtosis and serial auto-correlation coefficients with lags of 1, 21 and 63 trading days. In all tables and figures, the volatility measures are annualised and given in decimal form.

Sample		RVD	RVH	VIX	BSIV	CIV1	CIV2	CIV3	CIV4	MFIV
Full sample (January 1990 to December 2006)	Mean	0.149	0.150	0.191	0.165	0.134	0.163	0.172	0.178	0.185
	SD	0.071	0.066	0.064	0.058	0.048	0.058	0.062	0.063	0.064
	Skewness	1.500	1.428	0.983	1.017	1.009	1.042	1.064	1.069	1.080
	Kurtosis	5.913	5.254	3.795	3.955	3.958	4.046	4.096	4.116	4.137
	ρ_1	0.991	0.997	0.983	0.981	0.981	0.980	0.980	0.980	0.980
	ρ_{21}	0.650	0.758	0.827	0.830	0.837	0.827	0.823	0.821	0.822
	ρ_{63}	0.497	0.519	0.652	0.678	0.694	0.670	0.660	0.654	0.652
Sub-sample (January 1990 to December 1999)	Mean	0.138	0.139	0.185	0.157	0.126	0.155	0.164	0.170	0.177
	SD	0.063	0.057	0.059	0.051	0.041	0.052	0.055	0.057	0.058
	Skewness	1.878	1.629	1.134	1.117	1.025	1.171	1.230	1.258	1.284
	Kurtosis	8.983	7.132	4.526	4.830	4.590	5.048	5.182	5.277	5.327
	ρ_1	0.988	0.996	0.979	0.974	0.974	0.973	0.974	0.975	0.975
	ρ_{21}	0.586	0.736	0.806	0.799	0.805	0.796	0.792	0.790	0.794
	ρ_{63}	0.413	0.467	0.635	0.651	0.667	0.643	0.633	0.626	0.627
Sub-sample (January 2000 to December 2006)	Mean	0.163	0.164	0.199	0.177	0.145	0.175	0.183	0.189	0.196
	SD	0.079	0.075	0.070	0.065	0.054	0.065	0.068	0.069	0.070
	Skewness	1.091	1.107	0.760	0.775	0.774	0.793	0.804	0.799	0.803
	Kurtosis	3.824	3.698	3.063	3.033	3.029	3.080	3.114	3.103	3.116
	ρ_1	0.993	0.997	0.986	0.985	0.986	0.985	0.984	0.984	0.984
	ρ_{21}	0.696	0.761	0.844	0.847	0.850	0.846	0.844	0.844	0.843
	ρ_{63}	0.550	0.527	0.658	0.680	0.691	0.675	0.667	0.664	0.658

Table 6.2 Correlations for various volatility measures: RVD, RVH, VIX, BSIV, CIV1, CIV2, CIV3, CIV4 and MFIV. The sample period is January 1990–December 2006.

	RVD	RVH	VIX	BSIV	CIV1	CIV2	CIV3	CIV4	MFIV
RVD	1.000	0.955	0.855	0.857	0.854	0.857	0.858	0.859	0.859
RVH	0.955	1.000	0.898	0.899	0.896	0.899	0.899	0.899	0.899
VIX	0.855	0.898	1.000	0.988	0.981	0.990	0.992	0.993	0.993
BSIV	0.857	0.899	0.988	1.000	0.998	1.000	0.998	0.997	0.995
CIV1	0.854	0.896	0.981	0.998	1.000	0.997	0.994	0.991	0.988
CIV2	0.857	0.899	0.990	1.000	0.997	1.000	0.999	0.998	0.996
CIV3	0.858	0.899	0.992	0.998	0.994	0.999	1.000	1.000	0.998
CIV4	0.859	0.899	0.993	0.997	0.991	0.998	1.000	1.000	0.999
MFIV	0.859	0.899	0.993	0.995	0.988	0.996	0.998	0.999	1.000

measures obtained from the CME option futures market. As the VIX is constructed in a manner that, as argued earlier, effectively makes it a hybrid between a pure MFIV and a broad CIV measure, it is reassuring that it does tend to mimic the behaviour of these independently constructed series based on related derivatives data. This is further supported by the extremely high correlations between VIX, MFIV and CIV4 reported in Table 6.2. This suggests that we can study the qualitative links between the VIX and concepts such as (regular) MFIV and CIV through the corresponding features of the implied volatility measures obtained from the S&P500 futures option market.

Moving to the empirical features of the corridor implied variance based measures, which have not been explored in the literature hitherto, we have, by construction, a monotonically increasing pattern in the mean level of CIV as we progress from CIV1 to CIV4. In another manifestation of the large variance risk premium embedded in the options markets, we observe that the mean of the CIV2 measure, covering only 80% of the RND, is also significantly higher than the historical RV of the underlying asset. Moreover, not surprisingly, the narrower corridor volatility measures are more stable than the corresponding broader measures in terms of higher serial correlation and lower sample standard deviation, skewness and kurtosis. Note also that the RV measures, as expected, are more volatile than the implied measures. They have the highest standard deviation, skewness and kurtosis statistics of all of the series and they have the lowest serial correlation at monthly and lower frequencies where the measurement overlap ceases to have an effect. Such discrepancies are, of course, typical when comparing series that represent expectations of future realisations versus the actual *ex-post* realisations. The latter embody both an expected component, highly correlated with the implied volatility measures, and an unpredictable innovation term. The presence of the second component will naturally render the RV series comparatively erratic in nature.

The final volatility measure included in the analysis is the traditional ATM Black–Scholes measure, BSIV. Although this measure also incorporates a significant variance risk premium, it is an order of magnitude smaller than for the MFIV. In addition, it is noteworthy that BSIV is extremely highly correlated with the intermediate CIVs, especially CIV2. Nonetheless, it is more persistent than these mid-range corridor volatility measures and sports lower sample skewness and kurtosis. In fact, at monthly and lower frequencies only the CIV1 measure is more persistent than BSIV.

A last observation concerns the very strong degree of persistence in the volatility measures. The autocorrelation patterns decay extremely slowly and are well approximated by a hyperbolic shape in all instances, thus lending support to the hypothesis that the volatility process has long memory components. As this issue is not of direct relevance for our current study, we abstain from additional analysis of these features.

The summary statistics for the sub-samples are in line with those discussed above. As is also evident from the bottom panel of Figure 6.3, the average volatility is higher in the second sub-sample than the first, thus rendering the (right-skewed) volatility outliers less influential in the computation of the skewness and kurtosis for the second sub-sample. These separate sub-samples play a pivotal role in the forecast analysis below.[7]

In summary, the various implied volatility measures are all highly correlated although clearly not identical. Figure 6.4 displays the variation with time of the various CIV measures relative to MFIV and BSIV. The comparatively stronger coherence among the MFIV and the broader measures CIV3 and CIV4 as well as the very high correlation between BSIV and CIV2 is clearly visible in the top and bottom panels, respectively. Another common feature across the implied volatility measures is that they all embed a sizeable

Figure 6.4 The top panel plots the corridor variances CIV1–CIV4 scaled by MFIV. The bottom panel plots the corridor variances CIV1–CIV4 and MFIV scaled by BSIV.

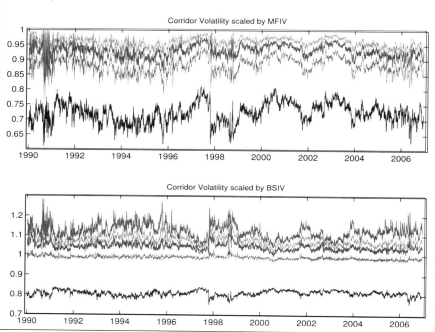

variance risk premium. Concurrent research, eg, Todorov (2007), concludes that the variance risk premium in the VIX tends to grow more than proportionally with the level of underlying volatility. The stationary and mean-reverting nature of RV and the pronounced mean reversion evident from the plots in Figure 6.4 then suggest that the variance risk premium associated with the tails of the RND are particularly volatile. If this line of reasoning has a degree of validity, MFIV may be a poorer predictor of future underlying volatility than alternative, less premium sensitive, implied volatility measures such as BSIV and CIV1. On the other hand, in a recent work Jiang and Tian (2005a) reached the exact opposite conclusion as they found their MFIV measure to dominate all other volatility forecasts, including the BSIV. As our understanding of the variance risk premium dynamics and its manifestation across the different implied volatility measures is related to this issue, we now turn to a direct investigation of the predictive ability of the various volatility indicators. Of course, the findings are also highly relevant for the more general volatility forecasting literature.

The relative forecast performance of implied volatility measures

There is no simple way to rank alternative volatility forecasts as the relative performance generally will depend on the intended use of the predictions. In other words, different loss functions applied to a given forecast error distribution will typically not provide identical rankings. Given this fundamental problem, we resort to the well-known root-mean squared forecast error (RMSE) criterion which is widely used, simple to implement and equipped with convenient statistical properties.

An intuitively appealing starting point from which to explore the predictive ability of the different candidate volatility measures is to include each separately within an in-sample forecast regression, also know as a Mincer–Zarnowitz regression. Letting the *ex-post* RV measure for month $t+1$ be given by y_{t+1} and the volatility predictor j, among a set of J candidate predictors, be denoted by $x_{j,t}, j = 1, \ldots, J$, these univariate regressions take the form

$$y_{t+1} = \alpha_j + \beta_j x_{j,t} + u_{j,t+1} \qquad (6.15)$$

where unbiased forecasts are subject to the constraint on the regression coefficients that $\alpha_j = 0$ and $\beta_j = 1$. Moreover, the regression R^2 captures the degree of variation in the *ex-post* RV explained by the forecast. Likewise, one may explore whether one predictor candidate, x_j, subsumes another, x_k, by including both in an encompassing regression of the form

$$y_{t+1} = \alpha_{jk} + \beta_j x_{j,t} + \beta_k x_{k,t} + u_{jk,t+1} \qquad (6.16)$$

where there is support for the hypothesis that x_j subsumes the information content in x_k if $\beta_j > 0$ and $\beta_k = 0$.

It is clear from our prior findings that the implied volatility measures generally will not be unbiased as they embed a sizeable premium related to equity market volatility risk. Nonetheless, they may well correlate strongly with future volatility and thus serve as useful indicators for prediction. Instead of imposing *a priori* restrictions on the character of the risk premiums, and thus the ensuing forecast biases, we allow the regressions to provide optimal (in-sample) regression coefficients for (linearly) transforming the specific volatility measures into forecasts of future RV for the underlying asset. One immediate concern is that this may induce a small-sample bias, or tendency for over-fitting, given the relatively short history of monthly volatility forecasts, the strong persistence in the realised and implied volatility measures and even the possibility of regime shifts. To assess robustness against such concerns, we split the full sample into an in-sample period of estimation, where the ordinary least-squares (OLS) regression coefficients are obtained, and an out-of-sample period, in which we keep the regression coefficients fixed, and use them to construct monthly volatility forecasts on the basis of the subsequent implied volatility measures constructed from available options data. In other words, no estimation or recalibration is performed in the out-of-sample period. If the in-sample results are reliable, there should be good coherence in the ranking of performance across the two distinct sample periods. We select the initial 10 years, covering 1990–1999, as the in-sample period and then explore robustness of the results in the seven-year out-of-sample period comprising the years 2000–2006. The separation into the estimation and out-of-sample forecast period is indicated by the vertical lines in Figure 6.3.

An additional complication is that the return variation concept often differs across studies depending on the intended application or research question. Most commonly, it is reported on an annual basis in units of standard deviation or volatility, as is standard for Black–Scholes implied volatility. This is also the convention adopted by the CBOE when publicising the VIX. Finally, it has a rationale within the stochastic volatility literature, as the ATM BSIV is approximately linear in the expected integrated volatility of the underlying asset up to expiry. Given the focus on return volatility in the literature, the majority of our exposition concentrates on forecast results for this concept of future monthly RV. However, the theory for MFIVs is developed for the return variance so a number of relations involving MFIV are more naturally couched in terms of variances. Finally, the small-sample properties of the predictive regressions are decidedly better when return variation is measured in log volatilities as this eliminates the main positive outliers and renders the various series close to Gaussian. As a consequence, many prior studies focus on this metric as well. For robustness and compatibility with earlier work, we therefore provide supplementary results for predictive regressions targeting the future monthly log-return volatility as well as the future monthly return variance. As our empirical results turn out to be fully consistent across these settings, we only provide a brief summary of these additional findings.

Results for the full set of predictive regressions along with selected encompassing regressions for future return volatility are given in Table 6.3, while the supplementary results for log-return volatility and return variance are reported in Tables 6.4 and 6.5. Focusing on the columns on the left-hand side of Table 6.3, we first note that the VIX provides the worst in-sample fit among all candidate implied volatility measures although it comes close to the theoretically related model-free and broad corridor implied measures, MFIV and CIV4. The slightly narrower corridor measure CIV3 seems to perform a bit better while the narrowest corridor measures CIV1 and CIV2 along with BSIV perform the best. However, overall the in-sample fit does not differ dramatically across the implied volatility measures so a more definitive conclusion must await the findings from the, in practice, more challenging out-of-sample evidence. As expected, all of the implied volatility forecasts vastly outperform the benchmark consisting of the lagged realised (historical) volatility measures, RVD and RVH, although the latter explain a fairly impressive 54% of the variation in subsequent monthly volatility. The fact that both the historical volatility indicators have a slope coefficient below unity and a significant positive intercept reflects the mean-reverting character of RV. More elaborate autoregressive time series models, estimated from a long history of daily RV measures, tend to perform well (see, for example, Andersen *et al* (2003)), but it is beyond the scope of the present chapter to pursue alternative time series volatility forecast procedures. We simply note that timely high-frequency conditioning information is lost when aggregating the daily RV series into monthly measures. As such, the historical volatility series, RVD and RVH, are mainly included to provide a simple and intuitive lower bound on the degree of volatility predictability over the sample.

Table 6.3 Volatility regressions: the results refer to predictive and encompassing regressions for future monthly RV, as measured by RVH. The explanatory (predictor) variables for each regression are listed in the left column. The estimation period is January 1990 to December 1999 and the out-of-sample forecast period is January 2000 to December 2006. Data was obtained for every trading day, so there is substantial overlap between successive observations on RV. Heteroscedasticity and autocorrelation consistent t-statistics are reported below the regression coefficients.

	In-sample estimation				Out-of-sample RMSE			
	α	β_1	β_2	R^2	All days	Low	Medium	High
RVD	0.05 (5.49)	0.62 (8.15)		46.75	31.91	16.47	26.81	44.15
RVH	0.04 (3.65)	0.74 (8.92)		54.05	30.23	13.91	25.62	42.12
VIX	0.00 (0.08)	0.75 (9.90)		60.25	27.98	10.52	26.45	38.08
BSIV	0.00 (0.36)	0.87 (10.79)		60.83	26.53	10.74	25.70	35.62
CIV1	0.00 (0.22)	1.09 (11.01)		60.79	26.11	10.78	25.39	34.97
CIV2	0.01 (0.55)	0.86 (10.79)		60.88	26.76	10.73	25.90	35.95
CIV3	0.01 (0.71)	0.80 (10.46)		60.59	27.15	10.72	26.21	36.56
CIV4	0.01 (0.70)	0.78 (10.34)		60.28	27.39	10.72	26.41	36.91
MFIV	0.01 (0.45)	0.76 (10.31)		60.34	27.58	10.83	26.58	37.18
RVD + RVH	0.04 (3.40)	−0.08 (−0.39)	0.82 (3.25)	54.13	30.28	13.88	25.72	42.17
RVH + VIX	0.01 (0.43)	0.19 (2.19)	0.59 (6.46)	60.91	27.42	10.53	25.70	37.40
RVH + CIV1	0.01 (0.60)	0.20 (2.04)	0.84 (8.26)	61.62	26.08	10.81	24.87	35.19
VIX + CIV1	0.00 (0.05)	0.30 (1.01)	0.67 (1.93)	61.15	26.47	10.51	25.54	35.64

Table 6.4 Log-volatility regressions: the results refer to predictive and encompassing regressions for future monthly log RV, as measured by log RVH. The explanatory (predictor) variables for each regression are the log of the variable listed in the left column. The estimation period is January 1990 to December 1999 and the out-of-sample forecast period is January 2000 to December 2006. Data was obtained for every trading day, so there is substantial overlap between successive observations on realised log volatility. Heteroscedasticity and autocorrelation consistent t-statistics are reported below the regression coefficients.

	In-sample estimation				Out-of-sample RMSE			
	α	β_1	β_2	R^2	All days	Low	Medium	High
RVD	−0.69 (−6.77)	0.65 (13.97)		53.34	12.70	9.39	11.59	16.08
RVH	−0.44 (−4.09)	0.78 (15.62)		61.48	11.60	8.19	10.71	14.84
VIX	−0.31 (−2.79)	1.00 (16.39)		65.25	10.93	6.95	10.86	13.80
BSIV	−0.18 (−1.71)	0.98 (17.71)		66.79	10.34	6.82	10.56	12.66
CIV1	0.04 (0.30)	0.98 (17.93)		67.21	10.17	6.79	10.44	12.37
CIV2	−0.19 (−1.79)	0.97 (17.73)		66.80	10.42	6.84	10.65	12.79
CIV3	−0.26 (−2.48)	0.96 (17.39)		66.29	10.58	6.87	10.78	13.05
CIV4	−0.29 (−2.75)	0.96 (17.14)		65.81	10.68	6.91	10.88	13.20
MFIV	−0.29 (−2.76)	0.98 (17.10)		65.64	10.76	6.90	11.00	13.30
RVD + RVH	−0.44 (−4.02)	−0.02 (−0.21)	0.81 (6.14)	61.48	11.61	8.19	10.72	14.85
RVH + VIX	−0.28 (−2.59)	0.29 (4.18)	0.67 (7.18)	66.78	10.52	6.86	10.37	13.25
RVH + CIV1	−0.02 (−0.21)	0.23 (3.42)	0.73 (9.67)	68.13	10.07	6.79	10.17	12.35
VIX + CIV1	0.00 (0.03)	0.12 (0.49)	0.86 (4.12)	67.23	10.19	6.75	10.43	12.44

Table 6.5 Variance regressions: the results refer to predictive and encompassing regressions for future monthly realised return variation, as measured by the squared value of RVH. The explanatory (predictor) variables for each regression are the squared values of the variables listed in the left column. The estimation period is January 1990 to December 1999 and the out-of-sample forecast period is January 2000 to December 2006. Data was obtained for every trading day, so there is substantial overlap between successive observations on realised return variation. Heteroscedasticity and autocorrelation consistent t-statistics are reported below the regression coefficients.

	In-sample estimation				Out-of-sample RMSE			
	α	β_1	β_2	R^2	All days	Low	Medium	High
RVD	0.01 (5.12)	0.51 (5.14)		37.51	68.27	24.04	52.52	97.04
RVH	0.01 (3.70)	0.66 (5.31)		43.07	65.98	19.17	51.81	93.88
VIX	0.00 (0.08)	0.60 (5.66)		50.82	59.21	11.27	53.28	82.44
BSIV	0.00 (0.38)	0.80 (6.25)		50.18	56.95	12.00	52.14	78.89
CIV1	0.00 (0.27)	1.26 (6.35)		49.18	56.36	12.10	51.61	78.05
CIV2	0.00 (0.57)	0.80 (6.28)		50.45	57.39	12.07	52.50	79.52
CIV3	0.00 (0.69)	0.70 (6.08)		50.74	58.06	12.07	52.99	80.50
CIV4	0.00 (0.69)	0.65 (6.06)		50.81	58.42	12.03	53.25	81.04
MFIV	0.00 (0.50)	0.62 (6.10)		51.43	58.66	12.20	53.39	81.39
RVD + RVH	0.01 (3.26)	−0.01 (−0.04)	0.67 (1.64)	43.05	65.99	19.13	51.84	93.89
RVH + VIX	0.00 (0.32)	0.13 (1.21)	0.50 (4.44)	51.20	58.92	11.42	52.51	82.21
RVH + CIV1	0.00 (0.69)	0.23 (1.80)	0.92 (5.41)	50.63	57.08	12.35	50.80	79.57
VIX + CIV1	0.00 (0.06)	0.50 (1.50)	0.21 (0.39)	50.87	58.33	11.29	52.82	81.08

Table 6.6 Volatility regressions: the results refer to predictive and encompassing regressions for future monthly RV, as measured by RVH. The explanatory (predictor) variables for each regression are listed in the left column. The estimation period is January 2000 to December 2006 and the out-of-sample forecast period is January 1990 to December 1999. Data was obtained for every trading day, so there is substantial overlap between successive observations on RV. Heteroscedasticity and autocorrelation consistent t-statistics are reported below the regression coefficients.

	In-sample estimation				Out-of-sample RMSE			
	α	β_1	β_2	R^2	All days	Low	Medium	High
RVD	0.05	0.71		54.70	26.00	30.04	21.83	19.83
	(5.46)	(13.85)						
RVH	0.04	0.77		57.94	23.86	27.99	19.23	18.24
	(3.88)	(11.99)						
VIX	−0.01	0.89		67.96	23.46	27.05	19.73	17.98
	(−1.62)	(15.07)						
BSIV	−0.01	0.96		68.39	22.16	26.26	18.07	16.18
	(−0.91)	(15.19)						
CIV1	−0.01	1.16		68.52	21.93	26.21	17.61	15.87
	(−0.66)	(15.07)						
CIV2	−0.01	0.97		68.15	22.24	26.33	18.20	16.24
	(−0.74)	(15.16)						
CIV3	−0.01	0.92		67.93	22.57	26.66	18.56	16.47
	(−0.71)	(15.18)						
CIV4	−0.01	0.90		67.74	22.79	26.82	18.86	16.72
	(−0.79)	(15.14)						
MFIV	−0.01	0.89		67.42	22.82	26.79	18.92	16.85
	(−1.28)	(14.97)						
RVD + RVH	0.04	0.09	0.68	57.98	23.94	28.09	19.37	18.23
	(3.92)	(0.36)	(2.57)					
RVH + VIX	−0.01	0.11	0.79	68.18	23.05	26.78	19.30	17.35
	(−1.27)	(0.88)	(5.90)					
RVH + CIV1	−0.00	0.11	1.03	68.74	21.74	26.01	17.52	15.62
	(−0.45)	(0.81)	(5.34)					
VIX + CIV1	−0.01	0.23	0.87	68.58	22.00	26.10	17.86	16.08
	(−0.88)	(0.47)	(1.37)					

The encompassing regressions provide additional insights. First, to the extent that lagged RV conveys relevant information it is captured entirely by the high-frequency-based measure RVH rather than the daily-return-based measure, RVD. The former has the superior in-sample fit, the encompassing regression including both measures adds no significant explanatory power to what is provided by RVH alone and the regression coefficient associated with RVD is now negative and insignificant. This is consistent with the findings in the literature that realised return variability is measured much more accurately by means of high-frequency return observations. This also supports our use of RVH as the *ex-post* measure of monthly realised return variation for the dependent variable on the left-hand side of the predictive regressions. Second, note that the extremely strong correlation among the implied volatility measures suggests that little can be gained by exploiting two of these simultaneously in the forecast regression setting. This turns out to be true. Results for a representative scenario using both CIV1 and VIX are reported in the table. This pair constitutes a serious candidate for constructing a combined measure as the two displays the lowest correlation among our implied volatility indicators. Nonetheless, the improvement of the in-sample forecast performance is slight and the coefficient on VIX is insignificant. In contrast, if the RVH measure is combined with CIV1 we obtain a larger increase in R^2 and both coefficients are significant. Hence, even if RVH in isolation represents a poorer volatility forecast than VIX, it adds more useful forecast information to the corridor variance measure than the VIX. Hence, the in-sample evidence suggests that, in terms of predictive relevance, the information embedded in the VIX is subsumed by our corridor variance measures while the historical volatility contains useful independent information.

We now turn to the pivotal out-of-sample evidence reported in the central and right columns of Table 6.3. The overall measure of forecast performance is the percentage (normalised) RMSE. If we let $\hat{y}_t$ denote a forecast for y_t, it is formally defined as

$$\text{RMSE} = \frac{\sqrt{E[(\hat{y}-y)^2]}}{\sqrt{E[y^2]}} \times 100$$

The middle column labelled "All days" covers the full out-of-sample period. The findings are consistent with the in-sample results but the relative ranking is even more evident. The narrow CIV measures and the BSIV continue to provide superior forecasts, with CIV1 now sporting the best overall performance. Forecast precision deteriorates monotonically as we move to CIV3, CIV4, MFIV and VIX. As before, the lagged monthly RVs perform significantly worse than all implied volatility measures.

The last three columns of the table document performance over sub-samples obtained by sorting the monthly forecasts in ascending order of ATM BSIV. Hence, results for a third of the monthly forecasts, corresponding to the lowest BSIV measures, are provided in the "Low volatility" column, results for the next third are in the "Medium volatility" column and results for the last third, associated with high BSIV measures, in the last column. First, we note that the historical volatility series perform particularly poorly in the extreme segments of the volatility distribution. It is apparent that the long backward-looking nature of the historical measures constitutes a major disadvantage in terms of providing timely signals concerning the current (and, likely, future) level of return volatility which is most problematic whenever the current volatility level is unusually high or low. Second, all measures perform comparably in the low-volatility regime in terms of normalised RMSE. The slightly better performance of VIX than the other implied volatilities is likely due to idiosyncratic sampling variation. In any case, the VIX and MFIV are the clear losers among the implied volatility measures for the higher volatility scenarios. In fact, the ranking across these two regimes is consistent with the overall findings as top performers listed in order are CIV1, BSIV, CIV2, CIV3, CIV4 and, finally, the two full-fledged model-free implied measures, MFIV and VIX.

The encompassing regressions largely confirm the observations drawn from the univariate out-of-sample predictive regressions. As the coefficients are fixed at values obtained from the estimation sample, it is now feasible, and indeed common, for the combined forecasts to underperform the univariate predictors. In particular, the VIX again adds no value beyond what is captured by CIV1 as the combined forecasts fare worse than the CIV1 forecasts. Moreover, the RVH continues to supplement CIV1 better than the VIX although the indicated improvement, relative to forecasts generated by CIV1 alone, is slight.

The two supplementary sets of results, based on the log-volatility and variance measures of the realised return variation and the corresponding measures for the predictor variables, serve to underscore the robustness of the main qualitative findings. This is especially evident in Table 6.4 where, remarkably, the ranking of the top five log-volatility forecasts is identical across all three volatility sorted sub-samples and also consistent with the ranking obtained for the volatility measures above, while CIV4, MFIV and VIX always perform worse and the historical realised log-volatility measures remain at the bottom. Moreover, the combination of CIV1 and RVH within one encompassing regression now appears even more successful in adding explanatory power beyond what is captured by CIV1 alone, while VIX remains subsumed by CIV1 in this setting. In contrast, the evidence is slightly less clear cut in the more noise-laden regression environment associated with Table 6.5. Even so, the out-of-sample findings still produce the same ranking among the implied forecasts as before.

One obvious concern with this comparative predictive analysis is that the conclusions may be driven by idiosyncratic features in the in-sample or out-of-sample periods. In particular, the forecast precision of some implied measures such as the VIX may be more sensitive to the discrepancy in average volatility across the sub-samples than others. As a final robustness check, we reverse the roles of the estimation and prediction sample. Hence, we run the in-sample regressions for the seven-year period 2000–2006, fix the regression coefficients at the point estimates obtained for this period, and then use historical RVs and observed implied volatilities over 1990–1999 to forecast RV in this "out-of-sample" period. The results reported in Table 6.6 provide strong confirmatory evidence. The ranking of forecast performance is identical to that obtained earlier. Furthermore, this ranking is uniform across the volatility sorted sub-samples. Moreover, in all instances, the combined forecast exploiting both CIV1 and RVH is superior to using the best single implied volatility predictor, CIV1, alone. Finally, the forecast information provided by the VIX measure continues to be subsumed by the information in CIV1.

CONCLUSION

This paper provides the first empirical study of CIV measure in the literature. We find that broad corridor CIV measures serve as good substitutes for MFIV with the advantage that CIV can be measured with better precision owing to the lack of liquid options quotes in the tails of the RND. On the other hand, narrow corridor CIV measures are more closely related to the concept of (ATM) BSIV. As such, they seem less sensitive to time variation in the market volatility risk premium which renders their time series behaviour relatively more stable and allows them to serve as a superior gauge for the future volatility of the underlying asset returns, not only relative to MFIV but also BSIV. Hence, our findings suggest that the best possible market-based implied volatility measure for volatility prediction may take the form of a CIV measure. Even so, there are indications that historical RV contains additional information for future volatility. It is an intriguing research question to determine how best to combine the implied and historically observed volatility measures for forecast purposes.

One general implication is that the MFIV measure should be interpreted strictly for what it seeks to represent, namely the market price of volatility exposure consistent with observed option prices. As such, it is a theoretically superior construction to the BSIV measure and it serves as a natural gauge for the pricing of broad asset categories with a strong exposure to general market risk. In contrast, in terms of direct indicators for future volatility, it must be recognised that MFIV combines volatility forecasting with pricing of the risk associated with volatility. Consequently, even if MFIV provides a pure market-based measure of the future return variation, the strong variation in the market pricing of volatility risk renders the linkage to the volatility process of the underlying asset tenuous. Nonetheless, our finding that the predictive content of the MFIV, and the VIX, is fully subsumed by the information conveyed by a narrow corridor CIV measure, or the BSIV, is new to the literature and contrary to some previous findings. However, our conclusion is based on a much longer time series and more carefully constructed volatility measures than existing studies of the relative predictive ability of VIX, or MFIV, and BSIV. The robustness of our finding is collaborated by the striking monotone improvement in forecast performance of the CIV measures as the corridor width is narrowed as well as the consistent results obtained across differently sorted subsamples.

In addition, we argue that the lack of liquid options in the tails of the RND induces inevitable measurement errors in MFIV which may be mitigated by restricting attention to a related CIV measure. Given how the VIX is actually constructed, this is in fact a fairly accurate descriptive of current practice. As such, explicit acknowledgment of the need and desirability of using a corridor measure in lieu of the full-fledged MFIV may motivate a modified implementation strategy which computes the measure on the basis of a predefined range of the RND rather than by means of a more error-prone random truncation procedure.

A constructive message of our study is that judiciously selected CIV measures can be exploited in a theoretically coherent and empirically tractable manner to further refine the information embedded in the derivatives markets. For example, combining complementary CIV measures should enable us to detect variation in the pricing of equity volatility risk across distinct future states of the world in a timely fashion. This will facilitate more detailed studies of the interaction between the pricing of equity volatility and the conditions of related financial markets. In particular, this may shed some new light on the well-documented, but poorly understood, linkages between the VIX index, the overall functioning and liquidity of the financial system and the pricing in global equity, credit and debt markets.

Finally, as long as the requisite option markets are sufficiently active, these tools are applicable across any asset class and horizon, irrespective of whether an official volatility index is being compiled and released or not. Hence, the notions of MFIV and CIV are not tied to equity-index volatility pricing and forecasting over a monthly horizon, but rather provide useful tools for quantifying and interpreting corresponding dynamic market features across diverse asset categories and maturities.

APPENDIX A. DERIVATION OF VALUE OF THE BARRIER VARIANCE UNDER BLACK–SCHOLES

One way to derive (6.12) is to write

$$E_0^Q[g(F_T)] = \int_0^\infty g(K)h_0(K)\,dK = -\int_0^\infty g'(K)H_0(K)\,dK$$

$$= \int_0^\infty \left(\frac{1}{K} - \frac{1}{B}\right) I_0 H_0(K)\,dK$$

$$= \int_0^B \frac{H_0(K)}{K}\,dK - \frac{P_0(B)}{B}$$

where $H_t(K)$ is the risk-neutral cumulative density function. For the Black–Scholes model,

$$H_0(K) = N(z), \quad z = z(K) := -\frac{\ln(F_0/K)}{\sigma\sqrt{\tau}} + \frac{1}{2}\sigma\sqrt{\tau}$$

The formula in (6.12) can now be obtained by noting that

$$\int_0^B \frac{H_0(B)}{K}\,dK = \int_0^y N(z)\sigma\sqrt{\tau}\,dz = \sigma\sqrt{\tau}(yN(y) - n(y))$$

and

$$\frac{P_0(K)}{B} = N(y) - \frac{F_0}{B}N(y - \sigma\sqrt{\tau})$$

APPENDIX B. CONSTRUCTION OF THE DATASET

To construct our dataset, we follow several steps.

1. For both options and futures we use settlement prices. Settlement prices (as opposed to closing prices) do not suffer from non-synchronous/stale trading of options and the bid–ask spreads. CME calculates settlement prices simultaneously for all options, based on their last bid and ask prices. As these prices are used to determine daily margin requirements, they are scrutinised carefully by the exchange and watched closely by traders. As a result, settlement prices are less likely to suffer from recording errors and they rarely violate basic no-arbitrage restrictions. In contrast, closing prices are generally less reliable and less complete.
2. In the dataset, we match all puts and calls by trading date t, maturity T and strike. For each pair (t, T), we drop very low (high) strikes for which put (call) price is less than 0.1.

To convert spot prices to forward prices, we approximate the risk-free rate r_f over $[t, T]$ by the rate of Treasury bills.

3. As the CME options are American-type options, their prices $P_t^A(K)$ and $C_t^A(K)$ could be slightly higher than prices of the corresponding European options $P_t(K)$ and $C_t(K)$. The difference, however, is very small for the short maturities that we focus on. This is particularly true for OTM and ATM options.[8] To infer the prices of European options $P_t(K)$ and $C_t(K)$, we proceed as follows. First, we discard all ITM options. That is, we use put prices for $K/F_t \leq 1.00$ and call prices for $K/F_t \geq 1.00$. Prices of OTM and ATM options are both more reliable and less affected by the early exercise feature. Second, we correct American option prices $P_t^A(K)$ and $C_t^A(K)$ for the value of the early exercise feature by using the approximation of Barone-Adesi and Whaley (1987).[9] Third, we compute the prices of ITM options through the put–call parity relationship

$$P_t(K) + F_t = C_t(K) + K$$

4. We check option prices for violations of the no-arbitrage restrictions. To preclude arbitrage opportunities, call and put prices must be monotonic and convex functions of the strike. In particular, the call pricing function $C_t(K)$ must satisfy:

(a) $C_t(K) \geq (F_t - K)^+$;
(b) $-1 \leq C_t'(K) \leq 0$;
(c) $C_t''(K) \geq 0$.

The corresponding conditions for the put pricing function $P_t(K)$ follow from put-call parity. When restrictions (a)–(c) are violated, we enforce them by running the so-called constrained convex regression (CCR); see Bondarenko (2000). Intuitively, CCR searches for the smallest (in the sense of least squares) perturbation of option prices that restores the no-arbitrage restrictions. For most trading days, option settlement prices already satisfy the restrictions (a)–(c). Still, CCR is a useful procedure because it allows one to identify possible recording errors or typos.

5. For each pair (t, T), we estimate RND using the PCA procedure of Bondarenko (2000, 2003). Armed with RND, we may obtain the put and call pricing functions as well as the other fundamental objects used in our analysis.

2. In reality, of course, the risk-free rate is non-zero. However, in the empirical tests below, we convert spot prices of options into forward prices (for delivery at time T). To obtain forward prices, spot prices are multiplied by $e^{r_f(T-t)}$, where r_f is the risk-free rate over $[t, T]$. For example, the forward put price is $P_t(K) = e^{r_f(T-t)} P_t^s(K)$, where $P_t^s(K)$ is the spot put price. A similar approach has been used by, for example, Dumas *et al* (1998).

3. See also Carr and Madan (1998), Demeterfi *et al* (1999) and Britten-Jones and Neuberger (2000).

4. This property is highlighted by, eg, Andersen and Bollerslev (1998), Andersen *et al* (2001), Barndorff-Nielsen and Shephard (2001, 2002) and Meddahi (2002).

5. Given the limited microstructure effects in the S&P500 futures market, the analysis of Andersen *et al* (2006a) indicates that this should work well in practice. Alternatively, one may utilise even higher-frequency intraday returns and exploit the robust procedures advocated recently by, eg, Bandi and Russell (2005), Zhang *et al* (2005) and Barndorff-Nielsen *et al* (2006).

6. Consecutive daily observations on the future monthly RV share 20 of the 21 trading day realised return variation measures that are cumulated to provide the monthly RV measure. Thus, only at the 21 trading day (monthly) frequency is the series not mechanically correlated.

7. The correlations among the volatility measures across the two sub-samples were nearly identical to the corresponding statistics for the full sample reported in Table 6.2. Hence, for brevity, we do not report these correlation statistics for the shorter sample periods.

8. As shown by Whaley (1986), the early exercise premium increases with the level of the risk-free rate, volatility, time to maturity, and degree to which an option is in-the-money.

9. It is important to point out that this correction is always substantially smaller than typical bid–ask spreads. In particular, the correction generally does not exceed 0.2% of an option price.

REFERENCES

Andersen, T. G. and T. Bollerslev, 1998, "Answering the Skeptics: Yes, Standard Volatility Models do Provide Accurate Forecasts", *International Economic Review*, **39**, pp 885–905.

Andersen, T. G., T. Bollerslev, F. X. Diebold and P. Labys, 2001, "The Distribution of Exchange Rate Volatility", *Journal of the American Statistical Association*, **96**, pp 42–55.

Andersen, T. G., T. Bollerslev, F. X. Diebold and P. Labys, 2003, "Modeling and Forecasting Realized Volatility", *Econometrica*, **71**, pp 579–625.

Andersen, T. G., T. Bollerslev and N. Meddahi, 2006a, "Realized Volatility Forecasting and Market Microstructure Noise", Working Paper, Kellogg School, Northwestern University, Duke University and Imperial College.

Andersen, T. G., P. H. Frederiksen and A. Staal, 2006b, "The Information Content of Realized Volatility Forecasts", Working Paper, Kellogg School of Management, Northwestern University.

Ang, A., R. J. Hodrick, Y. Xing and X. Zhang, 2006, "The Cross-section of Volatility and Expected Returns", *Journal of Finance*, **61**, pp 259–299.

Bakshi, G. S. and N. Kapadia, 2003, "Delta-hedged Gains and the Negative Market Volatility Risk Premium", *Review of Financial Studies*, **16**, pp 527–566.

Bakshi, G. S. and D. Madan, 2000, "Spanning and Derivative-Security Valuation", *Journal of Financial Economics*, **55**, pp 205–238.

Bakshi, G. S. and D. Madan, 2006, "A Theory of Volatility Spreads", *Management Science*, **52**, pp 1945–1956.

Bandi, F. and J. Russell, 2005, "Microstructure Noise, Realized Volatility, and Optimal Sampling", Working Paper, University of Chicago.

Banz, R. and M. Miller, 1978, "Prices for State-contingent Claims: Some Estimates and Applications", *Journal of Business*, **51**, pp 653–672.

Barndorff-Nielsen, O. E., P. R. Hansen, A. Lunde and N. Shephard, 2006, "Designing Realised Kernels to Measure the *Ex-post* Variation of Equity Prices in the Presence of Noise", Working Paper, Oxford University.

Barndorff-Nielsen, O. E. and N. Shephard, 2001, "Non-Gaussian OU Based Models and Some of Their Uses in Financial Economics", *Journal of the Royal Statistical Society B*, **63**, pp 167–241.

Barndorff-Nielsen, O. E. and N. Shephard, 2002, "Econometric Analysis of Realised Volatility and its Use in Estimating Stochastic Volatility Models", *Journal of the Royal Statistical Society B*, **64**, pp 253–280.

Barone-Adesi, G. and R. Whaley, 1987, "Efficient Analytical Approximation of American Option Values", *Journal of Finance*, **42**, pp 301–320.

Black, F. and M. Scholes, 1973, "The Pricing of Options and Corporate Liabilities", *Journal of Political Economy*, **81**, pp 637–654.

Bliss, R. R. and N. Panigirtzoglou, 2004, "Option-Implied Risk Aversion Estimates", *Journal of Finance*, **59**, pp 407–446.

Bollerslev, T., M. Gibson and H. Zhou, 2007, "Dynamic Estimation of Volatility Risk Premia from Option-Implied and Realized Volatilities", Working Paper, Duke University and Federal Reserve Board of Governors.

Bollerslev, T. and H. Zhou, 2007, "Expected Stock Returns and Variance Risk Premia", Working Paper, Duke University and Federal Reserve Board of Governors.

Bondarenko, O., 2000, "Recovering Risk-neutral Densities: A New Nonparametric Approach", Working Paper, University of Illinois at Chicago.

Bondarenko, O., 2003, "Estimation of Risk-neutral Densities Using Positive Convolution Approximation", *Journal of Econometrics*, **116**, pp 85-112.

Bondarenko, O., 2007, "Variance Trading and Market Price of Variance Risk", Working Paper, University of Illinois at Chicago.

Breeden, D. and R. Litzenberger, 1978, "Prices of State Contingent Claims Implicit in Options Prices", *Journal of Business*, **51**, pp 621–652.

Britten-Jones, M. and A. Neuberger, 2000, "Option Prices, Implied Price Processes, and Stochastic Volatility", *Journal of Finance*, **55**, pp 839–866.

Carr, P. and D. Madan, 1998, "Towards a Theory of Volatility Trading", in R. Jarrow (ed), *Volatility* (London: Risk Publications), pp 417-427.

Carr, P. and L. Wu, 2004, "Variance Risk Premia", Working Paper, New York University and Baruch College.

Demeterfi, K., E. Derman, M. Kamal and J. Zou, 1999, "More Than You Ever Wanted to Know About Volatility Swaps", Working Paper, Goldman Sachs, http://www.gs.com/qs/doc/volswaps.pdf.

Duan, J.-C. and C.-Y. Yeh, 2007, "Jump and Volatility Risk Premiums Implied by VIX", Working Paper, Rotman School of Management, University of Toronto.

Dumas, B., J. Fleming and R. Whaley, 1998, "Implied Volatility Functions: Empirical Tests", *Journal of Finance*, **53**, pp 2059–2106.

Dupire, B., 1993, "Model Art", *Risk* (September), pp 118–120.

Jiang, G. and Y. Tian, 2005a, "The Model-Free Implied Volatility and Its Information Content", *Review of Financial Studies*, **18**, pp 1305–1342.

Jiang, G. and Y. Tian, 2005b, "Gauging the 'Investor Fear Gauge': Implementation Problems in the CBOE's New Volatility Index and a Simple Solution", Working Paper, University of Arizona.

Meddahi, N., 2002, "A Theoretical Comparison Between Integrated and Realized Volatility", *Journal of Applied Econometrics*, **17**, pp 479–508.

Neuberger, A., 1994, "The Log Contract: A New Instrument to Hedge Volatility", *Journal of Portfolio Management* (Winter), pp 74–80.

Ross, S., 1976, "Options and Efficiency", *Quarterly Journal of Economics*, **90**, pp 75–89.

Todorov, V., 2007, "Variance Risk Premium Dynamics", Working Paper, Duke University.

Whaley, R., 1986, "Valuation of American Futures Options: Theory and Empirical Tests", *Journal of Finance*, **41**, pp 127–150.

Wu, L., 2004, "Variance Dynamics: Joint Evidence from Options and High-Frequency Returns", Working Paper, Baruch College.

Zhang, L., P. A. Mykland and Y. Aït-Sahalia, 2005, "A Tale of Two Time Scales: Determining Integrated Volatility with Noisy High-Frequency Data", *Journal of the American Statistical Association*, **100**, pp 1394–1411.

Part III

New Products Related to Trading Volatility

7

Second-Generation Volatility Products

Nicolas Mougeot

Deutsche Bank

The goal of this chapter is to introduce investors to sophisticated derivatives instruments that allow them to take views on volatility. Despite the fact that volatility-sensitive derivatives have been traded for years if not centuries, it is only recently that products giving pure exposure to volatility have appeared.

We start our overview by discussing the weaknesses of "traditional" methods of volatility investing. Although buying/selling straddles is an easy way to bet on volatility, the delta (ie, the portfolio's sensitivity to stock returns) ceases to be null once the stock moves away from its initial value.

One way to circumvent this problem is to delta-hedge the positions. However, as we demonstrate in the following, delta-hedging options does not yield pure exposure to volatility since the trader/investor then faces a further vega risk as well as a model/path dependency risk.

Variance swaps provide a pure view on volatility since they pay the difference between future realised variance and a pre-defined strike price. The rapid development of variance swaps reflects the simplicity with which they can be valued: under certain non-restrictive assumptions, the variance swap strike price can be shown to be equal to the value of an options portfolio that uses a continuum of strike prices and is inversely weighted by the square of the options' strike prices.

Variance swaps can be used in many ways, ranging from arbitraging realised versus implied volatility and dispersion trading, to hedging structured products or hedge fund strategies.

We also describe other volatility products that have been developed in recent years or even months. Gamma swaps are similar to variance swaps but with a notional that is a function of the asset price. Corridor and conditional variance swaps are two variants of variance that provide an asymmetric exposure to volatility while allowing investors to take positions on the skew.

VOLATILITY INVESTING: AN OLD STORY AND SOME RECENT INNOVATIONS

"Behold, there shall come seven years of great plenty in the whole land of Egypt. After which shall follow other seven years of so great scarcity, that all the abundance before shall be forgotten: for the famine shall consume all the land, and the greatness of the scarcity shall destroy the greatness of the plenty."

Genesis, Chapter 41

Chapter 41 of Genesis tells the story of an Egyptian Pharaoh. In his dream, the Pharaoh dreamed about seven cows, very beautiful and fat, which are then devoured by seven lean and skinny cows. The Pharaoh then called for all of the wise men of his country to interpret his dream. Joseph told Pharaoh that God wanted to let him know with this dream that Egypt would experience seven years of feast followed by seven years of famine. He therefore recommended Pharaoh to store corn as a hedge and the Pharaoh put Joseph in charge of administrating the hedging programme.

As Chance (1995) mentions, Joseph can in a way be considered as one of the first people to have used a derivatives instrument. Aristotle is also probably the first person to mention options in his *Politics* essay. Thales the Milesian, who anticipated great harvesting the following year, took options of olive presses and then rented them at a very high price a year after.

Investing in volatility contracts or volatility-sensitive products is therefore nothing new. As Chance (1995) points out, the first derivatives market – the Royal Stock Exchange in London – started forward trading in 1637. However, the growth of derivatives instruments has long been linked to the parallel development of mathematical tools for efficient pricing and hedging. Despite the breakthroughs presented by Bachelier (1900) in his PhD Thesis, trading in equity options only took off after the Black–Scholes model was published in 1973.

Contracts based on variance, such as variance swaps, were already being mentioned in the 1990s, but they only really took off after Carr and Madan developed an original pricing method in 2001.

While the emergence of variance swaps has allowed investors to take a pure position on volatility without taking on other risks, a second-generation of volatility products, including gamma corridor and conditional variance swaps, has appeared. These products provide investors with tools for taking positions on the skew/smile and efficiently trading dispersion.

The goal of this chapter is therefore to explain the methods of trading volatility, from straddles to variance swaps to second-generation products.

VOLATILITY AS AN ASSET CLASS: AN OVERVIEW
Introduction
While many authors have explored the topic of "volatility as an asset class", we believe that much of what has been written is based on false assumptions about how volatility can currently be traded.

The goal of this chapter is not to come up with a "set-in-stone" allocation between traditional asset classes and volatility, but to show investors how much value can be extracted from a series of new volatility products that allow them to directly invest in volatility.

Defining volatility
We define annualised variance as the average of the squared returns of a given asset, ie,

$$\text{Variance} = \frac{252}{T} \sum_{t=1}^{T} r_t^2$$

We define returns in log terms

$$r_t = \ln[P_t/P_{t-1}]$$

Volatility is the square root of variance:

$$\text{Volatility} = \sqrt{\frac{252}{T}\sum_{t=1}^{T} r_t^2}$$

Both variance and volatility are measures of equity risk, but it is common to refer to volatility because it is in the same unit as stock returns. Furthermore, if stock returns are normally distributed, returns lie within ± 2 standard deviations from the mean in 95% of cases. For example, if a stock yields a 10% average annual return with 15% volatility, the stock would have a 95% probability of lying between -5% and $+25\%$ in one year. The interval is symmetric if we use simple returns, ie, $r_t = \ln[P_t/P_{t-1}] - 1$. If we use log returns, the interval is -5% to $+28\%$.

Outright straddles or strangles positions

The simplest way to obtain an exposure to volatility is to buy or sell straddles or strangles. A straddle involves buying an at-the-money (ATM) call and an ATM put, while a strangle is a combination of one out-of-the-money (OTM) call and one OTM put.

Buying or selling a straddle or a strangle outright expresses a view on how much a stock or an index will move between today and maturity. Hence, it is a way to speculate on the terminal distribution of stock prices, not to capture the stock's day-to-day realised volatility. Since straddles are composed of a call and a put, their value rises with volatility and, as such, they provide a means for investors to get exposure to changes in implied volatility. Since the two options are ATM, straddles are initially quite expensive. In view of this, one way to decrease the premium paid upfront is to buy strangles since they combine two cheaper OTM options. However, an investor buying a strangle would require the stock price to move more in order to make money.

Taking volatility positions by delta-hedging options

In order to capture daily realised volatility, investors could buy or sell an option and delta-hedge it. Let us assume that at time t, the investor:

- sells an option, a call or a put, denoted by $O(S_t, T; \sigma_i)$, with maturity T, strike K as a percentage of spot price S and an initial implied volatility σ_i;

Figure 7.1 (a) Straddle and (b) strangle profiles at and before maturity. (Source: Deutsche Bank.)

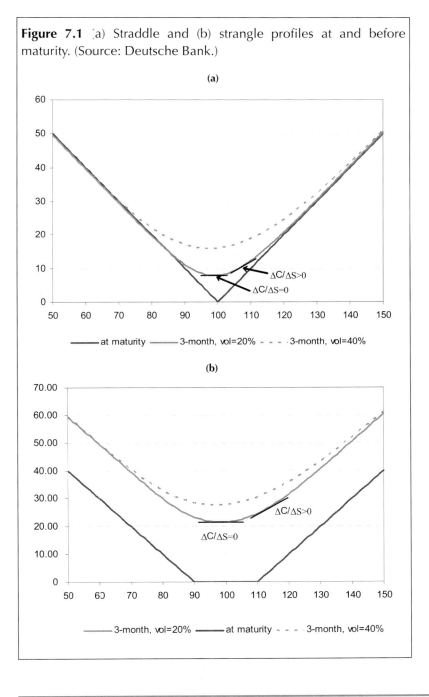

- buys Δ stocks in order to delta-hedge the position;
- borrows $-V(S_t, T; \sigma_i) + \Delta S$ to finance the position if necessary.

In order to remove the portfolio sensitivity to stock prices and obtain a pure exposure to volatility risk, the amount of stocks held, Δ, is periodically re-adjusted to ensure that the portfolio's sensitivity to the stock price remains null. This is what we call delta-hedging. At time t, Δ is thus equal to

$$\Delta_t = \frac{\partial}{\partial S} V(S_t, 0; \sigma)$$

Let us further assume that the option is delta-hedged at a constant implied volatility σ_h. The profit and loss (P&L) resulting from delta-hedging an option is, by definition, equal to the final cost of the option minus its initial cost minus the cost of delta-hedging the position. Under these assumptions, Mougeot (2004) showed that the P&L can be broken up into three components:

$$P\&L = \underbrace{(\sigma_i^2 - \hat{\sigma}^2)T g_0}_{1} + \underbrace{(\hat{\sigma}^2 - \sigma_h^2)T \left[g_0 - \frac{1}{T}\int_0^T g_t \, dt\right]}_{2}$$

$$+ \underbrace{\int_0^T (\hat{\sigma}^2 - \sigma_t^2) g_t \, dt}_{3}$$

where g_t is, by definition, equal to

$$g_t = \frac{e^{r(T-t)}}{2\sigma_h} \frac{\partial}{\partial \sigma} V(S_t, T-t; \sigma_h)$$

As Mougeot (2004) and Blanc (2004) highlight, these three components may be described as follows.

I. A "variance risk" component or a variance swap exposure for a notional amount equal to $T g_0$ and a variance strike equal to the square of the option implied volatility.

II. A "vega risk" factor, which stems from the fact that the option is hedged at the implied volatility σ_h instead of at the realised volatility $\hat{\sigma}$. This term is indeed null if the trader is able to hedge at the realised, but unknown, volatility.

III. A "volatility path dependency risk" or "model risk" factor that depends on the historical behaviour of realised volatility. Under the Black–Scholes assumption, the instantaneous volatility σ_t is constant and thus equal to the realised volatility between time t and T. However, should the volatility vary over time, $(\hat{\sigma}^2 - \sigma_t^2)$ will no longer be zero. As g_t is a decreasing function of time to maturity, this term will be positive if instantaneous, or intra-day, volatility rises during the life of the option. The term also depends on the true distribution of stock returns.

As a result, delta-hedging options does not provide a pure exposure to volatility, given that the P&L not only depends on variance risk but also on a vega risk which itself results from the fact that risk cannot be hedged at the (unknown future) realised volatility and that volatility may not be constant over time.

Indeed, delta-hedging options yields further risk sources not indicated above. The above analysis was performed without taking into account dividends and by assuming a constant interest rate.

Furthermore, the delta-hedging of options is impacted by transaction costs and liquidity issues. The above analysis does not take into account the fact that trading stocks is costly and that certain stocks and indices may lack liquidity. These issues paved the way for the introduction of new derivatives instruments that enable investors to take a pure view on volatility without bearing any other risks.

VARIANCE SWAP: A FIRST STEP TOWARDS VOLATILITY INVESTING

Variance swaps emerged in the 1990s as a means of circumventing the issues raised by taking volatility positions through the purchase of straddles/strangles or through delta-hedging options. Although variance swaps were initially considered as exotic products, over recent years, they have become flow products as a result of certain features that we will describe in greater detail in this section. These are:

- simple payouts;
- simple replication via portfolios of vanilla options.

Figure 7.2 Variance swap payout, where K^2_{vega} is the variance strike price, $\sigma^2_{realised}$ is the realised variance and N is the variance notional amount. (Source: Deutsche Bank.)

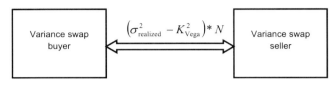

What is a variance swap?

A variance swap is a forward contract on realised variance. At maturity, it pays the difference between the realised variance and a predefined variance strike price multiplied by an agreed notional N.

Variance swaps are over-the-counter (OTC) products governed by a number of market conventions.

1. *Maturity.* Short-term as well as long-term variance swaps are available for investors on major indices (S&P500, €-Stoxx50, Nikkei225, etc) as well as on single stocks. The most liquid tenors are, in general, three-month to one-year for single stock variance swaps and three-month to two-year for index variance swaps. Even though variance swaps are OTC products, their maturities usually match listed option expiries, such as March 2007, June 2007 or December 2007.

2. *Strike price.* While the payout is function of variance, strike price is generally expressed as volatility and scaled by a factor of 100. Hence, if a variance swap has a volatility strike price equal to 20%, the variance used in the payout calculation is 400 (20 × 20).

3. *Notional.* A variance swap's notional is defined in variance units, but is often expressed as an approximate sensitivity to volatility. The notional in volatility terms, called the "vega" notional, approximates the P&L for a one volatility point difference between the volatility strike and the realised volatility. Variance and volatility notionals are related as follows:

$$\text{Notional}_{vega} = 2K_{vega} \times \text{Notional}_{variance}$$

where K_{vega} is the variance swap's volatility strike.

Hence, if the strike price expressed in volatility is 20%, and the variance notional is equal to US$2,500, then the equivalent vega notional is approximately US$100,000. It is worth keeping in mind that this approximation is only good when the future realised volatility is close to the volatility strike price. In addition, the vega notional is only given as an indication in a variance swap's termsheet while the effective final payout is a function of the variance notional.

Today, vega notionals for single-stock variance swaps typically range from US$25,000 to US$100,000, while vega notionals for index variance swaps commonly vary from US$100,000 to US$250,000.

4. *Volatility cap*. A dealer would typically hedge a variance swap using a strip of options that spans a range of strike prices. In theory, a trader would need a continuum of options at all strikes. In practice indeed, only a limited number of strikes are available and far OTM or in-the-money (ITM) options may not exist or may be illiquid.

The inability to perfectly replicate a variance swap in practice is why single stock variance swaps are often capped. A 2.5 cap on volatility means that the variance swap buyer can receive no more than 2.5 times the initial volatility strike. For example, if the volatility strike is equal to 20% and the cap is 50 (2.5 × 20), then the variance swap's buyer will receive at most Notional × ($50^2 - 20^2$) even if volatility is above 50% during the variance swap's life.

Table 7.1 displays an example of a hypothetical variance swap's payout in different market scenarios.

Pricing: the intuitive approach

Before examining variance swap pricing in detail, we shall explain the logic behind the mathematical derivation.

First, variance swap payout is, by definition, a function of the variance and is independent of the stock price level. However, the sensitivity of an option to variance depends on the stock price level. The sensitivity of an option to the variance, or variance vega, is centred around the strike price and will thus change daily according to changes in the stock price level.

Table 7.1 Variance swap's payout in different market scenarios. (Source: Deutsche Bank.)

Variance strike price in volatility terms	20%
Vega notional	€100,000
Variance notional	€2,500
Maturity	June 2007
Scenario 1	Realised volatility: 15% Payout: $2,500 \times (15^2 - 20^2) = -€437,500$
Scenario 2	Realised volatility: 20% Payout: $2,500 \times (20^2 - 20^2) = €0$
Scenario 3	Realised volatility: 25% Payout: $2,500 \times (25^2 - 20^2) = +€562,500$

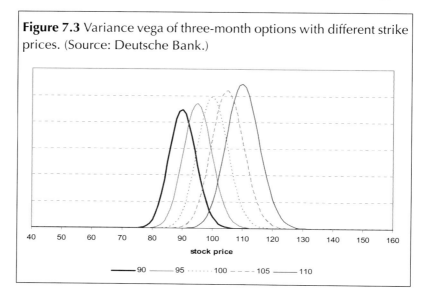

Figure 7.3 Variance vega of three-month options with different strike prices. (Source: Deutsche Bank.)

As Figure 7.3 shows, the variance vega declines as the stock price moves away from the strike price and is also an increasing function of the strike price. The goal is therefore to create an options portfolio with a constant variance vega.

This can be done by investing in a portfolio of options inversely weighted by the square of their strike prices. Figure 7.4 displays the variance vega of:

(a) a portfolio composed of three options with strike prices of 95% and 105%, and weighted $1/(95)^2$ and $1/(105)^2$, respectively; and
(b) a portfolio composed of 13 options with strike prices ranging from 70 to 130% and weighted from $1/(70)^2$ to $1/(130)^2$.

Figure 7.4 shows that the addition of options with strike prices away from ATM flattens variance vega and thus makes the portfolio sensitive to variance but invariant to stock price.

The Carr and Madan's formal pricing approach

Based on initial works by Neuberger (1994, 1996), Carr and Madan (1998) suggested a formal method for pricing variance swaps that has the advantage of requiring very few assumptions about stock price dynamics. Instead of defining a process for the stock price, Carr and Madan only assumed that markets are complete and that trading can take place continuously. As a result, their results hold for restrictive assumptions such as those underlying the Black–Scholes model and can also be extended to other models such as stochastic volatility.

First, Ito's lemma states that any smooth function $f(F_t)$ can be rewritten as

$$f(F_T) = f(F_0) + \int_0^T f'(F_t) \, dF_t + \frac{1}{2} \int_0^T F_t^2 f''(F_t) \sigma_t^2 \, dt \qquad (7.1)$$

Let us consider the following function:

$$f(F_t) = \ln(F_0/F_t) + \frac{F_t}{F_0} - 1$$

where F_t stands for the futures price. This function has a slope and a value equal to zero when $F_t = F_0$.

Therefore, we have

$$\frac{1}{2} \int_0^T \sigma_t^2 \, dt = \ln(F_0/F_T) + \frac{F_T}{F_0} - 1 - \int_0^T \left(\frac{1}{F_0} - \frac{1}{F_t} \right) dF_t \qquad (7.2)$$

Carr and Madan further assumed that a market exists for futures options of all strikes. In this case, they showed that any payout

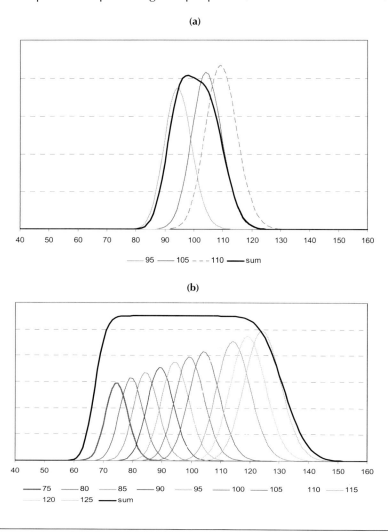

Figure 7.4 Straddle and strangle profiles at and before maturity: (a) three options; (b) combination of options with strike prices ranging from 70% to 130% inversely weighted by the square of their strike prices as a percentage of spot price. (Source: Deutsche Bank.)

SECOND-GENERATION VOLATILITY PRODUCTS

$f(F_T)$ of the futures price F_T can be broken up into

$$f(F_T) = \underbrace{f(\kappa)}_{1} + \underbrace{f'(\kappa)[(F_T - \kappa)^+ - (\kappa - F_T)^+]}_{2}$$
$$+ \underbrace{\int_0^\kappa f''(\kappa)(K - F_T)^+ \, dK}_{3} + \underbrace{\int_\kappa^\infty f''(\kappa)(F_T - K)^+ \, dK}_{4}$$
(7.3)

where κ is an arbitrary number. As Carr and Madan pointed out, the above terms can be interpreted as:

1. a position in $f(\kappa)$ discount bond;
2. a position in $f'(\kappa)$ calls with a strike price equal to κ minus $f'(\kappa)$ puts with the same strike price;
3. a static position in $f''(\kappa) \, dK$ puts at all strikes less than κ;
4. a static position in $f''(\kappa) \, dK$ calls at all strikes greater than κ.

In the absence of arbitrage, the above breakdown must prevail for initial values. Therefore, the initial value of the payout is equal to

$$V_f^0 = f(\kappa)B_0 + f'(\kappa)[C_0(\kappa) - P_0(\kappa)]$$
$$+ \int_0^\kappa f''(\kappa)P_0(\kappa) \, dK + \int_\kappa^\infty f''(\kappa)C_0(\kappa) \, dK$$

Carr and Madan thus proved that an arbitrary payout can be obtained from bond and option prices without making strong assumptions about the stochastic process driving the stock price.[1]

Applying Equation (7.3) to the function $f(F_t) = \ln(F_0/F_t) + (F_t/F_0) - 1$ and setting $\kappa = F_0$, we obtain

$$\ln(F_0/F_t) + \frac{F_T}{F_0} - 1 = \int_0^{F_0} \frac{1}{K^2}(K - F_T)^+ \, dK + \int_{F_0}^\infty \frac{1}{K^2}(F_T - K)^+ \, dK$$

Therefore, in order to receive $\int_0^T \sigma_t^2 \, dt$ at time T, a trader should buy a continuum of puts with strike prices ranging from 0 to F_0 and calls with strike prices ranging from F_0 to infinity. The initial cost is equal to

$$\int_0^{F_0} \frac{2}{K^2} P_0(K) \, dK + \int_{F_0}^\infty \frac{2}{K^2} C_0(K) \, dK \qquad (7.4)$$

The trader further needs to roll a futures position, holding at t:

$$-2\,e^{-rT}\left(\frac{1}{F_0} - \frac{1}{F_t}\right) \tag{7.5}$$

The net payout of (7.4) and (7.5) at maturity T is

$$\int_0^{F_0} \frac{2}{K^2}(K - F_T)^+ \, dK + \int_{F_0}^{\infty} \frac{2}{K^2}(F_T - K)^+ \, dK - 2\int_0^T \left(\frac{1}{F_0} - \frac{1}{F_t}\right) dF_t$$

$$= 2\left(\ln(F_0/F_t) + \frac{F_T}{F_0} - 1\right) - 2\int_0^T \left(\frac{1}{F_0} - \frac{1}{F_t}\right) dF_t$$

$$= \int_0^T \sigma_t^2 \, dt$$

Since the initial cost of achieving this strategy is given by (7.4), the fair forward value of the variance at time 0 should be equal to

$$V_f[\sigma_{0,T}^2] = \frac{2\,e^{rT}}{T}\left[\int_0^{F_0} \frac{1}{K^2} P_0(K)\, dK + \int_{F_0}^{\infty} \frac{1}{K^2} C_0(K)\, dK\right]$$

Variance-swap strike prices may thus be replicated by a continuum of puts and calls inversely weighted by the square of their strike price. Note that the above valuation is model-free since we did not have to state a specific process for the dynamic of the stock price in order to derive the formula. It is also worth mentioning that the above formula provides a market-based estimator of future realised volatility.

Why is volatility interesting?

Historically, volatility has been considered primarily as a risk measure or a pricing parameter in derivatives instruments. However, due to advances in financial engineering in the past decade we now think of it as an asset class in its own right, and one with the following interesting characteristics.

- Equity market volatility is negatively correlated with index returns. In particular, volatility tends to rise when stocks fall (see Figure 7.5).
- Volatility clusters: equity volatility is not constant over time. Historically, we have seen extended periods of high volatility followed by extended periods of low volatility (see Figure 7.6).

Figure 7.5 Volatility tends to rise when markets falls. (Source: Deutsche Bank, Bloomberg.)

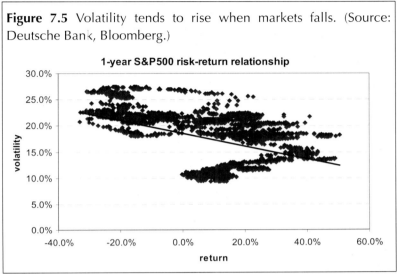

Figure 7.6 Volatility experiences high and low "regimes". (Source: Deutsche Bank, Bloomberg.)

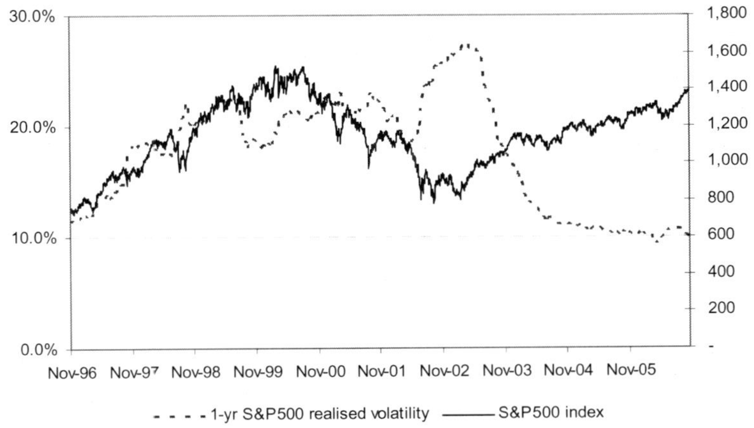

While returns may not be auto-correlated,[2] squared returns may be positively auto-correlated. Small magnitude returns tend to be followed by more small magnitude returns, and large magnitude returns tend to be followed by more large magnitude returns, but not necessarily with the same sign.

Since volatility tends to rise when stocks fall, volatility might seem promising in helping to diversify an equity portfolio. We will, however, demonstrate in the following that the situation is not that simple: it is important to discriminate between what is bought and what is sold. In doing so, it is important to specify what form of volatility is actually being bought or sold (eg, realised or implied), and to understand the terms of the instrument.

Investors can now gain realised volatility exposure via what has become a common product, a variance swap. In the case of a variance swap, the final value is the realised volatility of the underlying index or stock, and the initial price is the variance swap level, which is linked to implied volatility on the underlying. The following section explains variance swap into detail and shows how to calculate the performance of strategies based on that instrument.

From variance swap to forward-start variance swap

A close variant of the variance swap is the forward-start variance swap. A forward-start variance swap obligates its holder to enter into a variance swap at a later date at a pre-specified variance swap strike price. Forward-start variance swaps are often used to speculate on future movements of implied volatility while variance swaps may be more appropriate to trade the implied versus realised volatility spread.

For example, buying a six-month forward-start one-year variance swap with a strike price at 20% would obligate its holder to buy a one-year variance swap in six months at 20%. The swap does not yield any carry during the first six months and its mark-to-market value will evolve with implied volatility during that period. After six months, the investor can then compare the variance level set six months ago, ie, 20%, with the current level of a one-year variance swap. If the one-year variance swap strike price has risen, say to 25%, then the investor might unwind the position for a profit. A forward-start variance swap thus allows investors to bet on future movements in implied volatility without exposure to realised volatility as long as the position is unwound before or on the forward-start date.

Forward-start variance swap can be replicated using "plain vanilla" variance swaps with different maturities. Since variance is time-additive, the time-weighted average of the realised variances

SECOND-GENERATION VOLATILITY PRODUCTS

Figure 7.7 Forward-start variance swap pricing. (Source: Deutsche Bank.)

How to price a forward-start variance swap, with forward-start date T_1 and maturity T_2

$$\frac{1}{T_2}\sum_{t=0}^{T_2} r_t^2$$

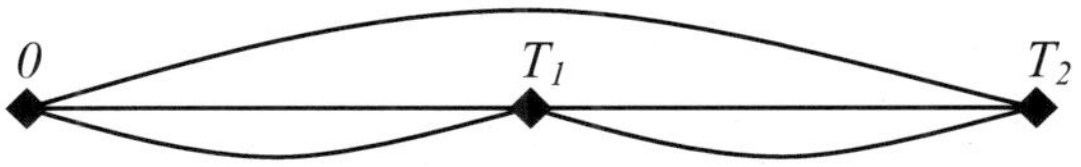

0 ——————— T_1 ——————— T_2

$$\frac{1}{T_1}\sum_{t=0}^{T_1} r_t^2 \qquad \frac{1}{T_2 - T_1}\sum_{t=T_1}^{T_2} r_t^2$$

$$\text{FwdVar}_{T_1,T_2} = \frac{T_2\,\text{Var}_{T_2} - T_1\,\text{Var}_{T_1}}{T_2 - T_1}$$

In volatility terms:

$$\sigma_{T_1,T_2} = \sqrt{\frac{T_2\sigma_{T_2}^2 - T_1\sigma_{T_1}^2}{T_2 - T_1}}$$

of a three-month variance swap and a three-month forward-start nine-month variance swap would be equal to the realised variance of a one-year variance swap, up to a scaling time factor. In absence of arbitrage, the equality holds true for variance swaps' levels.

Figure 7.7 illustrates the no-arbitrage pricing of forward-start variance swap between any two dates T_1 and T_2 using variance swaps with T_1 and T_2 maturities.

In the absence of arbitrage, the time-additive property of realised variance implies a similar relationship between variance swap strikes over different periods. As such, we use the expression in Figure 7.7 to determine the strike of a forward-strike variance swap from T_1 to T_2 based on strikes of "spot" variance swaps with T_1 and T_2 maturities.

Forward-start variance swap levels are thus sensitive to the term structure of implied volatility:

- upward sloping term structure → forward-start variance swap more expensive than spot variance swap;
- downward sloping term structure → forward-start variance swap cheaper than spot variance swap.

Returns from investing in variance swaps

A number of studies have looked at the impact of volatility on asset allocation by comparing index returns with volatility returns. Volatility returns are then calculated by observing implied or realised volatility at two different dates. Volatility, however, cannot be bought or sold as in the case of a stock or an index.

While implied volatility indices have been built for US and European indices such as S&P500, €-Stoxx50 and DAX30, one cannot directly invest in them. Investors can invest in futures on these indices but:

- liquidity is currently poor.

The behaviour of implied volatility indices and their futures differ significantly. Therefore, conclusions based on assumptions that amount to direct investment in the VIX, VDAX or VSTOXX should be viewed with caution.

- Further, taking a position in a variance swap is an implied/realised volatility relative value trade, not a pure long bet on realised volatility. If an investor only considers the relationship between an index's returns and its realised volatility, he excludes any reference to the initial variance swap's level.

To analyse the benefit of volatility investing, we therefore suggest looking at volatility returns that investors can actually capture by calculating the difference between variance swap strike prices and subsequent realised volatility.

For the purposes of treating volatility as an asset, we consider the purchaser of an asset to receive the "floating" leg of the trade and the invested capital to be the (forward) value of the fixed payment. "Selling" a variance swap means "receiving fixed" and being liable for the floating leg. Although in most cases it is only a scaling factor, we have treated allocation of capital during our backtests to mean allocating a constant variance notional to the fixed leg of the trade rather than maintaining constant vega exposure.

Let us denote the variance swap level in volatility terms by K_{vega} and the realised volatility between date 0 and T by $RV_{0,T}$. By definition, K_{vega} is the initial price and $RV_{0,T}$ is the unknown future payout, the same as in a futures contract on an index. Then the effective variance swap return is:[3]

$$\ln(RV_{0,T}/K_{vega})$$

For example, if the volatility strike price is equal to 25% and the subsequent realised volatility is 27%, the variance swap's return is equal to $\ln(27\%/25\%) = 7.7\%$.

Let us talk about risk

What is risk? We must address this philosophical question before we can measure risk. Asset managers often measure risk by calculating the standard deviation of portfolio returns. Standard deviation is a suitable risk measure as long as asset returns are normally distributed. If not, higher moments such as skew and kurtosis may also be relevant. Skew measures the symmetry of the returns distribution. Kurtosis measures whether the tails of the distribution are "fat" or not, ie, the likelihood of extreme versus modest outcomes.

When investing in derivatives, coming up with a definitive answer on how to measure the risk of certain derivatives instruments is sometimes complex because these products may be leveraged and may have asymmetric risk profiles with substantial tails. For variance swaps, traditional measures of risk such as standard deviation may not be the most appropriate.

The risk profile of a variance swap is asymmetric. From the buyer's perspective, its maximum loss is known and equal to the variance notional multiplied by the variance strike price. The seller, however, bares almost unlimited risk because volatility has no upside limit.

Figure 7.8 displays the distribution of historical overlapping returns of one-year variance swaps on the S&P500 index from November 1995 to November 2006 and a normal distribution with the same average return and standard deviation. Variance swap returns do not seem to have been normally distributed.

In order to assess the risk–return profile of variance swaps, we suggest calculating risk not only by using the volatility (or standard deviation) but also the semi-volatility.

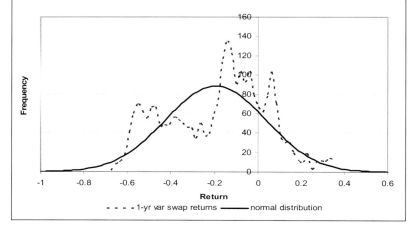

Figure 7.8 (Ab)normality of variance swaps returns. The graph displays the historical distribution of one-year variance swaps overlapping returns using data from November 1995 to November 2006, rolling every day. The normal distribution is drawn by taking the same return and standard distribution. (Source: Deutsche Bank.)

Semi-volatility is the standard deviation of returns that fall below the average return. It is one measure of downside risk:

$$\text{semi-volatility} = \sqrt{\frac{252}{N\,\text{days}_{r \leq \bar{r}}} \sum_{t=1}^{T} (r_t - \bar{r})^2 1_{r_t \leq \bar{r}}}$$

Two useful and complementary measures of performance are:

- the Sharpe ratio, the excess return[4] of the strategy divided by its volatility; and
- the semi-Sharpe ratio, the excess return of the strategy divided by its semi-volatility.[5]

VOLATILITY INVESTING IN PRACTICE
The economic value of shorting variance swaps

In the previous section, we saw that equity market returns and volatility are negatively correlated. This fact has led several previous studies to conclude that long variance swaps can help to diversify and enhance performance of equity portfolios.

Here, we first demonstrate the presence of a negative variance risk premium, which implies that systematically shorting variance swaps would have been on average a profitable strategy during the 1995–2006 period.

Based on Deutsche Bank's proprietary implied volatility database, we estimate S&P500 variance levels from November 1995 to November 2006 for one-month and one-year maturities as well as six-month forward-start six-month variance swap levels. For the estimations, we follow the methodology suggested by Derman *et al* (1999). We describe the methodology, including assumptions for dividend and bond yields, in Appendix A.

Since a variance swap is a forward contract on variance, we compare its return with the returns of a forward contract on the S&P500, for which the initial price is

$$F = e^{(r-d)T} S_0$$

where r is the swap rate corresponding to the forward maturity, d is the historical dividend yield and T is the time to maturity.

While we have taken precautions to generate realistic backtests, our analysis does not include transaction costs. Current bid–ask spreads for variance swaps on major indices such as the S&P500 and the €-Stoxx50 are roughly 30 to 50 bps (basis points) depending on the liquidity, but they were wider historically. Furthermore, variance swaps hedging methods were not well established until recent years, so pricing was not consistent.

Table 7.2 reports a risk–return analysis for forwards, variance swaps and forward-start variance swaps on the S&P500 index from 1995 to 2006.

Risk and return of one-year S&P500 index forwards
Over the past 10 years, the S&P500 index has risen 8.5% on average per year with annual volatility of 17.8%. This yields a Sharpe ratio close to 0.5 that we will use to benchmark other products' returns. The S&P500's semi-volatility has been slightly lower than its volatility, implying a higher semi-Sharpe ratio.

Risk and return of one-month and one-year variance swaps
Buying one-month or one-year variance swaps would have made an average loss of 19.3% and 66.8% per trade, respectively. Inversely, systematically selling variance swaps would have

Table 7.2 Historical simulations of S&P500 index forward and variance swap performances from November 1995 to November 2006 (overlapping periods, not annualised).

	One-year forward	One-year variance swap	One-month variance swap	Six-month forward start six-month variance swap	One-month forward start one-month variance swap
Average	8.5%	−19.3%	−33.4%	3.6%	0.9%
Median	10.0%	−15.4%	−34.4%	3.0%	−1.2%
Minimum	−33.0%	−67.5%	−108.1%	−46.2%	−43.1%
Maximum	50.6%	37.3%	46.8%	63.3%	81.8%
Volatility	17.8%	23.1%	25.7%	17.4%	17.4%
Semi-volatility	14.1%	44.1%	54.7%	13.5%	14.0%
Sharpe ratio	0.48	−0.83	−4.49	0,29	0.17
Semi-Sharpe ratio	0.60	−0.44	−2.11	0.38	0.22
Correlation with forward returns		−28.0%	−36.4%	−23.2%	−75%

implied a profit (excluding transaction costs). This is a well-known characteristic of variance and referred to as the variance risk premium. It is consistent with findings of several academic studies.[6] Multiple reasons can be advanced to explain the variance risk premium.

- Variance swaps display an asymmetric payout. The buyer of a variance swap has a limited loss if volatility falls to zero, equal to K^2 multiplied by the notional. The seller, however, has an unlimited potential loss because volatility is unbounded on the upside. As such, sellers may demand a premium to take on that risk.
- Index variance swaps may reflect a risk premium related to correlation. Even if there was no variance risk premium priced in single stocks variance swaps, index variance swaps levels could still exhibit a negative variance risk premium. This explanation, highlighted for example by Driessen et al (2006), arises from the fact that correlation between stock constituents may be stochastic. As such, the market would price a correlation risk resulting in an implied correlation on average higher than realised correlation. Index volatility, by definition, depends on correlation:

$$\sigma_I = \sqrt{\sum_{i=1}^{N} \omega_i^2 \sigma_i^2 + \sum_{i=1}^{N} \sum_{j \neq N} \omega_i \omega_j \sigma_i \sigma_j \rho_{i,j}}$$

where ω_i are the index weights and $\rho_{i,j}$ is the pairwise correlation (ie, the correlation between stocks i and j). Since ω_i are all positive numbers, increasing the correlation increases the index volatility. As such, sellers of index volatility might demand a premium for selling embedded correlation.

Not only would average returns of buying S&P500 variance swaps have been lower than of buying S&P500 forwards, but Table 7.2 shows that there would have also been greater volatility. In comparing the performance of selling variance swaps to buying index forwards, it makes a substantial difference whether we measure risk using volatility or semi-volatility. Historically, a short variance swap position would have had substantial downside risk, as reflected in a semi-volatility that is twice as high as the standard-deviation.

According to the Sharpe ratio, selling variance swaps provides a better risk–return trade-off than buying the S&P500 index. Using the semi-Sharpe ratio, however, the downside risk is emphasised, and buying the index appears more attractive.

Risk and return of forward-start variance swaps
The performance of the six-month forward-start six-month variance swap is calculated for a strategy of going long with the forward start variance swap and then unwinding it six months later by taking a short position in a six-month variance swap.[7] Over the past 10 years, following such a strategy would have produced a positive average return of around 3.6% (per trade, not annualised), before transaction costs. This historical positive outcome has to be taken with caution since the volatility of the strategy, 17%, has also been substantially historically high. It is nevertheless worth investigating where the positive performance comes from.

A first explanation could be that the market gets the direction of implied volatility's future movements right but on average incorrectly forecasts the magnitude of the change. Take, for example, the case of an upward-sloping implied volatility term structure. In such a situation, the six-month forward-start six-month implied volatility should be, by construction, higher than the spot six-month implied volatility, implying that the market anticipates a rise in implied volatility. If a long forward-start variance swap position unwound at the forward date realises a profit, it means that implied volatility has increased but by a wider margin than initially expected.

A second explanation could be that while implied volatility has declined over the past ten years, the slope of the implied volatility term structure has on average been slightly downward sloping as shown by Figure 7.9.

In order to fully understand the historical performance of forward-start variance swaps, we conduct the following decomposition:

Perf(six-month forward-start six-month variance swap)
$= \ln(K_{\text{6-month}_{t+6}} / K_{\text{6-month 6-month}_t})$
$= \ln(K_{\text{6-month}_{t+6}} / K_{\text{6-month}_t}) - \ln(K_{\text{6-month 6-month}_t} / K_{\text{6-month}_t})$

where:

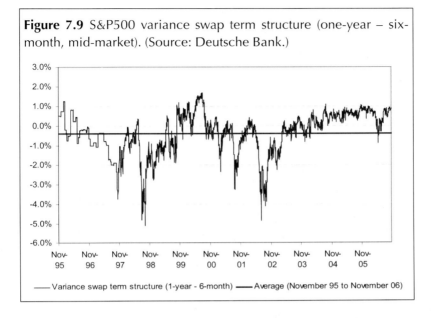

Figure 7.9 S&P500 variance swap term structure (one-year – six-month, mid-market). (Source: Deutsche Bank.)

- $K_{\text{6-month 6-month}_t}$ is the six-month forward-start six-month variance swap level at time t;
- $K_{\text{6-month}_t}$ is the six-month variance swap level at time t;
- $K_{\text{6-month}_{t+6}}$ is the six-month variance swap level at time $t+6$, ie, on the forward-start date, six months after initiating the trade (unwinding date).

Using the methodology described in Figure 7.7, we can calculate a mid-market six-month forward-start six-month variance swap level in variance terms as

$$K^2_{\text{6-month 6-month}_t} = 2 \times K^2_{\text{1-year}_t} - K^2_{\text{6-month}_t}$$

We can then rewrite the performance of the six-month forward-start six-month variance swap as

Perf(six-month forward-start six-month variance swap)
$$= \underbrace{\ln(K_{\text{6-month}_{t+6}}/K_{\text{6-month}_t})}_{\substack{\text{Returns attributable to changes}\\\text{in six-month variance swap level}}} - \underbrace{\tfrac{1}{2}\ln(2 \times K^2_{\text{1-year}_t}/K^2_{\text{6-month}_t} - 1)}_{\substack{\text{Returns attributable to steepness}\\\text{of the term structure}}}$$

This is a re-arrangement of the forward-start variance performance, knowing that

$$\tfrac{1}{2}\ln(K^2_{\text{1-year}}/K^2_{\text{6-month}_t}) = \ln(K_{\text{1-year}}/K_{\text{6-month}_t})$$

We can interpret the two components as follows.

- $\ln(K_{\text{6-month}_{t+6}}/K_{\text{6-month}_t})$ measures a "return" due to changes in "spot" variance swap level. If implied volatility should rise over the six months between the trade date and the forward-start date, this should be positive.
- $-\tfrac{1}{2}\ln(2 \times K^2_{\text{1-year}}/K^2_{\text{6-month}_t} - 1)$ measures a "return" due to the steepness of the "spot" variance swap term structure. It is positive if and only if $K_{\text{6-month}_t} > K_{\text{1-year}_t}$, ie, when the variance swap term structure is downward-sloping. As we have already mentioned, a downward-sloping variance swap term structure implies a forward-start variance swap level that is below the level of a "spot" variance swap with similar tenor. This component also has the great property of being known at the inception of the trade. However, as displayed by Figure 7.9, the variance swap term structure tends to be downward sloping:
  - in periods of market stress, when expectations of volatility are high in the short term, but people expect volatility to eventually fall back; or
  - when implied volatility declines.

In normal market conditions, the variance swap term structure in general slopes upward.

Buying a forward-start variance swap and unwinding it at the forward date therefore provides an exposure to changes in the "spot" variance swaps level and benefits from a more steeply downward-sloping variance swap term structure.

With this decomposition in mind, we split our historical sample into three different periods. The first period spans from November 1995 to December 1997, when volatility was rising. The second period spans from January 1998 to December 2002, when volatility experienced a high-volatility regime. The third period spans from January 2003 to November 2006, when volatility fell back to historically low levels. Results are displayed in Table 7.3.

- *November 1995 to December 1997.* During this period marked by rising volatility (both implied and realised), our historical backtest suggests that taking a long position into six-month forward-start six-month variance swap would have been profitable before transaction costs. About 40% of returns are explained by the variance swap term structure which was on average downward-sloping over the period (on average −0.7 volatility points between one-year and six-month variance swaps levels). Results from this period should be read carefully, because implied volatility data is not as high quality as at later dates, and variance swaps were not yet trading.
- *January 1998 to December 2002.* This was a high-volatility regime punctuated by a series of crises (LTCM/Ruble, Internet bubble bursting, 9/11, 2002 sell-off). S&P500 implied volatilities were above 20% for extended periods, spiking up to 35%. On average, returns from buying six-month forward-start variance swaps would have been positive although less so than during the preceding period. The average downward-sloping term structure accounts for about 80% of total returns.
- *January 2003 to November 2006.* During the most recent period, in which implied volatilities fell and combined with an upward-sloping variance swap term structure, buying a six-month forward-start variance swap would have produced a negative return.
- *November 1995 to November 2006.* Over the whole sample, the components of returns due to variance swap term structure steepness dominates the components of returns due to changes in "spot" variance swap levels.

Results are similar with one-month forward start one-month variance swaps with the exception of a much higher correlation between forward-start variance swap returns and S&P500 forward returns. This is due to the fact that short-term implied volatilities (reflected in short-dated variance swaps levels) are much more sensitive to index movements than longer-dated implied volatilities.

Figures 7.10 and 7.11 display the historical performance of a six-month forward-start six-month S&P500 variance swap and a portfolio combining US$1 invested in S&P500 index forwards and US50 cents invested in the forward-start variance swap

Table 7.3 Decomposition of S&P500 six-month forward-start six-month variance swap returns. (Source: Deutsche Bank.)

	November 1995 to November 2006			November 1995 to December 1997		
	Total return[a]	Return IV[b]	Return TS[c]	Total return[a]	Return IV[b]	Return TS[c]
Average	3.6%	0.2%	3.4%	16.0%	9.3%	6.7%
Median	3.0%	0.5%	2.5%	14.8%	11.0%	6.6%
Minimum	−46.2%	−45.7%	−17.8%	−0.4%	−21.6%	−17.8%
Maximum	63.3%	61.5%	40.1%	44.1%	39.9%	35.6%
Volatility	17.4%	16.9%	10.0%	8.8%	11.7%	10.0%
Semi-volatility	13.5%	16.6%	6.3%	11.3%	7.8%	6.6%
Sharpe ratio	0.29	0.02	0.48	2.57	1.12	0.94
Semi-Sharpe ratio	0.38	0.02	0.76	2.00	1.69	1.42

	January 1998 to December 2002			January 2003 to December 2006		
	Total return[a]	Return IV[b]	Return TS[c]	Total return[a]	Return IV[b]	Return TS[c]
Average	7.7%	1.3%	6.4%	−10.0%	−7.0%	−3.0%
Median	6.3%	0.5%	5.6%	−10.2%	−6.1%	−4.2%
Minimum	−32.2%	−45.7%	−15.9%	−46.2%	−45.0%	−13.9%
Maximum	63.3%	61.5%	40.1%	22.6%	27.8%	16.6%
Volatility	17.5%	18.5%	9.9%	11.3%	13.7%	6.4%
Semi-volatility	10.2%	16.0%	5.3%	19.9%	20.6%	8.3%
Sharpe ratio	0.62	0.10	0.91	−1.25	−0.72	−0.66
Semi-Sharpe ratio	1.06	0.11	1.71	−0.71	−0.48	−0.51

[a] Total return is calculated as $\ln(K_{6\text{-month}_{t+6}}/K_{6\text{-month}_t})$.
[b] Return IV stands for the return due to changes in variance swap level: $\ln(K_{6\text{-month}_{t+6}}/K_{6\text{-month}_t})$.
[c] Return TS stands for the return due to steepness of variance swap: $-\frac{1}{2}\ln(2 \times K_{1\text{-year}}^2/K_{6\text{-month}_t}^2 - 1)$.

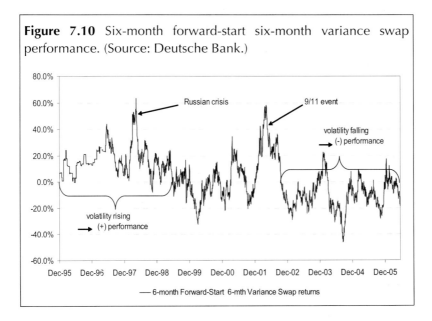

Figure 7.10 Six-month forward-start six-month variance swap performance. (Source: Deutsche Bank.)

(in vega notional). In other words, if US$50,000 is invested in S&P500 forwards (equivalent to 200 contracts) then US$25,000 in vega notional is invested in variance swaps. Figure 7.10 shows that in periods of market stress (eg, Russian crisis, 9/11, May 2005 market correction), buying forward-implied volatility would have been profitable because implied volatility rose sharply.

Figure 7.11 suggests that forward-start variance swaps would have historically provided a good hedge against market crises. Adding a forward-start variance swap to a position in S&P500 futures helped to reduce S&P500 losses in times of crises. The following section explores the combination of S&P futures and volatility derivatives in greater detail.

Combining volatility and equity

Given the preceding observations, investors need to assess whether they should:

- buy variance swaps because realised volatility is negatively correlated with index returns; or
- sell variance swaps because implied volatility trades at a premium versus future realised volatility; or

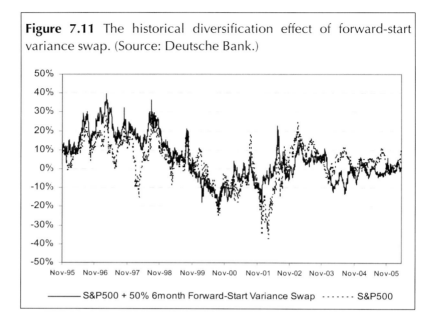

Figure 7.11 The historical diversification effect of forward-start variance swap. (Source: Deutsche Bank.)

- buy forward-start variance swaps, unwinding the positions at the forward-start dates, to take a view on implied volatility's future movements.

We believe that the appropriate choice depends on each investor's objective. Is an asset manager looking to invest in volatility in order to diversify his portfolio? Is he looking to hedge his portfolio against rare but significant market downturns?

To assess the benefits of introducing variance swaps into a stock portfolio, we assume that an investor starts with a position in S&P500 forwards. Then, we analyse the performance of the addition of variance swaps with a weight ranging from -100% to $+100\%$. A 0% weight implies no variance swap position, a $+100\%$ weight implies a long variance swap position with a vega notional equivalent to the notional invested in the S&P500 forwards and a -100% weight implies a short variance swap position with a vega notional equivalent to the notional invested in the S&P500 forwards.

As a complement to the standard-deviation and the Sharpe ratio to assess the risk and performance of a derivatives portfolio, we also present an analysis using the semi-volatility and the semi-Sharpe ratio, hence putting emphasis on downside risk.

SECOND-GENERATION VOLATILITY PRODUCTS

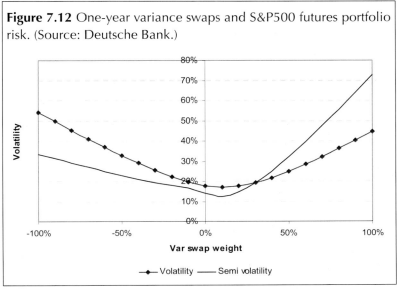

Figure 7.12 One-year variance swaps and S&P500 futures portfolio risk. (Source: Deutsche Bank.)

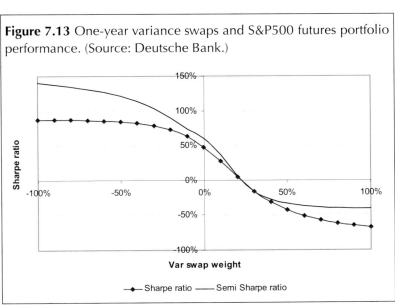

Figure 7.13 One-year variance swaps and S&P500 futures portfolio performance. (Source: Deutsche Bank.)

Figure 7.12–7.19 report results for trading one-month and one-year variance swaps as well as six-month forward-start six-month variance swaps from November 1995 to November 2006.

215

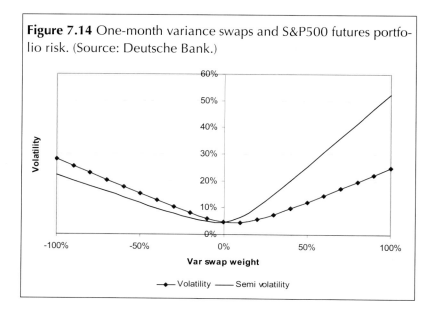

Figure 7.14 One-month variance swaps and S&P500 futures portfolio risk. (Source: Deutsche Bank.)

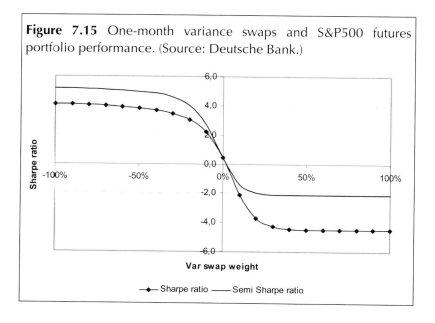

Figure 7.15 One-month variance swaps and S&P500 futures portfolio performance. (Source: Deutsche Bank.)

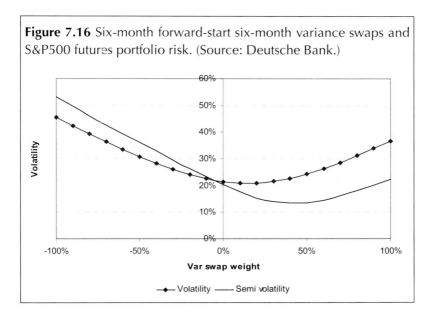

Figure 7.16 Six-month forward-start six-month variance swaps and S&P500 futures portfolio risk. (Source: Deutsche Bank.)

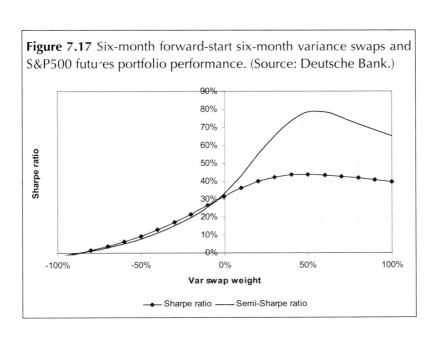

Figure 7.17 Six-month forward-start six-month variance swaps and S&P500 futures portfolio performance. (Source: Deutsche Bank.)

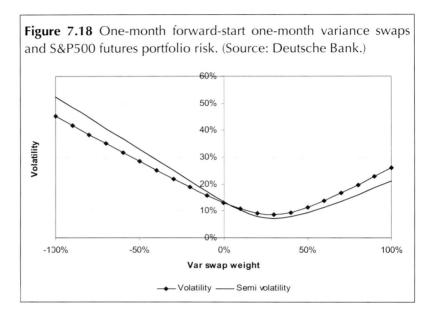

Figure 7.18 One-month forward-start one-month variance swaps and S&P500 futures portfolio risk. (Source: Deutsche Bank.)

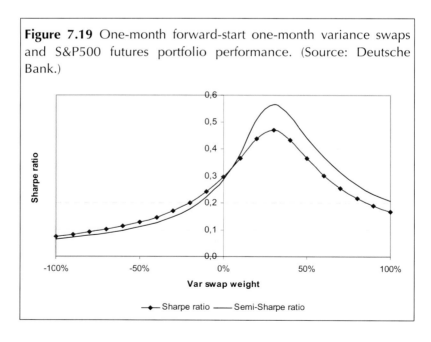

Figure 7.19 One-month forward-start one-month variance swaps and S&P500 futures portfolio performance. (Source: Deutsche Bank.)

First, let us evaluate the common belief that taking a long variance swap position helps to diversify a stock portfolio. Figures 7.12–7.15 show that historically, overlaying an equity portfolio with long one-month or one-year variance swaps would have reduced the Sharpe ratio. In fact, the Sharpe ratios become quickly negative as investors buy more variance swaps. This is in part because the negative variance risk premium more than offsets the benefits of negative correlation between equity returns and equity volatility. Furthermore, the risk, and especially the downside risk as measured by the semi-volatility, jumps up to 100%, comparing poorly to the 17.8% annual volatility of S&P500 futures.

A short position in variance swaps, however, significantly increases the Sharpe ratio although with higher volatility and semi-volatility. We reach similar conclusions using either one-month or six-month swaps. Hence, our historical backtests suggest that investors should have historically favoured selling variance swaps based on using Sharpe or Semi-Sharpe ratios to measure their investment performance.

Introducing long forward-start variance swaps into the equity portfolio provided a different outcome historically. Doing so would have reduced the risk of the portfolio while increasing the return, hence delivering a higher semi-Sharpe ratio. In our historical simulation, the maximum semi-Sharpe ratio is achieved by taking a position in six-month forward-start six-month variance equal to roughly 50% of the notional invested in S&P500 futures. We obtain similar results for one-month forward-start one-month variance swaps but with a lower optimal weighting in the forward-start variance swaps.

The "optimal" variance swap weightings generated in these exercises should not be viewed as prescriptions for specific investment amount since, in practice, the optimal investment in forward-start variance swaps would depend on several factors such as the composition of the investor's actual portfolio, his risk limit and his risk appetite. The exercises do show, however, that forward-start variance swaps are worth considering as hedging instruments against extreme market events and for stand-alone performance.

SECOND-GENERATION VOLATILITY PRODUCTS
Gamma swaps

As discussed previously, the gamma exposure of variance swaps is insensitive to the level of the underlying asset. In the event the stock price rises or declines, the gamma exposure depends solely on the initial value of the portfolio. Variance swaps are thus said to have constant "cash" gamma exposure.

However, it is often more useful to have a constant "share" gamma exposure than a "cash" one. In general, investors focus on the number of portfolio units they manage and not on the initial cash value of their portfolio. Gamma swaps are by definition products that answer to this need.

Gamma swaps have the following payout:

$$\text{Payout}_{\text{gamma swap}} = (\text{Gamma} - K_{\text{Gamma}}) \times N$$

where

$$\text{Gamma} = \frac{252}{T} \sum_{i=1}^{T} \left[(\ln(S_i/S_{i-1}))^2 \frac{S_i}{S_0} \right]$$

K_{Gamma} is the strike and N the notional amount. In continuous-time, the gamma swap payout is equal to

$$\Gamma_{0,T} = \frac{1}{T} \int_0^T \sigma_t^2 S_t / S_0 \, dt$$

Gamma swaps are thus equivalent to variance swaps whose nominal is proportional to the level of the underlying asset.

The intuitive and formal approaches to gamma swap pricing

Pricing gamma swaps is as easy as pricing variance swaps. We have already shown that whereas the variance swap vega should be independent of the stock price, the gamma swap vega should be a linear function of the stock price. The aim is to create an options portfolio whose vega will be a linear function of the stock price. As Figure 7.20 illustrates, an option portfolio using a continuum of strike prices and inversely weighted by their strike prices provides a vega that is linear with respect to the stock price.

Carr and Madan's formal approach may also be applied to gamma swap pricing. Assuming constant interest rate and no dividend payment, the value – or the strike price – of a gamma swap is

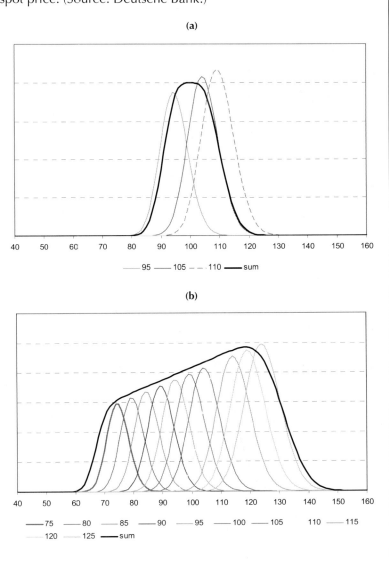

Figure 7.20 Option-portfolio variance vega: (a) three options; (b) combination of options with strike prices ranging from 70% to 130% inversely weighted by their strike prices as a percentage of spot price. (Source: Deutsche Bank.)

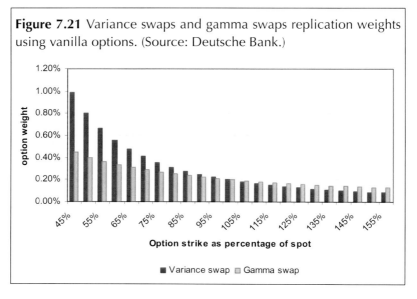

Figure 7.21 Variance swaps and gamma swaps replication weights using vanilla options. (Source: Deutsche Bank.)

given by

$$V_f[\Gamma_{0,T}] = \frac{2\,e^{rT}}{TS_0}\left[\int_0^{F_0}\frac{1}{K}P_0(K)\,dK + \int_{F_0}^{\infty}\frac{1}{K}C_0(K)\,dK\right]$$

The gamma swap's strike price may thus be replicated by a continuum of puts and calls inversely weighted by their strike prices.

Empirical differences between gamma swaps and variance swaps
By virtue of their payout and insofar as squared returns $(\ln(S_i/S_{i-1}))^2$ are weighted by the performance of the stock S_i/S_0, gamma swaps underweight big downward index moves relative to variance swaps. This means that if the distribution of stock returns is skewed to the left, gamma swaps minimise the effect of a crash, thereby making it easier for the trader to hedge. In this case, hedging does not require additional caps, unlike variance swaps which need to be capped.

Gamma swap strike prices should thus be lower than variance swap strike prices. Figure 7.22 shows the strike prices of six-month variance and gamma swaps on the €-Stoxx50. The gamma swap strike price would systematically have been slightly lower than the variance swap strike price by 1.03 volatility points on average.

The gamma swap payout is slightly delta-positive, given that it is a function of the performance of the stock since inception.

Figure 7.22 Six-month gamma and variance swap strike prices on the €-Stoxx50 index: (a) three options; (b) combination of options with strike prices ranging from 70% to 130% inversely weighted by their strike prices as a percentage of spot price. (Source: Deutsche Bank.)

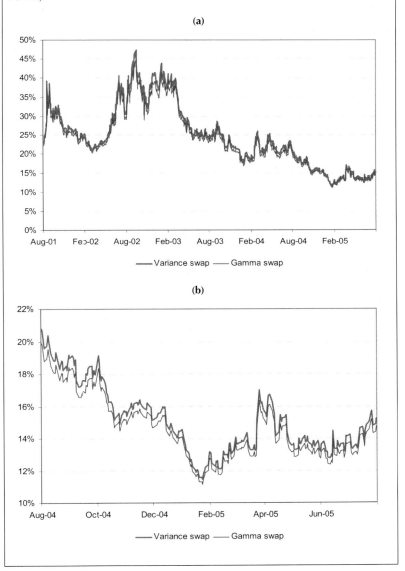

Efficient dispersion trading using gamma swaps

As we pointed out before, dispersion is calculated by the difference between the realised index volatility and the market-cap weighted sum of the realised volatility of its constituents. The dispersion between time 0 and T is thus described by

$$\text{Dispersion}_t = \sum_{i=1}^{N} \alpha_{i,t} \sigma_{i,t}^2 - \sigma_{I,t}^2$$

where $\alpha_{i,t}$ is the weight of stock i in the index. By definition, it changes over time as stock prices change and is equal to

$$\alpha_{i,t} = n_i S_{i,t} / I_t$$

If an investor trades dispersion using variance swaps weighted by the initial weights of the stocks in the index, he faces the risk of a possible change in weights over time until maturity of the variance swap. Gamma swaps, however, offer a more efficient way to trade dispersion. If one sells a gamma swap on the index and buys $n_i S_{i,0} / I_0$ (or $\alpha_{i,0}$) gamma swaps on each stock i, the payout at maturity should be equal to

$$\text{P\&L}_T = \sum_{i=1}^{N} \frac{n_i S_{i,0}}{I_0} \frac{1}{T} \int_0^T \sigma_{i,t}^2 S_{i,t} / S_{i,0} \, dt - \frac{1}{T} \int_0^T \sigma_{I,t}^2 I_t I_0 \, dt$$

Rearranging the terms, we obtain

$$\text{P\&L}_T = \frac{1}{T} \int_0^T \left(I_t / I_0 \sum_{i=1}^{N} \alpha_{i,t} \sigma_{i,t}^2 \right) dt - \frac{1}{T} \int_0^T \sigma_{I,t}^2 I_t / I_0 \, dt$$

$$= \frac{1}{T} \int_0^T \frac{I_t}{I_0} \text{Dispersion}_t \, dt$$

The payout is thus equal to the average dispersion over the period $[0, T]$ weighted by index performance.

Corridor variance swaps

Corridor variance swaps are a variant of variance swaps that only take into account daily stock variations when the stock is in a specific range.

The payout is equal to

$$\text{Payout}_{\text{Corridor}} = K^2 - K_{\text{Corr}}^2$$

where K^2 is the initial strike price and K^2_{Corr} is described by

$$K^2_{\text{Corr}} = \frac{252}{T} \sum_{i=1}^{T} (\ln(S_i/S_{i-1}))^2 1_{S_t \in [\kappa - \Delta; \kappa + \Delta]}$$

Hence, squared returns are counted in if the stock price lies within a pre-specified range $[\kappa - \Delta; \kappa + \Delta]$.

Corridor variance swaps therefore enable bets to be taken on the pattern of the stock. If the stock moves sideways and stays within the defined range, K^2_{Corr} will be high. If the stock moves sharply upward or downward and leaves the range quickly, K^2_{Corr} will be low.

Up and down corridor variance swaps
Financial engineering never stops producing new products and up corridor variance swaps are an example of such innovation. Up corridor variance swaps are a variant of corridor variance swaps and have the following payout:

$$\text{Payout}_{\text{up}} = K^2 - K^2_{\text{upcorr}}$$

where K^2 is the initial strike price and K^2_{upcorr} is described by

$$K^2_{\text{upcorr}} = \frac{252}{T} \sum_{i=1}^{T} (\ln(S_i/S_{i-1}))^2 1_{S_t > B}$$

Hence, squared returns are counted in if and only if the stock price lies above a predefined level denoted by B. Indeed, one can also define a down corridor variance swap whose payout would be defined by

$$K^2_{\text{downcorr}} = \frac{252}{T} \sum_{i=1}^{T} (\ln(S_i/S_{i-1}))^2 1_{S_t < B}$$

Aggregating a down corridor variance swap and an up corridor variance swap yields the classic variance swap. This particular payout has several advantages:

- it enables investors to bet on volatility or to hedge a position up to a certain level that may be defined by the overall risk structure of a derivatives book;

- it is cheaper than a variance swap as only returns associated with a stock higher than B will be taken into account.

Another reason why this swap is cheaper is that no purchases of expensive OTM puts are required to replicate it. Figure 7.23 provides a comparison of the payouts of one-year variance swaps and one-year ATM down corridor variance swaps on the S&P500 since 1976. The ATM down corridor variance swap has a threshold level B equal to the initial level of the index, while only returns associated with an index level below the threshold are counted in.

The ATM down corridor variance swap systematically yields a lower payout and should thus be cheaper than the variance swap. Furthermore, Figure 7.23 shows that the down corridor variance swap's payout is negatively correlated with the market trend. With squared returns not counted in when the market rises, the down corridor variance swap offers a lower strike price. This is confirmed by the statistics reported in Table 7.4. As a result, up and down corridor variance swaps enable a combined view to be taken on volatility, correlation and market direction.

Pricing corridor variance swaps can be achieved using the Carr and Madan's methodology. In such a case a corridor variance swap that ranges between A and B (A and B being either numbers or infinite) is statically replicated by a portfolio of a continuum of options with strike prices spanning from A to B, each weighted by the inverse of its strike price squared,[8] where strikes are expressed as a percentage of spot price.

Up and down conditional variance swaps

Up conditional variance swaps are a variant of up corridor variant swaps, whose payout is described by

$$\text{Payout}_{\text{upcond}} = (K^2 - K^2_{\text{upcond}}) \frac{1}{T} \sum_{i=1}^{T} 1_{S_i > B}$$

where K^2 is the initial strike price and K^2_{upcond} is described by

$$K^2_{\text{upcond}} = \frac{252}{\sum_{i=1}^{T} 1_{S_i > B}} \sum_{i=1}^{T} (\ln(S_i S_{i-1}))^2 1_{S_t > B}$$

Figure 7.23 Comparison of variance swaps and down corridor variance swaps on the S&P500 index: (a) three options; (b) combination of options with strike prices ranging from 70% to 130% inversely weighted by their strike prices as a percentage of spot price. (Source: Deutsche Bank.)

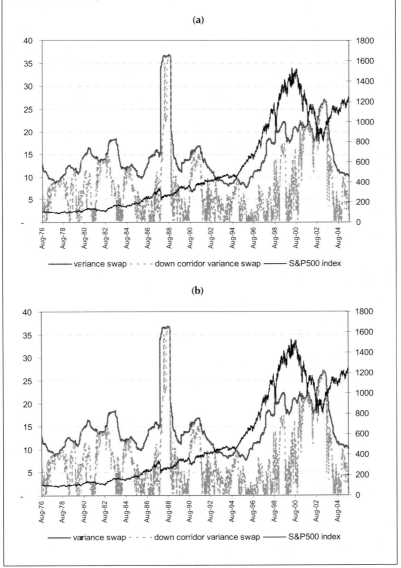

Table 7.4 Comparison of one-year variance swaps with one-year ATM up and down corridor variance swaps (in volatility terms). (Source: Deutsche Bank.)

	Variance swap	Up corridor variance swap	Down corridor variance swap	Variance up corridor	Variance down corridor
Average	14.91	10.69	8.10	4.22	6.81
Minimum	7.56	0.00	0.00	0.00	0.00
Maximum	36.84	32.92	36.82	36.82	27.14
Correlation with one-year S&P500 returns	−31%	50%	−69%	−73%	64%

SECOND-GENERATION VOLATILITY PRODUCTS

Similarly, a down conditional variance swap can be structured as

$$\text{Payout}_{\text{downcond}} = (K^2 - K^2_{\text{downcond}}) \frac{1}{T} \sum_{i=1}^{T} 1_{S_i < B}$$

where K^2 is the initial strike price and K^2_{downcond} is described by

$$K^2_{\text{downcond}} = \frac{252}{\sum_{i=1}^{T} 1_{S_i > B}} \sum_{i=1}^{T} (\ln(S_i/S_{i-1}))^2 1_{S_t < B}$$

The conditional variance swap payout is such that if the stock price never trades above the threshold B, it will be null whereas the up corridor variance swap payout would be equal to K^2. It also enables bets to be taken on very specific volatility behaviour. Take the case of an index whose initial value is 100. If the index stands above 100 for a few days with a high volatility, say 40% annualised, and then drops below 100, an ATM up conditional variance swap will yield a much higher payout than an ATM up corridor variance swap, given that the payout's floating leg is divided by the number of days the index stays above the threshold (above 100 in this case). As a result, timing is less of an issue for an investor who buys a conditional variance swap rather than a corridor variance swap.

Conditional variance swaps are slightly more complex volatility-related products and there is no decomposition of its payout into plain vanilla options. However, take the case of an up conditional variance with threshold B. Its payout can be decomposed as

$$\text{Payout}_{\text{upcond}}$$

$$= (K^2_{\text{upcond}} - K^2) \frac{\sum_{i=1}^{T} 1_{S_t \geq B}}{T}$$

$$= \left(\frac{252}{\sum_{i=1}^{T} 1_{S_t \geq B}} \sum_{i=1}^{T} [(\ln(S_i/S_{i-1}))^2 1_{S_t \geq B}] - K^2 \right) \frac{\sum_{i=1}^{T} 1_{S_t \geq B}}{T}$$

$$= \underbrace{\frac{252}{T} \sum_{i=1}^{T} [(\ln(S_i/S_{i-1}))^2 1_{S_t \geq B}]}_{\text{corridor variance swap's payout}} - \underbrace{\frac{K^2}{T} \sum_{i=1}^{T} 1_{S_t \geq B}}_{\substack{\text{payout of } K^2/T \text{ binary options} \\ \text{with maturities ranging from 1 to } T}}$$

A conditional variance swaps can therefore be priced using vanilla options (to replicate the corridor variance swap) and binary options.

229

CONCLUSION

Recent advances in financial engineering have supported the development of new derivatives instruments based on volatility or variance. Once reserved for banks' proprietary trading desk and volatility hedge funds, variance swap and its variants are now used by other types of less-sophisticated investor such as pension funds, asset managers or treasurers. They allow for a better diversification of equity portfolio while targeting returns in very specific market environments.

Banks currently battle over innovation and new products are now launched at a fast pace, for example trading not only volatility as an asset class but also the option skew or the market correlation.

APPENDIX A. VARIANCE SWAP REPLICATION

As shown previously, a variance swap can be replicated by a strip of options across a continuum of strikes. Each option is weighted by the square of the inverse of its strike expressed as a percentage of spot. Based on this replication, we can derive the strike of a variance swap:

$$K_{VAR} = \frac{2}{T} e^{rT} \left[\int_0^{F_0} \frac{1}{K^2} P(K, T) \, dK + \int_{F_0}^{\infty} \frac{1}{K^2} C(K, T) \, dK \right]$$

In practice, however, options are not available at all strikes. Also, there is often poor liquidity in options with deep out-of-the-money or in-the-money strikes. Furthermore, strikes are listed at discrete intervals, not continuously.

Derman *et al* (1999) suggest a discrete approximation of a variance swap strike price using a piecewise linear function. We use this methodology to estimate historical variance swap strike prices from November 1995 to November 2006 also making the following assumptions.

- We calculate options prices using the Black–Scholes–Merton model.
- We source implied volatilities from Deutsche Bank's proprietary database.
- We incorporate into our replicating options "strip" strikes ranging from 40% to 160% of spot at 5% increments.

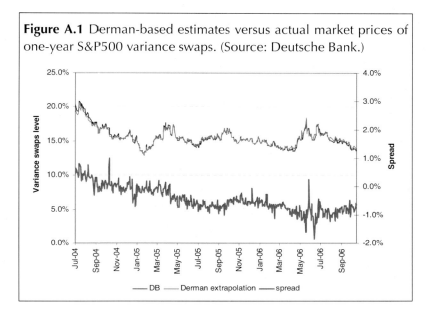

Figure A.1 Derman-based estimates versus actual market prices of one-year S&P500 variance swaps. (Source: Deutsche Bank.)

- Given that implied volatility below 70% and above 130% is inconsistently historically available, we assume a flat skew below 70% and above 130% when data is unavailable.
- For discounting, we use the US swap rate that corresponds to the option's maturity.
- We proxy for the expected dividend yield with the one-year historical dividend yield of the underlying asset.

To check whether these assumptions provide reasonable strike prices for variance swaps, we compare our approximation with market observed prices that are available from April 2004 until now. Figure A.1 shows the Derman-based estimates, market observed variance saps levels and the spread between the two series. On average, the difference is 0.001 volatility points with a minimum of −0.9 and a maximum of 1.2 volatility points. Our methodology approximates mid-market prices, so our analyses do not include transaction costs.

1 A more complete proof of the result can be found in Carr and Madan (1998).
2 Auto-correlation measures the correlation of a variable at time t with the same variable but lagged.
3 The same return can be calculated in variance terms and is by construction twice the volatility returns.

4   By construction, the return of the forward contract equals the excess return of the index: $r_{\text{forw}} = \ln(S_T/F_0) = \ln(S_T/\exp(r_f T) \times S_0) = r_S - r_f T$.

5   This is also known as the Sortino Ratio.

6   For US evidence, see, for example, Bondarenko (2004). For European evidence, see Wallmeier and Hafner (2006). From an option's perspective, see Coval and Shumway (2001).

7   When we hereafter refer to buying a forward-start variance swap, we mean buying the swap and unwinding the position on the forward-start date.

8   For a thorough analysis of variance swap pricing, see Carr and Madan (1998).

REFERENCES

Black, F. and M. Scholes, 1973, "The Pricing of Options and Corporate Liabilities", *Journal of Political Economy*, **81**, pp 637–654.

Blanc, N., 2004, "Index Variance Arbitrage: Arbitraging Component Correlation", Technical Studies, BNP Paribas.

Bondarenko, O., 2004, "Market Price of Variance Risk and Performance of Hedge Funds", Working Paper, University of Illinois at Chicago.

Carr, P. and D. Madan, 2001, "Towards a Theory of Volatility Trading", in R. Jarrow (ed), *Volatility: New Estimation Techniques for Pricing Derivatives* (London: Risk Publications), pp 417–427.

Chance, Don M., 1995, "A Chronology of Derivatives", *Derivatives Quarterly*, **2**(Winter), pp 53–60.

Coval, J. and T. Shumway, 2001, "Expected Options Returns", *Journal of Finance*, **56**, pp 983–1009

Derman, E., M. Kamal, J. Zou and K. Demeterfi, 1999, "A Guide to Volatility and Variance Swaps", *The Journal of Derivatives* (Summer), pp 1–32

Driessen, J., P. Maenhout and G. Vilkov, 2006, "Option-implied Correlations and the Price of Correlation Risk", Working Paper, INSEAD.

Mougeot, N., 2004, "Volatility Investing Handbook", Technical Paper, BNP Paribas.

Neuberger, A., 1994, "The Log Contract: A New Instrument to Hedge Volatility", *Journal of Portfolio Management* (Winter), pp 74–80.

Neuberger, A., 1996, "The Log Contract and other Power Contracts", in I. Nelken (ed), *The Handbook of Exotic Options* (New York: McGraw-Hill), pp 200–212.

Wallmeier, M. and R. Hafner, 2006, "Volatility as an Asset Class: European Evidence", Working Paper, University of Fribourg.

8

Exchange-traded Volatility: CBOE and CFE VIX and Variance Derivatives

John Hiatt, Catherine Shalen

CBOE[1]

BRIEF HISTORY

In 1993, the Chicago Board Options Exchange (CBOE) introduced the CBOE Volatility Index or VIX, often called the "fear gauge" because of its ability to capture the level of uncertainty in the marketplace. The VIX is an index that infers 30-day expected stock market volatility from stock index options. Robert Whaley (1993), who helped design the index, immediately proposed trading derivatives on the VIX. However, the VIX was derived from Black–Scholes prices of at-the-money options. This original version of the VIX was difficult to replicate and arbitrage.

In 2003, CBOE revised the calculation of VIX with the help of market participants to reflect new theoretical developments.[2] The work of Neuberger, among others, showed that total realised variance (squared volatility) over a period of time can be synthesised by hedging a properly calibrated portfolio of out-of-the-money European-style options expiring at the end of the period. It follows that the price of this portfolio is the risk-neutral expectation or price of variance. The current VIX is the square root of the price of 30-day variance. It is calculated from the prices of S&P500 options (SPX) instead of S&P100 options (OEX), as was done previously. This is for two reasons.

---

1 Provided as a courtesy by Chicago Board Options Exchange, Incorporated.

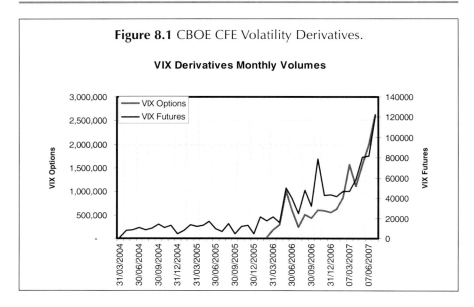

Figure 8.1 CBOE CFE Volatility Derivatives.

Table 8.1 CBOE CFE Volatility Derivatives.

Volatility type	CBOE/CFE contract
30-day implied volatility	VIX futures (S&P500)
	VIX options (S&P500)
	VXD futures (DJIA)
	RVX futures (Russell 2000)
	RVN futures (Nasdaq 100)
Realised variance	3-month S&P500 variance futures
	1-year S&P500 variance futures

First, SPX options are the largest index options market in the US, as measured by average daily trading volume. Second, OEX options are American-style while SPX options are European-style.

The changes in the calculation of the VIX and the launch of the CBOE Futures Exchange (CFE) ushered the launch of VIX futures contracts. Futures on realised S&P500 variance and futures on DJIA-implied volatility soon followed. The next contracts CBOE introduced were options on the VIX, listed in February 2006. VIX options have had an unprecedented success, reaching a record volume of 325,577 contracts on 11 July, 2007.

Figure 8.2 Bloomberg's screen for 10 July, 2006.

```
                        Contract Table
CBOE  SPX  VOLATILI                          Monitoring enabled
                   Pricing Date: 6/22/07
CBOE Futures Exchange                      ---LATEST AVAILABLE---    2
Grey date = options trading                  44948      2150   Previous
            Last   Change   Time    Bid  1  Ask   OpenInt  TotVol  Close
 1)VIX  spot 15.79  +1.58  12:53                      0       0   14.21
 2)UXN7 Jul07 15.63  +.56  12:53   15.63   15.65   10663   1654   15.07
 3)UXQ7 Aug07 15.78  +.40  12:51   15.70   15.87   18328    344   15.38
 4)UXU7 Sep07 15.80  +.30  12:43   15.71   15.86    2899     23   15.50
 5)UXV7 Oct07 15.83  +.26  12:46   15.73   15.90    1616     58   15.57
 6)UXX7 Nov07 15.91  +.16  12:49   15.85   15.94    8476     24   15.75
 7)UXZ7 Dec07 15.83  +.08  12:45   15.80   15.97    1102     13   15.75
 8)UXG8 Feb08 15.89  +.09  12:38   15.90   16.03    1450     12   15.80
 9)UXK8 May08 16.07  +.17  12:36   16.07   16.19     414     20   15.90
10)UXM8 Jun08 16.03  +.22  12:38   16.00   16.16       0      2   15.81
11)UXQ8 Aug08                                           0      0
```

BENEFITS OF EXCHANGE-TRADED VOLATILITY

CBOE's and CFE's expanding volatility complex is the first central marketplace for volatility and the first market for implied volatility; only realised volatility is actively traded over the counter. The complex pools investors from different segments of the financial markets and aggregates their expectations of stock index volatility. The confluence of expectations results in fair and representative prices that are continuously disseminated to data vendors. Bloomberg's screen, reproduced as Figure 8.2, displays the 22 June, 2007 prices of VIX futures with successive expiration dates and the underlying index, VIX. On this date, VIX was 15.79 and the price of November 2007 futures was 15.91. This indicates that the market expected 30-day volatility to remain virtually unchanged between 22 June and the expiration of the November contract. In other words, the market expected volatility to average 15.79% between 22 June, and 22 July, 2007 and 15.91% between 21 November, and 21 December, 2007.

Historical information on the different volatility contracts since their inception is also publicly available from the data vendors.

Exchange trading provides other benefits besides greater pricing and informational efficiencies. First, the concentration of volume in a small number of standardised contracts increases liquidity and reduces transaction costs. Second, trading volatility on an exchange virtually eliminates counterparty risk. The guarantees provided by clearing houses owned by or affiliated to derivative exchanges have successfully prevented financial crises on these exchanges. Investors trading CBOE's and CFE's volatility contracts are protected by the clearing safeguards of the Options Clearing Corporation, a triple-A-rated company that acts as an intermediary to all transactions. Third, the contiguous trading of futures on implied and realised volatility and of options on implied volatility simplifies arbitrage. It also reduces its cost because of advantageous cross-margining between the different contracts.

WHO TRADES, WHY AND HOW?

The VIX acquired a large following in the decade that followed its introduction. Investors viewed and continue to view VIX as a technical indicator capable of predicting market movements. VIX futures and options therefore generate a lively interest from both institutional and retail customers.

Initially, a significant portion of volume was tied to the over-the-counter volatility market, but participants now come from more diverse backgrounds. To be more specific, VIX futures and options are drawing in volatility and credit desks at investment banks, mutual funds, hedge funds, option market makers and a few high-end retail investors. Investment banks are the main source of volume, with over 90% of their flow on behalf of customers. The main selling points for these various types of users are the fact that implied volatility rises instantly when markets become stressed; the greater effectiveness of using VIX derivatives to hedge volatility compared with SPX options that require continuous delta-hedging; the convenience of a single trading facility for SPX options and VIX derivatives; and the transparency of exchange trading.

The dominance of institutional traders makes for frequent large trades in the form of block trades and crossing orders. Trades of 10,000 to 20,000 option contracts or 1,000 to 2,000 futures contracts are not unusual. As is normal for novel derivative contracts, the patterns of trading evolve with the maturity of the market. They also evolve with market conditions. VIX futures transactions were initially all outright positions but calendar spreads later became popular. Over the year following the introduction of VIX options, trading shifted from the back to the front months. Option transactions are now divided between outrights, call spreads, ratio spreads and straddles.

Volatility traders at investment banks are the principal users of VIX derivatives. They hedge VIX-based structured products sold to customers over the counter, strip out the volatility exposure of correlation strategies, or speculate on volatility. There is also a healthy flow of volume from credit desks eager to buy volatility in any shape or form as an antidote to widening credit spreads. This is especially true of desks that specialise in high-yield credits that historically have the highest correlations with index volatility. Arbitrageurs between the credit and equity markets trade VIX derivatives to offset volatility risk. Similar to credit-portfolio managers, mutual-fund managers find VIX derivatives helpful to insure against extreme adverse returns. More generally, these managers buy VIX derivatives as another "asset class" to diversify equity portfolios.

A variety of hedge funds trade CBOE and CFE derivatives. Much like credit funds, distressed-equity funds find the contracts useful for portfolio insurance. Other hedge funds that are directionally neutral, such as long-short funds, trade VIX derivatives to manage their volatility risk. For hedge funds that specialise in trading volatility, VIX derivatives and variance futures offer additional tools to implement different speculative and risk-management strategies. For example, they might short variance futures to reap the premium between implied and realised volatility, buy or sell VIX derivatives when they spot mispricing, or trade calendar spreads to play the term structure of futures prices. There are hedge funds that trade the front months of VIX options to speculate on or hedge "vol-vol", the volatility of volatility, much as an equity or index option trader uses options to hedge the volatility of the underlying.

Maintaining long-term protection against credit, equity or volatility risk requires rolling contract positions from expiration to expiration. The optimal rolling schedule and volatility contract – VIX futures, realised variance futures or VIX options – depend on the costs of rolling and on the risk premiums embedded in the prices of the different contracts. For example, rolling VIX futures quarterly tends to be less expensive than rolling them monthly. The trade-off is greater basis risk because the nearby futures are the most tightly correlated with variations in credit spreads. When VIX options became available, trading desks also realised that various option structures such as call spreads could be less expensive hedges than long VIX futures positions.

CBOE AND CFE VOLATILITY CONTRACTS

CBOE and CFE volatility contracts enable investors to trade two different types of volatility: implied volatility, which looks to the future, and realised volatility, which looks to the past. VIX futures, VXD futures and VIX options that settle to implied volatility are in the first category. Three-month and one-year variance futures that settle to realised variance and are in the second. The design of the different contracts and the market factors that influence their pricing are important to know for volatility traders.

CFE VIX futures
What VIX futures prices represent
VIX futures settle on a monthly basis to the value of the CBOE VIX. The price of a VIX futures contract therefore reflects a market forecast of the future level of VIX, specifically the value of VIX at the futures expiration. And, since VIX itself is an index that forecasts S&P500 volatility over the next 30 calendar days, the price of VIX futures is a forecast of a forecast of future volatility, or, equivalently, a forecast of forward 30-day volatility. This is in contrast to VIX, which is a forecast of spot 30-day volatility.

Let's illustrate with an example. Suppose that, at the close of 4 August, 2006, VIX is equal to 14.46. This means that the market expects S&P500 volatility to average 14.46% between 4 August, and 3 September, 2006, 30 days later. Also suppose that the price of September 2006 futures is 15.42 or a VIX forecast of 15.42% for 13 September, 2006, when the futures expire. This implies that on 4 August, 2006, the market expects volatility will average 15.42% in the 30 days between 13 September and 20 October, 2006.

Speculation and arbitrage
Investors with a different view of forward volatility from the consensus forecast encapsulated by VIX futures prices can take positions in VIX futures. For example, if on 4 August, 2006, you had believed that the price of the September futures was too low because September and October are frequently such stormy months, you could have bought September 2006 VIX futures to

lock in the 15.42% volatility. If VIX had been greater than 15.42% on 13 September, eg, 16.73%, the position would have earned US$13,100 (US$1,000 * (16.73 − 15.42)). Alternatively, the position might have been sold at a profit at any time between 4 August, and 13 September, 2006 if the futures price increased.

More generally, investors can buy or sell VIX futures with any listed expiration date to bank on what they think the market will think about the expiration value of VIX between now and the futures expiration date. Six near-contracts and several additional months in the February quarterly cycle are usually listed. Successive VIX futures can be stripped in various combinations to fit expectations regarding the fluctuations of future implied volatility around its perceived mean.

Note that 20 October, 2006 is the third Friday of October 2006, and the third Friday is when S&P500 options usually expire. This is not a coincidence. All VIX futures contracts, including the September 2006 contract, expire exactly 30 calendar days before a SPX option expiration in the next calendar month. This final settlement schedule guarantees that the value of VIX used to settle the futures is calculated from a portfolio of SPX options expiring on a single date. On other days VIX is interpolated linearly from the prices of SPX options expiring at multiple dates that bracket 30 calendar days. This scheme facilitates arbitrage between the futures and SPX options at the futures expiration.

Because of the ongoing arbitrage between VIX futures and SPX options, the forecast of forward volatility embedded in VIX futures prices blends the expectations of participants in both markets. Traders can relate SPX option prices and VIX futures prices to detect arbitrage violations that may arise because of differing supply-and-demand pressures in the two markets.

Term structure
Similar to the term structure of SPX-implied volatilities, the term structure of VIX futures prices is shaped by traders' expectations about forward volatilities. On 13 June, 2006 volatility reached a local peak, and both term structures changed from upward to downward-sloping. The market must have believed that volatility would drop back down. By 16 June, both term structures reversed course, presumably because investors reverted to their prior belief,

Figure 8.3 VIX futures under different term structures of S&P500 implied volatility.

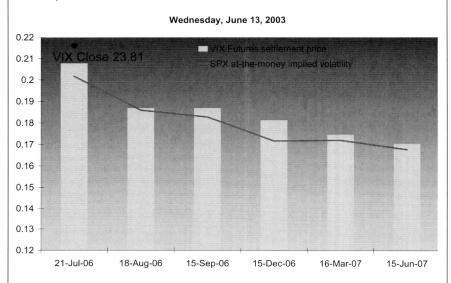

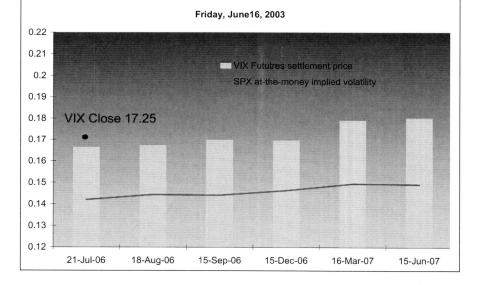

volatility seemed low by historical standards. The sensitivity of volatility to market moods and investors' uncertainty about the exact timing of mean reversions, not to mention uncertainty about the mean level of volatility itself, can easily produce such flip-flops in the term structure.

Volatility
The historic volatilities of near-term VIX futures prices have generally been higher than the volatilities of the S&P500 and most of its component stocks. Figure 8.4 shows the realised volatilities of VIX futures with those of Google, IBM and the S&P500 in 2005. What the chart also reveals is that VIX futures have been much less volatile than the VIX itself. This is the norm, and for two reasons. The first is that VIX forecasts nearby volatility, while VIX futures prices forecast forward volatilities. The volatility of a forecast varies with the flow of information, and this flow often increases as one nears the date of disclosure of the forecast variable. Put another way, the closer VIX futures are to expiration, the more uncertainty is resolved about the expiration value of VIX, and hence the more volatile is the futures price.

The second reason why VIX futures prices are less volatile than VIX is that VIX is mean-reverting and that it rarely wanders outside a band ranging approximately from 10% to 45%. It means that a shock to VIX generates ever smaller shocks in expected future values of VIX. The volatility and "dollar" volatility of VIX futures prices therefore dampen with the time to expiration.

VIX futures, VIX, and realised volatility
VIX, near-term VIX futures and past realised volatility all tend to move together. The covariation of VIX and VIX futures prices is not based on the sort of "carry" arbitrage that ties stock index futures prices and the underlying stock index. To replicate the return of stock index futures, an investor can buy the underlying stock index, finance the purchase and carry the position to the futures expiration date. But, just as a rate of interest or a rate of inflation cannot be carried, VIX cannot be carried to replicate a forward value of VIX.

The real reason why VIX futures prices often track the VIX and both in turn track realised volatility is that volatility is persistent. Expectations about volatility in forthcoming months often parallel

Figure 8.4 VIX futures under different term structures of S&P500 implied volatility.

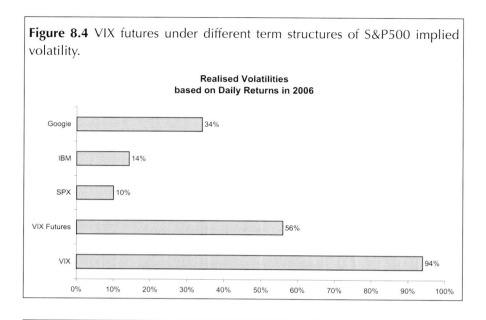

Figure 8.5 VIX futures under different term structures of S&P500 implied volatility.

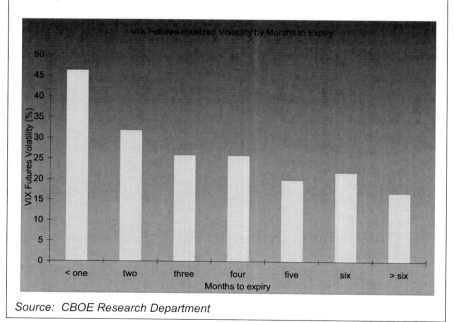

Source: CBOE Research Department

Table 8.2 Daily US dollar variation of VIX futures October 2005–August 2006.

Time to expiration		Daily dollar variation
1 month	Average	US$349.15
	Minimum	US$37.50
	Maximum	US$1,611.25
2 months	Average	US$192.98
	Minimum	US$25.56
	Maximum	US$720.00
3 months	Average	US$196.98
	Minimum	US$3.33
	Maximum	US$880.00
4 months	Average	US$156.37
	Minimum	US$7.50
	Maximum	US$685.00

Source: CFE

expectations about nearby volatility; moreover, both expectations are often strongly influenced by recent realised volatility. This relationship can break down during financial crises when volatility reaches extreme values that are not likely to persist for long. More generally, VIX futures prices tend to rise above or fall below VIX when volatility is well below or above its recent historical average and more likely to revert to the mean. This phenomenon was much in evidence in the first couple of years after the launch of VIX futures. The prices of successive futures contracts consistently decreased from listing date to expiration. The resulting gains to investors who were short VIX futures could be interpreted as a negative risk premium for volatility. Alternatively, the shorts profited from the longs' mistaken belief that volatility was bound to rise.

VIX futures during market upheavals

VIX has always surged during financial crises and the prices of nearby VIX futures will probably do the same. Even at a volatility of 15%, a historically moderate level, the correlation between S&P500 returns and VIX futures returns approaches –1. The negative correlation implies that VIX futures are effective to hedge against moderate to severe market downturns.

Fair value

A theoretical value of VIX futures[3] can be calculated based on the method used to derive VIX. The 4 August, price of September 2006 VIX futures is equal to $E_{\text{Aug 4}}\sqrt{E_{\text{Sep 13}} \text{Var}[\text{Sep 13, Oct 20}]}$, where the term under the square root is the value of VIX on 13 September, 2006. Since variance is additive the expected 30-day forward variance between 13 September, and 20 October, 2006 is equal to:

$$E_{\text{Aug 4}} FV = E_{\text{Aug 4}} \text{Var}[\text{Sep 13, Oct 20}]$$
$$= E_{\text{Aug 4}} \text{Var}[\text{Aug 4, Oct 20}] - E_{\text{Aug 4}} \text{Var}[\text{Aug 4, Sep 13}]$$

Both expected variances in this difference can be calculated from the prices of out-of-the money S&P500 options using the same methodology as for the calculation of VIX. Taking the square root of the difference is not quite what we need, which is the expected value of the square root of VIX. To get us there, we need to subtract the variance of the futures price from the expected forward variance. This adjusts for the concavity of the square root function. In percentage points, the theoretical value of VIX futures is thus:

$$100\sqrt{(365/30)(E_{\text{Aug 4}}FV - E_{\text{Aug 4}}\text{Var}[\text{VIX}_{\text{Sep 13}}])}$$

A technical detail about VIX futures to keep in mind is that they settle to a special opening quotation (SOQ) of the VIX at expiration. The SOQ is calculated from the opening prices of the different option series that enter into the calculation of the VIX. As for S&P500 futures, the SOQ method of settlement is used to help arbitrageurs unwind cash and futures positions at the same price, and as for S&P500 futures it induces some discrepancy between the cash and futures settlement price. Cash VIX is calculated from contemporaneous option prices, whereas the VIX SOQ is calculated from a sequence of opening option prices. The difference in construction implies that the final settlement price of VIX derivatives often deviates from the contemporaneous value of VIX. This deviation is akin to the familiar discrepancy between a stock index and the special opening quotation used as final settlement price of derivatives on the stock index.

CBOE VIX options

VIX options are standard European-style options based on VIX. Their multiplier is US$100, and like VIX futures, VIX options are quoted on the same scale as VIX. The notional size of the options is thus one-tenth the size of the futures. Similar to VIX futures, VIX options expire 30 calendar days prior to a SPX option expiration and settle to the value of VIX, or, more precisely, the Special Opening Quotation of VIX. Prior to expiration, the price of a VIX call represents the risk-neutral expectation of the spread between forward volatility and the strike of the option, and conversely for the put. An important feature to note in this regard is that since spot VIX does not represent the expected value of forward VIX, VIX is not the at-the-money strike of VIX options. The at-the-money strike is the price of forward volatility, and is equal to the price of VIX futures with the same expiration as the option. The term structure of VIX options – price levels as well as realised volatilities – exhibits the same patterns as the term structure of VIX futures and S&P500 options. Similar to VIX futures, VIX options can be used to hedge credit and equity portfolios, or to speculate on volatility.

Speculation and arbitrage

VIX options offer the opportunity to trade on more defined views of the probable range of VIX at expiration. To illustrate, on 22 June, 2007, CBOE had VIX options expiring in July, August, September, October, November, February 2008 and May 2008, with strikes spaced at 1 and 2.5 point intervals from 10 to 35. Going long a September 2007 call at a strike of 15 would have been a speculation that VIX would rise above 15 at the September expiration. In the same vein, a November 2007 strangle position short one call at a strike of 17 and short one put at a strike of 12 would have been a speculation that VIX would range between 12 to 17 at the November expiration. Straddles and call spreads are some other popular option combinations. Since VIX options and VIX futures prices are both conditioned on the estimated probability distribution of forward volatility, the two contracts can be arbitraged or combined to create structured exposures. Volatility is permanently stuck in what stock index analysts call a trading range. For example, a structure which can become effective when volatility appears stuck in what stock index analysis call a trading range is a buy-write portfolio long VIX futures and short VIX calls.

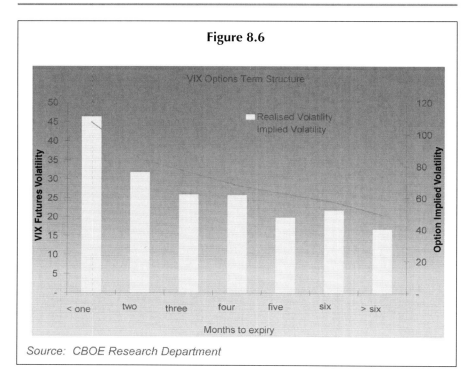

Figure 8.6

Source: CBOE Research Department

Implied volatility

The implied volatility of VIX options tends to be much higher than the realised volatility of expected forward volatility – as measured by the realised volatility of VIX futures prices. It is also higher than the implied volatility of the S&P500 and the implied volatility of the average equity option. Another characteristic feature of the implied volatility of VIX options is that it decreases with the time to expiration. This downward-sloping term structure reflects the lower realised volatility of longer-dated VIX futures.

The VIX option implied volatilities in the chart below are derived from the Black option model. An arresting feature of the chart is that unlike the familiar downward "smirk" of S&P500 Black–Scholes implied volatilities, the Black skew of VIX option implied volatilities increases with the strike price. Also, note that its slope steepens inversely with the maturity of the options. As for the smirk of S&P500 implied volatilities, the probable explanation for the upward skew is the estimation error stemming from applying a lognormal distribution to a distribution that is asymmetric

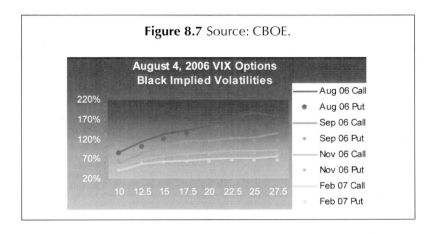

Figure 8.7 Source: CBOE.

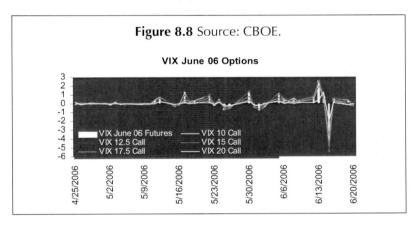

Figure 8.8 Source: CBOE.

and kurtotic. In the case of S&P500 returns, the distribution is leptokurtic, and its left tail has fattened considerably since the crash of 1987. The distribution of VIX returns is the mirror image – it has a fatter right tail – first because extreme negative returns are accompanied by extreme volatilities, and second because the probability of volatilities in the neighbourhood of zero is low.

VIX options and VIX futures
VIX option prices move lock in step with those of VIX futures but with different sensitivities or "deltas" depending on their strike. From April 2006 to June 2006, for example, variations of the June 2006 10 call tracked the June 2006 futures more closely than those of the 20 call.

CFE realised variance futures

Realised variance futures are the exchange counterparts of realised variance swaps traded over the counter. CFE lists three and 12-month variance futures that settle respectively to estimates of the total S&P500 variance realised in the three and 12 months preceding the third Friday of the contract month. As for S&P500 variance swaps, the estimate of realised variance used as final settlement price is calculated as a multiple of the annualised sum of squared daily log returns of the S&P500 over the previous three or 12 months.

To express this more formally, let us denote the S&P500 log return from date $t-1$ to date t by $R_t = \ln(S_t/S_{t-1})$, where S_t is the value of the S&P500 at date t. CFE three-month June 2006 variance futures settle to

$$10^4 * \text{VAR}_{\text{Mar}}^{\text{Jun}} = 10^4 * \frac{252}{N} \sum_{t=1}^{N} R_t^2$$

where N is the expected number of S&P500 returns tabulated over the three months preceding the June 2006 expiration. If the average volatility realised during those three months is 25.17%, the realised variance is 0.06335 and the final settlement price is quoted as 633.50 variance points. The contract multiplier is US$50. Hence a 0.0001 change in realised variance moves the futures price by 1 variance point and the contract value by US$50.

To frame this in volatility terms, recall that variance is the square of volatility, hence a 1% move in volatility translates to a $(1+2\sigma)*10^{-4}$ move in variance or US$50 * $(1+2\sigma)$ in the value of a variance futures. For example, if volatility increases from $\sigma = 15\%$ to 16%, a long futures gains US$1,550 = 50 * $(1+2*15)$. At a 15% volatility, what the over-the-counter markets calls a US$100,000 "vega" exposure (an exposure with a US$100,000 payout per 1% increase in volatility) has the same payout as approximately 64.52 variance futures. More generally, a US$100,000 "vega" exposure is equivalent to $2000/(2\sigma+1)$ 3-month variance futures contracts.

RUC and IUG

RUG and IUG are the tickers for the realised and implied volatility components implicit in the price of realised variance futures. The price of realised variance futures is a weighted sum of

RUG and IUG, eg $\text{VAR}^{\text{Mar}}_{\text{Jun}} = wRUG + (1-w)IUG$. To illustrate how to read RUG and IUG, consider the June 2006 three-month realised variance futures that were listed on 21 April, 2006. This contract was to settle on 16 June, 2006 to the annualised sum of daily variances from 17 March, to 16 June, 2006. From 21 April, 2006 to 17 March, 2006 no term of the sum was observable. Hence the futures price was entirely composed of the risk-neutral expectation of the three-month total variance. RUG was equal to zero and the futures price was equal to IUG. Note in passing that one could also extrapolate the expected variance from the prices of March, April and May VIX futures. On 17 March, 2006, IUG and the futures prices were equal. Both were also theoretically equal to the price of a three-month over-the-counter variance swap. Each business day that elapsed after 17 March, 2006 contributed a term to the realised component of the total variance. The unrealised or implied component was represented by IUG. At expiration, 16 June, 2006, every term of the sum was realised. At this juncture, IUG was equal to zero and the futures price was equal to RUG. CFE disseminates RUG and IUG daily at the close.

Looking at the history of June 2006 three-month variance futures, one finds that the futures price is consistently greater than the realised variance. This is consistent with empirical studies of implied and realised volatility that suggest volatility carries a negative risk premium. A second finding is that the average forecasting error of the futures price relative to the realised three-month volatility is less than half the forecasting error of a naïve forecast derived by linear extrapolation of the resolved component of the variance.

Successive variance futures contracts can be stripped to synthesise a position on longer-term realised variance. For example, a strip of June 2006, September 2006, December 2006 and March 2007 variance futures constitutes a one-year variance contract. An alternative to this strip is a position in CFE's 12-month realised variance futures expiring in March 2007. This contract settles to the realised variance from March 2006 to March 2007, or $10^{4}*$ $\text{VAR}^{\text{Mar07}}_{\text{Mar06}} = (252/N) \sum_{t=1}^{N} R_t^2$. Since the 12-month variance futures multiplier is also US$50, the contract size is a quarter of the size of the three-month variance futures. If current volatility is σ and it increases by an average 1% over the contract year, a 12-month

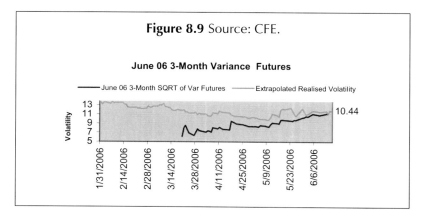

Figure 8.9 Source: CFE.

variance futures gains US$50 * (2σ + 1), while a strip of three-month variance futures contracts gains 4* $ 50 * (2σ + 1).

CONCLUSION

Exchange-traded volatility derivatives have significantly eased the task of managing volatility risk by bringing transparency, clearing guarantees and a greater choice of contracts to investors. CBOE's and CFE's futures and options based on VIX – the benchmark for implied volatility – have inspired several new speculative and arbitrage strategies. As market participants become more familiar with these innovative contracts and learn how to trade them, they ready themselves for the next wave of products based on the volatility of other asset classes.

2 Goldman Sachs played an important role in redesigning the index and supporting the launch of exchange-listed volatility products.

3 Bruno Dupire derived this theoretical value.

REFERENCES

Whaley, Robert E., 1993, "Derivatives on Market Volatility: Hedging Tools Long Overdue", *Journal of Derivatives* **1**, Fall, pp 71–84.

9

Investment Strategies Using the Volatility Index (case study of the Korean market)

Chul Min Kim
Hyundai Securities

In the Korean market, there is not currently any official volatility index. According to KRX, the Korea Exchange, within a couple of years, they plan to launch the volatility index based on KOSPI200 options, the most actively traded option in the world.

Even though there is not currently any official volatility index in Korea now, we can calculate the volatility index using the KOSPI200 option prices. Here, we calculate the unofficial volatility index based on KOSPI200 options, analyse its characteristics and simulate an investment strategy using it. For the sake of simplicity, I have named the calculated volatility index Voldex.

VOLATILITY INDEX IN KOREA

In Figure 9.1, you can see the volatility index of Korea market based on KOSPI200 options from the start of 1999 to mid-2007. As you can see, volatility implied in KOSPI200 options has been significantly decreased during the period and can also see a couple of sharp soaring periods like September 2001.

MAJOR CHARACTERISTICS OF VOLATILITY INDEX

The Korean stock market has enjoyed a rally from 2003, as can be seen in Figure 9.2. As of 31 July, 2007 the YTD return of the KOSPI200 index is 31.8%. Currently the volatility index itself seems

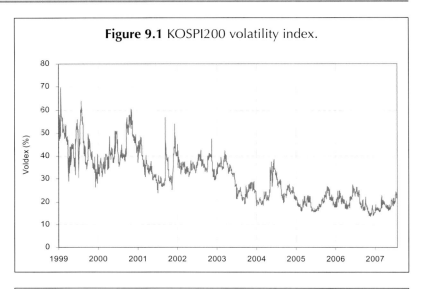

Figure 9.1 KOSPI200 volatility index.

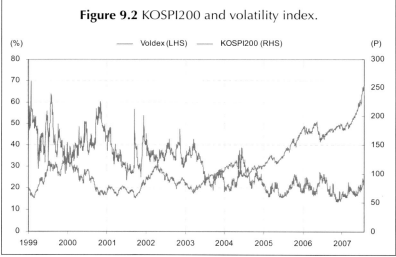

Figure 9.2 KOSPI200 and volatility index.

to hit the bottom at the end of 2006 and it has been slowly increasing during 2007.

RELATIONSHIPS WITH STOCK MARKETS

Let us think about the relationships between the volatility index and the stock market. The volatility index is originally extracted from the underlying index option prices and the option prices reflect

INVESTMENT STRATEGIES USING THE VOLATILITY INDEX (CASE STUDY OF THE KOREAN MARKET)

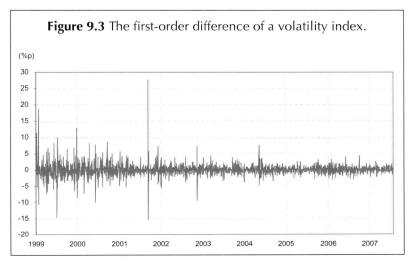

Figure 9.3 The first-order difference of a volatility index.

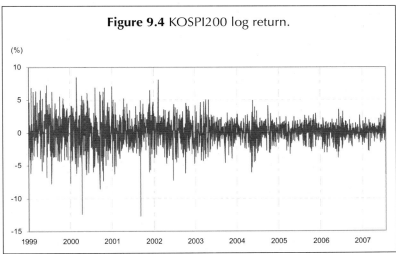

Figure 9.4 KOSPI200 log return.

the market participants' future expectation of the volatility. Hence, when the most market participants expect the high volatility in the near future, the volatility index is up.

In Figure 9.5 we made a scatter plot with the first-order difference of the volatility index and KOSPI200 log return, both in daily. As you can see, there is a negative relationship between these two. When the volatility index is down, the underlying stock market tends to be up.

253

Figure 9.5 Relationship between the volatility index and its underlying stockmarket index.

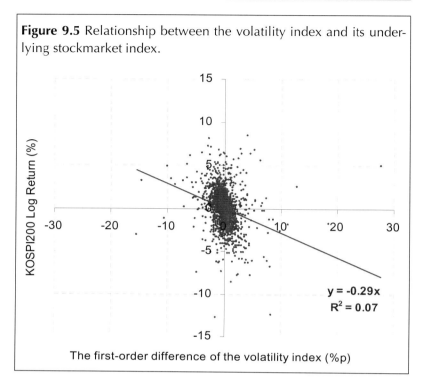

Figure 9.6 is another chart that shows the relationship between the volatility index and the forward stock market return. What we see in this chart is that, when the volatility index is very high, the 30-day future stock market return is also positive. It is well known that the volatility index is the fear gauge and also the contrary indicator. When the volatility index is unusually at a high level, it is time to buy the underlying stocks or take a long position on the stock market. Conversely, when the volatility index is very low, it is likely that the volatility will be rising and consequently the stock market will experience some amount of loss.

INVESTMENT STRATEGIES USING VOLATILITY INDEX

Using its basic characteristics of mean-reverting and the relationship with the stock market, the underlying equity index, we can develop various investment strategies. Here we develop a simple investment strategy using the volatility index as an indicator to buy or sell the underlying equity index.

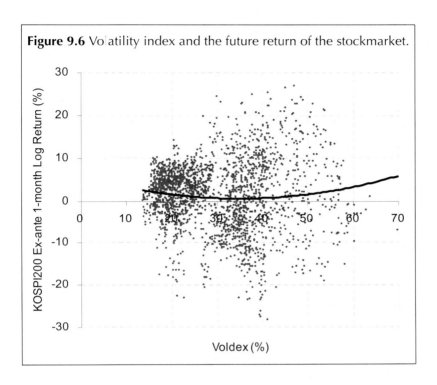

Figure 9.6 Volatility index and the future return of the stockmarket.

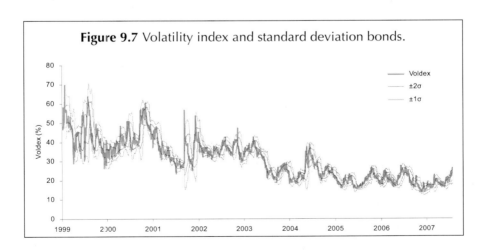

Figure 9.7 Volatility index and standard deviation bonds.

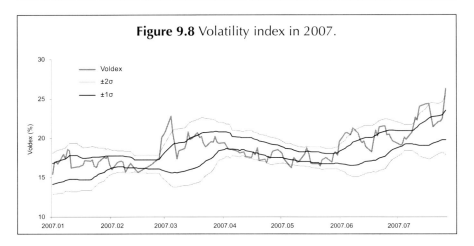

Figure 9.8 Volatility index in 2007.

Table 9.1 Trading record.

Number	Entry		Exit		Holding period	Return (%)
	Date	Price (pt)	Date	Price (pt)		
1	07-03-06	181.23	07-03-07	182.36	1	0.062
2	07-06-07	223.17	07-06-12	219.94	5	−1.45
3	07-07-12	242.86	07-07-20	251.45	8	3.54
	Total number of trade					3
	Total return (%)					2.67

In Figure 9.7, we can see the volatility index and its 30-day moving standard deviations. There are plus or minus one standard deviation and plus or minus two standard deviations. Considering the mean-reverting nature of the volatility index, we can assume that, when it is far from its mean, it will try to come back to it.

With this idea in mind, we test the performance of the strategy that buy and sell the underlying equity index according to the signals. In Figure 9.8, you can see the volatility index and its 30-day moving standard deviations in 2007. The volatility index is moving up and down and obviously it shows some mean-reverting activity.

Here we enter the long position on the underlying equity index (KOSPI200) when the volatility index is below the lowest line (minus two standard deviations) and exit the long position when the volatility index is above the lowest line.

Applying this criteria, there were three trades in 2007 and you can see the summary in Table 9.1. Position-holding periods are relatively short, between one and eight days, and the absolute returns per trade are 0.62%, −1.45% and 3.54%.

Even though we have simulated only about seven months in 2007, we can easily extend this strategy, a kind of channel-break trading not using the underlying time series itself but using the volatility index, to long-term period.

10

Risk Premium, Pricing and Hedging for Variance Swaps

Srdjan D. Stojanovic

University of Cincinnati

INTRODUCTION

The classical Black–Scholes theory of pricing (and hedging) of financial contracts assumes market completeness, ie, the tradability of all randomness in the model, which means that it is assumed that all economic factors considered are tradable or perfectly correlated to some other tradables. Once the market completeness assumption is relaxed, we are in the realm of incomplete markets. Incomplete markets consist of tradables for which at least some of the factors are not perfectly correlated with the tradables.

The incomplete markets literature can be classified into (at least) two camps. The classical works do not consider the issue of determination of the risk premium (due to the non-hedgeable risks), but rather assume one, leaving it to be determined statistically. The more recent works concentrate on actual determination of the risk premium consistent with the pricing model and investor's risk aversion.

In the literature on incomplete markets, with risk premium determination, two major pricing methodologies were established recently: "indifference derivative pricing" and "neutral derivative pricing". The first assumes that the financial contract considered for pricing is not tradable, or at least that it is illiquid. The second assumes, on the contrary, that the financial contract considered for pricing is perfectly tradable, or at least that it is liquid. The two methodologies therefore complement each other.

In a recent series of works, relying only on analytic methods, ie, relying on partial differential equations (PDE) methods, which means without any reliance on abstract probability, the author has established a theory of simultaneous ("neutral") pricing of multiple types of (liquid) tradable financial derivative contracts under multidimensionality of risks in incomplete markets, including markets with non-hedgeable interest rate risks. The non-hedgeable risk premium is determined by the selection of the investor's risk aversion parameter, and characterised via an additional non-linear PDE. The derived pricing PDE system may possibly be viewed as the "ultimate" extension of the famous Black–Scholes PDE. A hedging formula of the same generality was also derived. Furthermore, both results were derived as corollaries of the discovered formula for a matrix inverse, therefore called the "fundamental matrix of derivatives pricing and hedging".

Here we briefly recall the general theory and apply it in the case of volatility derivatives. In particular, we derive explicit formulae for the price and for the hedge for variance swaps, under the assumption that the non-hedgeable volatility risk is priced according to the hyperbolic absolute risk aversion (HARA), ie, power utility of wealth function, and more precisely, by its perpetual version/simplification (see Stojanovic (2005b) for the case of the constant absolute risk aversion (CARA), ie, exponential utility pricing). We also discuss the obtained result noting, for example, that, if the correlation between the price of the tradable (say, equity) and its volatility is negative, then the developed theory predicts that the variance swaps are more expensive under the "bull" market conditions than under the "bear" market conditions.

SIMPLE ECONOMIES, MARKETS AND OPTIMAL PORTFOLIO THEORY
Simple economies and markets
Following Stojanovic (2005b), we give the following definition.

Definition 10.1 A simple economy (often referred to also as just an economy) $\mathfrak{E}$ consists of a finite set of dynamic factors, tradables (often with a non-empty intersection), and an interest rate, denoted by $A(t) = \{A_1(t), \ldots, A_m(t)\}$, $S(t) = \{S_1(t), \ldots, S_k(t)\}$ and $r(t)$, respectively. The factors and tradables are assumed to obey Itô stochastic differential equation (SDE) dynamics

$$dA(t) = b(t, A(t))dt + c(t, A(t)) \cdot dB(t)$$
$$dS(t) = S(t)(a_s(t, A(t)) - (t, A(t)))dt + S(t)\sigma_s(t, A(t)) \cdot dB(t)$$
(10.1)

and that $\sigma_s \cdot \sigma_s^T > 0$ (which is thought of as market non-redundancy condition; this condition also implies that tradables $S(t)$ can, and will, also be referred to as the risky assets). If the interest rate is stochastic (non-deterministic), then it has to be declared as one of the factors.

In the above, $B(t) = \{B_1(t), \ldots, B_n(t)\}$ is a standard n-dimensional Brownian motion, the vector-valued function $b(t, A)$ is the m-vector of factor-drifts, $c(t, A)$ is $m \times n$ factor-diffusion matrix, $a_s(t, A)$ is the k-vector of appreciation rates for the tradables (before dividends), (t, A) is the k-vector of dividend rates of the corresponding assets and $\sigma_s(t, A)$ is the volatility $(k \times n)$-matrix. The set of all tradables can also be referred to as the market $\mathfrak{M} = \{S(t), t \in \mathbb{R}\}$. Functions $a_s, \sigma_s, b, c,$ (and r, the interest rate, if not included in A) are called market coefficients.

The notation in (10.1) may be a bit confusing. For example, $S(t)\sigma_s(t, A(t))$ is by definition obtained by multiplying components of $S(t)$ with the rows of matrix $\sigma_s(t, A(t))$, while $\sigma_s(t, A(t)) \cdot dB(t)$ is the usual matrix–vector product. Note that vectors, such as $S(t) = \{S_1(t), \ldots, S_k(t)\}$, are always understood as one-dimensional arrays, so that they cannot, and need not, be transposed. On the other hand $\{S(t)\}$ is a "row-vector", while $\{S(t)\}^T$ is a "column vector", and they are both two-dimensional arrays, ie, matrices. It may also be interesting to note that $(S(t)\sigma_s(t, A(t))) \cdot dB(t) = S(t)(\sigma_s(t, A(t)) \cdot dB(t))$.

Complete and incomplete markets
Definition 10.2 A market $\mathfrak{M}$ in a simple economy $\mathfrak{E}$ is said to be complete (in the simple economy $\mathfrak{E}$) if

$$c \cdot (\mathbb{I}_n - \sigma_s^T \cdot (\sigma_s \cdot \sigma_s^T)^{-1} \cdot \sigma_s) \cdot c^T = {}_m$$
(10.2)

(where $\mathbb{I}_n$ is the n-dimensional identity matrix, $_{j \times k}$ is the $(j \times k)$-zero matrix, and $_m := {}_{m \times m}$). Otherwise, market $\mathfrak{M} \subset \mathfrak{E}$ is said to be incomplete.

It can be shown (see Stojanovic (2006b)) that market $\mathfrak{M}$ in a simple economy $\mathfrak{E}$ is complete if and only if

$$\text{SpanOfRows}[c] \subseteq \text{SpanOfRows}[\sigma_s] \qquad (10.3)$$

ie, if "all factor-randomness is tradable".

Optimal portfolio theory for multi-factor, multi-tradable SDE markets under HARA and CARA utilities

General wealth-utility: Monge–Ampère type portfolio PDE

Consider a simple economy (10.1), and let $\Pi(t, X, A) = \Pi(t) = \{\Pi_1, \ldots, \Pi_k\}$ be a (self-financing) portfolio trading strategy ($\Pi(t)$ is the vector of the cash value of investments into the risky assets $S(t)$) amounting to $X(t) = X^{\Pi}(t)$, the corresponding wealth process (the total portfolio value, consisting of cash, and the cash value of the investments in the risky assets). Then, as is well known (see, eg, Stojanovic (2003)), the wealth evolution equation is equal to

$$dX(t) = (\Pi(t, X(t), A(t)) \cdot (a_s(t, A(t)) - r(t, A(t)))$$
$$+ r(t, A(t))X(t))dt + \Pi(t, X(t), A(t)) \cdot \sigma_s(t, A(t)) \cdot dB(t)$$
$$dA(t) = b(t, A(t))dt + c(t, A(t)) \cdot dB(t) \qquad (10.4)$$

and it is to be controlled: (Merton's problem) for a given utility function ψ, find $\varphi(t, X, A)$ and a portfolio strategy $\Pi^*(t, X, A)$ such that

$$\varphi(t, X, A) = \sup_{\Pi} E_{t,X,A} \psi(X^{\Pi}(T)) = E_{t,X,A} \psi(X^{\Pi^*}(T)) \qquad (10.5)$$

for $t < T$.

Let $\nabla_\varphi = \{\partial \varphi / \partial A_1, \ldots, \partial \varphi / \partial A_m\}$ denote the gradient of φ and let $\nabla \nabla \psi$ denote the Hessian matrix. Then the Hamilton–Jacobi–Bellman (HJB) PDE associated to the stochastic control problem (10.5) becomes

$$0 = \underset{\Pi}{\text{Max}} \left[\frac{\partial \varphi}{\partial t} + \frac{\partial \varphi}{\partial X} (\Pi \cdot (a_s - r) + rX) \right.$$
$$+ b \cdot \nabla \varphi + \frac{1}{2} \frac{\partial^2 \varphi}{\partial X^2} \Pi \cdot \sigma_s \cdot \sigma_s^T \cdot \Pi$$
$$\left. + \frac{1}{2} \text{Tr}(c \cdot c^T \cdot \nabla \nabla \varphi) + \Pi \cdot \sigma_s \cdot c^T \cdot \nabla \left(\frac{\partial \varphi}{\partial X} \right) \right] \qquad (10.6)$$

together with the terminal condition

$$\varphi(T, X, A) = \psi(X) \qquad (10.7)$$

The HJB PDE (10.6) can be simplified into a Monge–Ampère type PDE (see Stojanovic (2005b, 2006b)):

$$\frac{\partial^2 \varphi}{\partial X^2} \frac{\partial \varphi}{\partial t} - \frac{1}{2}\left(\frac{\partial \varphi}{\partial X}\right)^2 (a_s - r) \cdot (\sigma_s \cdot \sigma_s^T)^{-1} \cdot (a_s - r) + rX \frac{\partial^2 \varphi}{\partial X^2} \frac{\partial \varphi}{\partial X}$$
$$+ (b \cdot \nabla \varphi)\frac{\partial^2 \varphi}{\partial X^2} - \frac{\partial \varphi}{\partial X}(a_s - r) \cdot (\sigma_s \cdot \sigma_s^T)^{-1} \cdot \sigma_s \cdot c^T \cdot \left(\nabla \frac{\partial \varphi}{\partial X}\right)$$
$$- \frac{1}{2}\left(\nabla \frac{\partial \varphi}{\partial X}\right) \cdot c \cdot \sigma_s^T \cdot (\sigma_s \cdot \sigma_s^T)^{-1} \cdot \sigma_s \cdot c^T \cdot \left(\nabla \frac{\partial \varphi}{\partial X}\right)$$
$$+ \frac{1}{2}\left(\frac{\partial^2 \varphi}{\partial X^2}\right) \mathrm{Tr}(c \cdot c^T \cdot \nabla \nabla \varphi)$$
$$= 0 \qquad (10.8)$$

If PDE (10.7)–(10.8) is solved, the stochastic control problem (10.5), ie, Merton's problem, is solved by means of the optimal portfolio strategy given by the formula

$$\Pi^\star(t, X, A)$$
$$= -\frac{1}{\partial^2 \varphi / \partial X^2}\left(\frac{\partial \varphi}{\partial X}(a_s - r) + \left(\nabla \frac{\partial \varphi}{\partial X}\right) \cdot c \cdot \sigma_s^T\right) \cdot (\sigma_s \cdot \sigma_s^T)^{-1}$$
$$(10.9)$$

This is true for any utility of wealth $\psi(X)$. Unfortunately, PDE (10.8), although much simpler than (10.6), is still quite difficult. It can be solved numerically in general (see Stojanovic (2003, 2005b) for examples). Yet, if explicit solutions are sought, one needs to specialise with respect to the utility of wealth $\psi(X)$, as discussed in the next section.

HARA portfolio PDE – the risk premium PDE
In the case of the HARA utility of wealth $\psi(X) = X^{1-\gamma}/(1-\gamma)$, and assuming $0 < \gamma \neq 1$ (if $\gamma = 1$, the problem is almost trivial, which we shall refer to colloquially as "logarithmic utility is trivial"), we look for the solution of (10.8) in the form

$$\varphi(t, X, A) = \frac{X^{1-\gamma}}{1-\gamma} e^{g_\gamma(t,A)} \qquad (10.10)$$

Parameter γ is called the relative risk aversion.

Plugging (10.10) into (10.8), we derive (see Stojanovic (2005b)) a PDE characterising function $g_\gamma(t, A)$ in (10.10)

$$\frac{\partial g_\gamma}{\partial t} + \frac{1}{2}\mathrm{Tr}(c \cdot c^\mathrm{T} \cdot \nabla\nabla g_\gamma)$$
$$+ \left(b - \frac{\gamma-1}{\gamma}(a_s - r) \cdot (\sigma_s \cdot \sigma_s^\mathrm{T})^{-1} \cdot \sigma_s \cdot c^\mathrm{T}\right) \cdot \nabla g_\gamma$$
$$+ \frac{1}{2}\nabla g_\gamma \cdot c \cdot \left(\mathbb{I}_n - \frac{\gamma-1}{\gamma}\sigma_s^\mathrm{T} \cdot (\sigma_s \cdot \sigma_s^\mathrm{T})^{-1} \cdot \sigma_s\right) \cdot c^\mathrm{T} \cdot \nabla g_\gamma$$
$$= \frac{\gamma-1}{\gamma}\left(\frac{1}{2}(a_s - r) \cdot (\sigma_s \cdot \sigma_s^\mathrm{T})^{-1} \cdot (a_s - r) + r\gamma\right) \qquad (10.11)$$

for $t < T$, with the terminal condition

$$g_\gamma(T, A) = 0 \qquad (10.12)$$

while the optimal portfolio strategy (10.9) simplifies to

$$\Pi_\gamma^{H,\star}(t, X, A) = \frac{X}{\gamma}(a_s - r + \nabla g_\gamma \cdot c \cdot \sigma_s^\mathrm{T}) \cdot (\sigma_s \cdot \sigma_s^\mathrm{T})^{-1} \qquad (10.13)$$

Remark 10.1 In addition to its obvious importance in the optimal portfolio theory, PDE (10.11)–(10.12) will be of fundamental importance in the theory of pricing (and, consequently, also for hedging) of financial contracts. When applied in such a context, Equations (10.11)–(10.12) will be referred to as the risk premium PDE.

Remark 10.2 Denote by $g_{\gamma,T}$ the solution of (10.11)–(10.12) emphasising the dependence on T, the investment horizon. It is an important problem in portfolio optimisation, and also in pricing, to consider the perpetual problem, ie, to send $T \to \infty$. An important remark is that it is not possible to send $T \to \infty$ in (10.11), ie, $g_{\gamma,T}$ does not converge to any function as $T \to \infty$; see Stojanovic (2006a) for details (see also Stojanovic (2005b, 2006b)). Nevertheless, instead of g_γ we require ∇g_γ in (10.13) and, surprisingly, $\lim_{T\to\infty} \nabla g_{\gamma,T}$ does exist. The corresponding financial intuition is that the optimal portfolio strategy stabilises for very long-term investing. This is also going to be very important in pricing, when we approximate the risk premium with its perpetual version, in order, for example, to be able to derive explicit pricing formulae, or to solve more complicated problems (see the section "Volatility derivatives for Heston's economies").

OPTIMAL PORTFOLIO-BASED PRICING AND HEDGING
Problem of neutral derivative pricing posed

Consider $\mathfrak{E}$, a simple economy (10.1). Following Howison *et al* (2004) and Stojanovic (2005b) (see Stojanovic (2006a) for perpetual contracts), we give the following definition.

Definition 10.3 A finite set of dividend paying European contingent claims (contracts) in a simple economy $\mathfrak{E}$, expiring at time $T \leq \infty$ (if $T = \infty$, ie, if the contract never expires, the contract is said to be perpetual), is a set of tradables in an (extended) auxiliary simple economy $\mathfrak{E}_a$, with prices $V(t) = \{V_1(t), \ldots, V_l(t)\}$, for $t < T$, with the terminal payout equal to

$$V(T) = \{V_1(T), \ldots, V_l(T)\} = \{v_1(A(T)), \ldots, v_l(A(T))\} = v(A(T))$$
(10.14)

and with the dividend payments of

$$\mathcal{D}(t) = \mathcal{D} = \{\mathcal{D}_1, \ldots, \mathcal{D}_l\} = \{\mathcal{D}_1(A(T)), \ldots, \mathcal{D}_l(A(T))\}, \quad \text{for } t < T$$

So, the tradables in the auxiliary economy are $\{S(t), V(T)\} = \{S_1(t), \ldots, S_k(t), V_1(T), \ldots, V_l(T)\}$, with same factors $A(t) = \{A_1(t), \ldots, A_m(t)\}$ as in $\mathfrak{E}$. We denote by a_a, σ_{s_a}, b, c the market coefficients of the auxiliary economy $\mathfrak{E}_a$.

In the above, $\mathcal{D} = \{\mathcal{D}_1, \ldots, \mathcal{D}_l\}$ is the vector of dividends paid by considered contracts ($\mathcal{D}_j$ is the amount of currency paid per unit time, ie, per year, per unit jth contract). This is different from the way dividend rates are accounted for in (10.1), where they are accounted for as "percentages" of the security prices, while dividend $\mathcal{D}$ is accounted for in the units of currency. Note that the option payout as well as the dividend is a function of factors A, and not of tradables S, so that if they are functions of a tradable underlying, as most often is the case, then such a tradable has to be declared as a factor as well, in which case $A \cap S \neq \emptyset$. This, of course, is not a restriction of any kind.

The problem of the pricing and hedging of such contracts in the case $l = 1, \mathcal{D} = 0, T < \infty$ was solved by the present author in Stojanovic (2007). The case $l = 1, T \leq \infty$ was solved by the present author in Stojanovic (2006a). The case $l \geq 1, T \leq \infty$ was solved by the present author in Stojanovic (2007).

Consider a self-financing portfolio strategy $\Pi(t, X, A) = \{\Pi_1, \ldots, \Pi_k, \Pi_{k+1}, \ldots, \Pi_{k+1}\}$ in the auxiliary economy $\mathfrak{E}_a$, where $\{\Pi_1, \ldots, \Pi_k\}$ is the cash value of the investments into the market $\mathfrak{M} \subset \mathfrak{E}$, and $\{\Pi_{k+1}, \ldots, \Pi_{k+1}\}$ are the cash values of investments into the considered contracts. For a given utility function ψ, let $\Pi^\star_\psi(t, X, A) = \{\Pi^\star_{\psi,1}, \ldots, \Pi^\star_{\psi,k}, \Pi^\star_{\psi,k+1}, \ldots, \Pi^\star_{\psi,k+1}\}$ denote the solution of Merton's problem (10.5).

Definition 10.4 ("Neutral derivative pricing"; cf. Kallsen (2002))
For a given utility function ψ, for any dividend payment $\mathcal{D}$ and for any terminal payout $v(A)$, the ψ-fair option vector price $V_\psi(t, X, A) = V_\psi = \{V_{\psi,1}, \ldots, V_{\psi,l}\}$ is defined as a (smooth) solution of the system of equations $\Pi^\star_{\psi,k+j}(t, X, A) = 0, j = 1, \ldots, l$, with the (vector) terminal condition $V_\psi(T, X, A) = v(A)$. If $\psi = \psi^H_\gamma$, then vector function $V_\gamma(t, A) := V_{\psi^H_\gamma}(t, X, A)$ is called the HARA fair price. If $\psi = \psi^C_\eta$, then vector function $V_{\psi^C_\eta}(t, X, A)$ is called the CARA fair price.

It is very important to note a feature of the price in Definition 10.4, as declared in Definition 10.3, that it is assumed that the considered contracts are tradable. So, the pricing theory that follows is suitable for liquid contracts. This should be contrasted with the so-called "indifference" pricing, appropriate only for pricing of non-tradable, or at least illiquid contracts (eg, over-the-counter (OTC) contracts).

Further vector calculus notation used
We commented briefly in sections "Simple economies and markets" and "General wealth-utility: Monge–Ampère type portfolio PDE" about some vector calculus notation. As we shall state some of the results in the case of multiple contracts (to be priced and hedged), we need some further notation. The vector of derivative prices is going to be denoted by $V(t, A) = V = \{V_1, \ldots, V_l\}$. The gradient ∇ of scalar functions was already introduced, while

$$\nabla V = \nabla\{V_1, \ldots, V_l\} := \{\nabla V_1, \ldots, \nabla V_l\}$$
$$= \left\{\left\{\frac{\partial V_1}{\partial A_1}, \ldots, \frac{\partial V_1}{\partial A_m}\right\}, \ldots, \left\{\frac{\partial V_1}{\partial A_1}, \ldots, \frac{\partial V_1}{\partial A_m}\right\}\right\} \quad (10.15)$$

which is a matrix. Similarly, a Hessian of a scalar function was already introduced, while $\nabla\nabla V$ is a vector of Hessian matrices

(a three-dimensional array, ie, rank 3 tensor)

$$\nabla\nabla V = \nabla\nabla\{V_1,\ldots,V_l\} = \nabla\{\nabla V_1,\ldots,\nabla V_l\}$$
$$= \{\nabla\nabla V_1,\ldots,\nabla\nabla V_l\} \tag{10.16}$$

We denote by $\text{Tr}(A_j)$ the usual trace of a matrix A_j, while we define the operator "tr" to be applied at a rank 3 tensor $A = \{A_1,\ldots,A_l\}$, where A_j are matrices, as

$$\text{tr}(\{A_1,\ldots,A_l\}) := \{\text{Tr}(A_1),\ldots,\text{Tr}(A_l)\} \tag{10.17}$$

Also, a dot product "·" of a rank 3 tensor α and a matrix β is a rank 3 tensor $\alpha \cdot \beta$ defined via $(\alpha \cdot \beta)_{i,j,k} := \sum_q \alpha_{i,j,q} \beta_{q,k}$.

Applying the above notion, the vector Itô chain rule for $V(t, A(t))$ can be written (see Stojanovic (2007)) as

$$\frac{dV}{V} = \frac{\partial V/\partial t + \frac{1}{2}\text{tr}(\nabla\nabla V \cdot c \cdot c^T) + \nabla V \cdot b}{V} dt + \frac{\nabla V}{V} \cdot c \cdot dB(t) \tag{10.18}$$

where, for example, a vector is divided by a vector componentwise, etc. (see Stojanovic (2007)).

The fundamental matrix of derivatives pricing and hedging

From (10.18) we can read the market coefficients for the auxiliary economy $\mathfrak{E}_a$:

$$a_a = \left\{\varrho_s, \frac{\partial V/\partial t + \frac{1}{2}\text{tr}(\nabla\nabla V \cdot c \cdot c^T) + \nabla V \cdot b + \mathcal{D}}{V}\right\},$$

$$\sigma_a = \begin{pmatrix} \sigma_s \\ \frac{\nabla V}{V} \cdot c \end{pmatrix} \tag{10.19}$$

Preparing to compute the optimal portfolio strategy (10.13) in the case of the auxiliary economy $\mathfrak{E}_a$, in order to apply Definition 10.4, we compute

$$\nabla g_\gamma \cdot c \cdot \sigma_a^T = \nabla g_\gamma \cdot c \cdot \begin{pmatrix} \sigma_s^T & c^T \cdot \left(\frac{\nabla V}{V}\right)^T \end{pmatrix}$$
$$= \left\{\nabla g_\gamma \cdot c \cdot \sigma_s^T, \nabla g_\gamma \cdot c \cdot c^T \cdot \left(\frac{\nabla V}{V}\right)^T\right\} \tag{10.20}$$

Remark 10.3 To see why in (10.20) it suffices to take g_γ characterised by (10.11), instead of, say, $(g_a)_\gamma$, as characterised by an appropriately modified Equation (10.11), to account for the market coefficients of the auxiliary economy $\mathfrak{E}_a$, see Stojanovic (2005b).

To proceed further in getting ready to apply Definition 10.4 (see (10.13)), we shall need $(\sigma_a \cdot \sigma_a^T)^{-1}$, the inverse of the matrix

$$\sigma_s \cdot \sigma_a^T = \begin{pmatrix} \sigma_s \cdot \sigma_s^T & \sigma_s \cdot c^T \cdot \left(\frac{\nabla V}{V}\right)^T \\ \frac{\nabla V}{V} \cdot c \cdot \sigma_s^T & \frac{\nabla V}{V} \cdot c \cdot c^T \cdot \left(\frac{\nabla V}{V}\right)^T \end{pmatrix} \tag{10.21}$$

Theorem 10.1 ("The fundamental matrix of derivatives pricing and hedging") Suppose that matrix $\mathfrak{X} = \nabla V \cdot c \cdot (\mathbb{I}_n - \sigma_s^T \cdot (\sigma_s \cdot \sigma_s^T)^{-1} \cdot c^T \cdot (\nabla V)^T$ is invertible. Then $\sigma_a \cdot \sigma_a^T$ is invertible and, moreover, its inverse $(\sigma_a \cdot \sigma_a^T)^{-1}$ is given by the explicit formula

$(\sigma_a \cdot \sigma_a^T)^{-1}$
$= \begin{pmatrix} (\sigma_s \cdot \sigma_s^T)^{-1} + (\sigma_s \cdot \sigma_s^T)^{-1} \cdot \sigma_s \cdot c^T \cdot (\nabla V)^T \cdot \mathfrak{X}^{-1} \cdot \nabla V \cdot c \cdot \sigma_s^T \cdot (\sigma_s \cdot \sigma_s^T)^{-1} \\ -(V\mathbb{I}_l) \cdot \mathfrak{X}^{-1} \cdot \nabla V \cdot c \cdot \sigma_s^T \cdot (\sigma_s \cdot \sigma_s^T)^{-1} \end{pmatrix}$

$\begin{pmatrix} -(\sigma_s \cdot \sigma_s^T)^{-1} \cdot \sigma_s \cdot c^T \cdot (\nabla V)^T \cdot \mathfrak{X}^{-1} \cdot (V\mathbb{I}_l) \\ (V\mathbb{I}_l) \cdot \mathfrak{X}^{-1} \cdot (V\mathbb{I}_l) \end{pmatrix}$

(10.22)

Remark 10.4 Formula (10.22) was proved by the present author in Stojanovic (2007). The problem of finding the fundamental matrix of derivative pricing and hedging in the case $V = \{V_1\}$ was solved by the present author in Stojanovic (2005b).

Problem of neutral derivative pricing solved

Using Theorem 10.1, after some calculations (see Stojanovic (2006b)), we get ($*$ stands for an entry of no importance)

$(a_a - r + \nabla g_\gamma \cdot c \cdot \sigma_a^T) \cdot (\sigma_a \cdot \sigma_a^T)^{-1}$

$= \Big\{ *, \Big(\frac{\partial V}{\partial t} + \frac{1}{2} \text{tr}(\nabla \nabla V \cdot c \cdot c^T)$

$+ \nabla V \cdot (b - (a_s - r) \cdot (\sigma_s \cdot \sigma_s^T)^{-1} \cdot \sigma_s \cdot c^T)$

$+ \nabla V \cdot c \cdot (\mathbb{I}_n - \sigma_s^T \cdot (\sigma_s \cdot \sigma_s^T)^{-1} \cdot \sigma_s) \cdot c^T \cdot \nabla g_\gamma - rV + \mathcal{D} \Big)$

$\cdot \mathfrak{X}^{-1} \cdot (V\mathbb{I}_l) \Big\}$ (10.23)

which, according to Definition 10.4, requesting that

$$\Pi_\gamma^{H,*}(t, X, A) = \frac{X}{\gamma}(a_a - r + \nabla g_\gamma \cdot c \cdot \sigma_a^T) \cdot (\sigma_a \cdot \sigma_a^T)^{-1} = \{*, 0\} \tag{10.24}$$

implies the following corollary.

Corollary 10.1 ("The ultimate Black–Scholes type PDE") Under the HARA utility of wealth (with relative risk aversion $\gamma > 0$), the general Black–Scholes type system of (pricing) PDEs for a set of (tradable) contracts with prices $V = \{V_1, \ldots, V_l\}$, paying dividends $\mathcal{D} = \{\mathcal{D}_1, \ldots, \mathcal{D}_l\}$ and with the terminal payouts $v = \{v_1, \ldots, v_l\}$, in any simple economy $\mathfrak{E}$, with market coefficients a_s, σ_s, b, c and interest rate r, reads as

$$\frac{\partial V}{\partial t} + \frac{1}{2} \mathrm{tr}(\nabla \nabla V \cdot c \cdot c^T) + \nabla V \cdot (b - (a_s - r) \cdot (\sigma_s \cdot \sigma_s^T)^{-1} \cdot \sigma_s \cdot c^T)$$
$$+ \nabla V \cdot c \cdot (\mathbb{I}_n - \sigma_s^T \cdot (\sigma_s \cdot \sigma_s^T)^{-1} \cdot \sigma_s) \cdot c^T \cdot \nabla g_\gamma - rV = -\mathcal{D} \tag{10.25}$$

for $t < T \leq \infty$, with the terminal condition (if $T < \infty$)

$$V(T, A) = v(A) \tag{10.26}$$

where ∇g_γ is characterised via (10.11)–(10.12).

Remark 10.5 If $T = \infty$, then terminal condition (10.26) is irrelevant or, equivalently, not needed (see Stojanovic (2006a) for a very relevant example of perpetual financial contracts).

Remark 10.6 If $\nabla r = 0$, ie, if interest rate is deterministic, the CARA price can be found as well by sending $\gamma \to \infty$ in (10.25) and, more importantly, in a modified version of (10.11); see Stojanovic (2005b) for details. On the other hand, if $\nabla r \neq 0$, the CARA price may fail to exist (see Stojanovic (2005b)).

Remark 10.7 Of course, if the market is complete, ie, if $c \cdot (\mathbb{I}_n - \sigma_s^T \cdot (\sigma_s \cdot \sigma_s^T)^{-1} \cdot \sigma_s) \cdot c^T =$ no matter what ∇g_γ is, the pricing equation (10.25) is independent of γ and, therefore, the price is unique. On the other hand, if $c \cdot (\mathbb{I}_n - \sigma_s^T \cdot (\sigma_s \cdot \sigma_s^T)^{-1} \cdot \sigma_s) \cdot c^T \neq$, ie, if market is incomplete, for example, we still can have $\nabla g_\gamma = 0$ (if $g_\gamma = g_\gamma(t)$), so that the price may be unique in incomplete markets as well.

Remark 10.8 The vector

$$(\mathbb{I}_n - \sigma_s^T \cdot (\sigma_s \cdot \sigma_s^T)^{-1} \cdot \sigma_s) \cdot c^T \cdot \nabla g_\gamma$$
$$= \sqrt{\mathbb{I}_n - \sigma_s^T \cdot (\sigma_s \cdot \sigma_s^T)^{-1} \cdot \sigma_s} \cdot c^T \cdot \nabla g_\gamma \qquad (10.27)$$

will be referred to as the (non-hedgeable) risk premium. For an intuitive meaning of the risk premium see Stojanovic (2005a,b, 2006b) and the section "Risk premium (variance swaps)" below.

Optimal portfolio-based hedging – the most conservative hedging

As in Stojanovic (2005b) (see also Stojanovic (2003)), recalling (10.4), we consider the wealth-variance

$$\mathfrak{W}^\Pi(t) := \lim_{dt \to 0} \frac{(dX^\Pi(t))^2}{dt}$$
$$= \Pi(t, X(t), A(t)) \cdot \sigma_s(t, A(t)) \cdot \sigma_s(t, A(t))^T$$
$$\cdot \Pi(t, X(t), A(t)) \geq 0 \qquad (10.28)$$

and the problem of wealth-variance minimisation: find Π_∞ such that, for all t,

$$\mathfrak{W}^{\Pi_\infty}(t) = \min_\Pi \mathfrak{W}^\Pi(t) \qquad (10.29)$$

Of course, if there are no constraints on the portfolio, then the wealth-variance minimising portfolio strategy is trivial, ie, $\Pi_\infty = 0$ (zero investment into the risky assets – only cash is held). Let $\mu = \mu(t, A)$ be an $(l \times k)$-matrix valued function and let $\xi = \xi(t, A)$ be an l-vector valued function. We refer to constraints such as

$$\mu(t, A) \cdot \pi(t, A, X) = \xi(t, A)X \qquad (10.30)$$

as affine (portfolio) constraints. It can be shown (see Stojanovic (2003)) that the wealth-variance minimising portfolio strategy under the affine constant (10.30) is equal to

$$\Pi_\infty(t, X, A) = X(\sigma_s \cdot \sigma_s^T)^{-1} \cdot \mu^T (\mu \cdot (\sigma_s \cdot \sigma_s^T)^{-1} \cdot \mu^T)^{-1} \cdot \xi \qquad (10.31)$$

Consider now a self-financing portfolio strategy $\Pi(t, X, A) = \{\Pi_1, \ldots, \Pi_k, \Pi_{k+1}, \ldots, \Pi_{k+l}\}$ in the auxiliary economy $\mathfrak{E}_a$, where $\{\Pi_1, \ldots, \Pi_k\}$ is the cash value of the investments into the market $\mathfrak{M} \subset \mathfrak{E}$, and $\{\Pi_{k+1}, \ldots, \Pi_{k+l}\}$ is the cash values of investments into considered contracts, with an already determined fair price

$V_\gamma = V_\gamma(t, A) = V(t, A) = \{V_1(t, A), \ldots, V_l(t, A)\}$. Set

$$\mu = (_{l \times k} \quad \mathbb{I}_l) \qquad (10.32)$$

and

$$\xi(t, A) = V(t, A)\kappa = \{V_1(t, A)\kappa_1, \ldots, V_l(t, A)\kappa_l\} \qquad (10.33)$$

where μ is $l \times (k + l)$ matrix, and $\kappa = \{\kappa_1, \ldots, \kappa_l\} \in \mathbb{R}^l$. After some calculations, and again using Theorem 10.1, we conclude (see Stojanovic (2007) for details) that

$$\begin{aligned}\Pi_\infty(t, X, A) &= X(\sigma_a \cdot \sigma_a^T)^{-1} \cdot \mu^T \cdot (\mu \cdot (\sigma_a \cdot \sigma_a^T)^{-1} \cdot \mu^T)^{-1} \cdot \xi \\ &= X\{-(\sigma_s \cdot \sigma_s^T)^{-1} \cdot \sigma_s \cdot c^T \cdot (\nabla V)^T \cdot \kappa, V\kappa\}\end{aligned} \qquad (10.34)$$

This implies (the hedging formula (10.35) was established by the present author in Stojanovic (2005b) for the case $l = 1$ and in Stojanovic (2007) for the case $l \geq 1$) the following.

Corollary 10.2 The most conservative hedging of $\kappa = \{\kappa_1, \ldots, \kappa_l\}$ contracts with prices $V = \{V_1, \ldots, V_l\}$, in any simple economy $\mathfrak{E}$, is given by the formula

$$\Pi_\infty^{\mathfrak{h}}(t, A) = -(\sigma_s \cdot \sigma_s^T)^{-1} \cdot \sigma_s \cdot c^T \cdot (\nabla V)^T \cdot \kappa \qquad (10.35)$$

Remark 10.9 The hedging formula (10.35) reduces to the Black–Scholes hedging formula in the case of complete markets (see Stojanovic (2003, p. 439). See Stojanovic (2005b) for the discussion of consistency of (10.35) with other approaches to hedging in incomplete markets.

Remark 10.10 The risk aversion affects (the most conservative) hedging formula (10.35) only through the price V. Furthermore, the price V does not have to be determined using the above "neutral derivative pricing" methodology, ie, the hedged contracts do not have to be liquid. For example, if an illiquid contract is priced using an "indifference pricing" methodology, then such an "indifference" price V should be used in formula (10.35).

VOLATILITY DERIVATIVES FOR HESTON'S ECONOMIES
Heston's model
Our purpose here is to apply the general theory of pricing and hedging, reviewed above, in the case of volatility derivatives and,

in particular, in the case of variance swaps. Our emphasis is on determination of the risk premium. For alternative approaches to the pricing and hedging of volatility derivatives we refer to Howison *et al* (2004), Swishchuk (2000) and Windcliff *et al* (2006).

In the framework reviewed above, pricing, even for simple payout contracts such as futures, is a more difficult problem than the portfolio optimisation since portfolio optimisation is a subproblem of the pricing problem – finding the risk premium is only the first step. So, the model employed has to be manageable for both subproblems, from the point of view of finding the risk premium and from the point of view of solving the pricing equation. One such model is Heston's model (introduced in Heston (1993)).

Suppose that the economy is described simply through a single tradable with price $Y(t)$ and a non-tradable factor, $s(t)$ (price-variance), via a SDE system

$$\frac{dY(t)}{Y(t)} = (\mathfrak{a}_0 + \lambda_s s(t) - 1)dt + \sqrt{s(t)}\, dB_1(t)$$

$$ds(t) = \alpha(s_0 - s(t))dt + \beta\sqrt{s(t)}\left(\rho_{2,1} dB_1(t) + \sqrt{1 - \rho_{2,1}^2}\, dB_2(t)\right)$$
(10.36)

where $\mathfrak{a}_0, \lambda_s, 1$ (the dividend rate), $\alpha \geq 0$, $s_0 \geq 0$, β, $\rho_{2,1}$ are assumed to be known constants. Volatility derivatives have payouts of the form

$$\varphi\left(\int_{t_0}^{T} (s(\tau))d\tau\right)$$
(10.37)

for some given functions and φ. For example, variance swaps are realised via $(s) = s$ and

$$\varphi(\mathcal{I}) = \frac{\mathcal{I}}{T - t_0} - K^2$$
(10.38)

where K is the strike. Indeed, a variance swap is a forward contract on annualised variance σ_R^2:

$$\sigma_R^2 = 252 \frac{1}{n-2} \sum_{i=1}^{n-1} \log^2\left(\frac{Y(t_{i+1})}{Y(t_i)}\right)$$

$$= 252 \frac{1}{n-2} \sum_{i=1}^{n-1} (\log(Y(t_{i+1})) - \log(Y(t_i)))^2$$

$$= 252 \frac{1}{n-2} \sum_{i=1}^{n-1} (d\log(Y(t_i)))^2$$
(10.39)

where $Y(t_i)$ are the daily closing prices of the underlying tradable, 252 is the annual number of trading days and n is the number of days from the trade date to and including the maturity date. The contract payout is equal to

$$\text{payout} = \sigma_R^2 - K^2 \qquad (10.40)$$

where K is the strike. When entering the swap (at time $t = t_0$) the strike K is usually set at a level so that counter parties do not have to exchange the cashflows – the fair strike. We shall denote the fair strike by K_F.

A continuous-time version of (10.39) can be easily seen to be

$$\varphi\left(\int_{t_0}^T \mathsf{s}(t)\mathrm{d}t\right) = \frac{1}{T-t_0}\int_{t_0}^T \mathsf{s}(t)\mathrm{d}t - K^2$$

$$= \frac{1}{T-t_0}\int_{t_0}^T (\mathrm{d}\log(Y(t)))^2 - K^2 \approx \sigma_R^2 - K^2 \quad (10.41)$$

Indeed, using Itô's chain rule and (10.36)

$$\mathrm{d}\log(Y(t)) = (\mathfrak{o}_0 + \lambda_s \mathsf{s}(t) - 1)\mathrm{d}t + \sqrt{\mathsf{s}(t)}\,\mathrm{d}B_1(t) - \tfrac{1}{2}\mathsf{s}(t)\mathrm{d}t \quad (10.42)$$

and, therefore,

$$(\mathrm{d}\log(Y(t)))^2 = (\sqrt{\mathsf{s}(t)}\,\mathrm{d}B_1(t))^2 = \mathsf{s}(t)\mathrm{d}t \qquad (10.43)$$

proving (10.40).

Payouts like (10.37) are non-Markovian if considered in the context of the system (10.36). Nevertheless, system (10.36) can be extended in a way so that payouts of the form (10.37), including variance swaps, become Markovian. For example, consider a stochastic process $\mathcal{I}(t)$ defined by

$$\mathcal{I}(t) = \int_{t_0}^t (\mathsf{s}(\tau))\mathrm{d}\tau \qquad (10.44)$$

or, equivalently, by

$$\begin{aligned}\mathrm{d}\mathcal{I}(t) &= (\mathsf{s}(t))\mathrm{d}t \\ \mathcal{I}(t_0) &= 0\end{aligned} \qquad (10.45)$$

We can realise (10.36) and (10.45) as a simple economy $\mathfrak{E}$ with the tradable $S(t) = \{Y(t)\}$, and with factors $A(t) = \{Y(t), \mathsf{s}(t), \mathcal{I}(t)\}$, with constant interest rate r, and market coefficients

$$a_s = \{ \mathfrak{o}_0 + \lambda_s \mathfrak{s} \}, \quad \sigma_s = (\sqrt{\mathfrak{s}} \quad 0)$$
$$b = \{ Y(\mathfrak{o}_0 + \lambda_s \mathfrak{s} - 1), \alpha(\mathfrak{s}_0 - \mathfrak{s}), (\mathfrak{s}) \}$$
$$c = \begin{pmatrix} Y\sqrt{\mathfrak{s}} & 0 \\ \sqrt{\mathfrak{s}}\, \beta \rho_{2,1} & \sqrt{\mathfrak{s}}\, \beta \sqrt{1 - \rho_{2,1}^2} \\ 0 & 0 \end{pmatrix} \qquad (10.46)$$

We note that
$$\sigma_s \cdot \sigma_s^T = (\mathfrak{s}) \qquad (10.47)$$
and
$$c \cdot (\mathbb{I}_2 - \sigma_s^T \cdot (\sigma_s \cdot \sigma_s^T)^{-1} \cdot \sigma_s) \cdot c^T = \begin{pmatrix} 0 & 0 & 0 \\ 0 & \mathfrak{s}\beta^2(1 - \rho_{2,1}^2) & 0 \\ 0 & 0 & 0 \end{pmatrix} \qquad (10.48)$$

so that this market is non-redundant for $\mathfrak{s} > 0$, and incomplete for $\mathfrak{s}\beta^2(1 - \rho_{2,1}^2) > 0$.

As an example, specialising to variance swaps, ie, assuming that

$$(\mathfrak{s}) = \mathfrak{s} \qquad (10.49)$$

and if, for example, $\mathfrak{o}_0 = r$, and if the rest of the data is equal to

$$\begin{aligned} r &= 0.05, \quad \lambda_s = 0.1, \quad {}_1 = 0.01, \quad \alpha = 2, \quad \mathfrak{s}_0 = 0.1 \\ \rho_{2,1} &= 1/2, \quad T = 1, \quad t_0 = 0 \end{aligned} \qquad (10.50)$$

a single randomly generated Monte-Carlo market/factor trajectory is shown in Figure 10.1.

Risk premium PDE

As the risk premium PDE (10.11) does not depend on a particular contract payout, the present and next sections are applicable irrespective of whether we are considering variance swaps or some other more complicated volatility contracts.

To find the risk premium we have to solve the risk premium PDE (10.11)–(10.12) or, at least, the perpetual version of the risk premium (see Remark 10.2). As pricing is simpler in such a case, in order to be able to find an explicit formula for the price, we confine ourselves to finding the perpetual risk premium. (The reader is

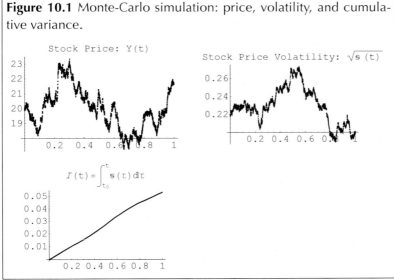

Figure 10.1 Monte-Carlo simulation: price, volatility, and cumulative variance.

referred to Liu (2005) (cf. also Stojanovic (2006b)) for the time-dependent risk premium, but, unfortunately, only for the case when $\varpi_0 = r$.)

To that end, we first note that the risk premium PDE (10.11) in the present problem becomes (we use an alternative notation for partial derivatives; for example, $g^{(0,0,1,0)}(t,Y,s,\mathcal{I}) = \partial g(t,Y,s,\mathcal{I})/\partial s$)

$$g^{(1,0,0,0)}(t,Y,s,\mathcal{I}) + g^{(0,0,0,1)}(t,Y,s,\mathcal{I})s$$
$$+ g^{(0,0,1,0)}(t,Y,s,\mathcal{I})\frac{(s_0-s)\alpha\gamma + \beta(\gamma-1)(r-\varpi_0 - s\lambda_s)\rho_{2,1}}{\gamma}$$
$$+ g^{(0,1,0,0)}(t,Y,s,\mathcal{I})\frac{Y(r(\gamma-1)+\varpi_0 - \gamma_1 + s\lambda_s)}{\gamma}$$
$$+ g^{(0,2,0,0)}(t,Y,s,\mathcal{I})\frac{Y^2 s}{2} + g^{(0,1,1,0)}(t,Y,s,\mathcal{I})Ys\beta\rho_{2,1}$$
$$+ g^{(0,0,2,0)}(t,Y,s,\mathcal{I})\frac{s\beta^2}{2} + \frac{s\beta^2(\gamma-(\gamma-1)\rho_{2,1}^2)}{2\gamma}g^{(0,0,1,0)}(t,Y,s,\mathcal{I})^2$$
$$+ \frac{Ys\beta\rho_{2,1}}{\gamma}g^{(0,0,1,0)}(t,Y,s,\mathcal{I})g^{(0,1,0,0)}(t,Y,s,\mathcal{I})$$
$$+ \frac{Y^2 s}{2\gamma}g^{(0,1,0,0)}(t,Y,s,\mathcal{I})^2 = \frac{\gamma-1}{\gamma}\left(\frac{(-r+\varpi_0+s\lambda_s)^2}{2s} + r\gamma\right)$$
(10.51)

VOLATILITY AS AN ASSET CLASS

for $t < T$, with $g(T, Y, s, \mathcal{I}) = 0$. Hypothesising that there exists a solution independent of Y and $\mathcal{I}$, ie, assuming that $g = g(t, s)$, Equation (10.51) simplifies to

$$g^{(1,0)}(t,s) + g^{(0,1)}(t,s)\frac{(s_0 - s)\alpha\gamma + \beta(\gamma-1)(r - \varpi_0 - s\lambda_s)\rho_{2,1}}{\gamma}$$

$$+ g^{(0,2)}(t,s)\frac{s\beta^2}{2} + \frac{s\beta^2(\gamma - (\gamma-1)\rho_{2,1}^2)}{2\gamma}g^{(0,1)}(t,s)^2$$

$$= \frac{\gamma-1}{\gamma}\left(\frac{(-r + \varpi_0 + s\lambda_s)^2}{2s} + r\gamma\right) \quad (10.52)$$

for $t < T$, and $s > 0$, with $g(T, s) = 0$. Recalling Remark 10.2, we know that the steady state solution for (10.52) does not exist and, yet, we can find the steady state for $\nabla g = \{g^{(0,1)}(t,s)\}$. Indeed, differentiating Equation (10.52) with respect to s, and then making a substitution

$$g(t, s) = \int h(s)\mathrm{d}s \quad (10.53)$$

we obtain an equation characterising $h(s)$:

$$\frac{\beta^2(\gamma - (\gamma-1)\rho_{2,1}^2)}{2\gamma}h(s)^2 + \frac{s\beta^2(\gamma - (\gamma-1)\rho_{2,1}^2)}{\gamma}h(s)h'(s)$$

$$- \frac{\alpha\gamma + \beta(\gamma-1)\lambda_s\rho_{2,1}}{\gamma}h(s) + \frac{s\beta^2}{2}h''(s)$$

$$+ \frac{(\beta^2 - 2s\alpha + 2s_0\alpha)\gamma + 2\beta(\gamma-1)(r - \varpi_0 - s\lambda_s)\rho_{2,1}}{2\gamma}h'(s)$$

$$= -\frac{\gamma-1}{2s^2\gamma}(r^2 - 2\varpi_0 r + \varpi_0^2 - s^2\lambda_s^2) \quad (10.54)$$

We look for the solution of (10.54) in the form

$$h(s) = {}_0 + \frac{-1}{s} \quad (10.55)$$

Making the substitution (10.55) in (10.54), we obtain

$$\left(\frac{(\gamma-1)(r - \varpi_0)^2}{2\gamma} + \frac{(\beta^2 - 2s_0\alpha)\gamma - 2\beta(\gamma-1)(r - \varpi_0)\rho_{2,1}}{2\gamma}{}_{-1}\right.$$

$$\left. + \frac{\beta^2((\gamma-1)\rho_{2,1}^2 - \gamma)}{2\gamma}{}_{-1}^2\right)\frac{1}{s^2} - \frac{(\gamma-1)\lambda_s^2}{2\gamma}$$

$$- \frac{\alpha\gamma + \beta(\gamma-1)\lambda_s\rho_{2,1}}{\gamma}{}_0 + \frac{\beta^2(\gamma - (\gamma-1)\rho_{2,1}^2)}{2\gamma}{}_0^2 = 0 \quad (10.56)$$

and therefore, finally, we end up with two quadratic equations characterising $_0$ and $_{-1}$:

$$\frac{\gamma-1}{\gamma}\frac{\lambda_s^2}{2} + \left(\alpha + \frac{\gamma-1}{\gamma}\beta\lambda_s\rho_{2,1}\right)_0 + \frac{\beta^2}{2}\left(\frac{\gamma-1}{\gamma}\rho_{2,1}^2 - 1\right)_0^2 = 0 \tag{10.57}$$

and

$$\frac{\gamma-1}{\gamma}\frac{(\mathfrak{o}_0-r)^2}{2} + \left(\frac{\beta^2}{2} - \mathfrak{s}_0\alpha + \frac{\gamma-1}{\gamma}\beta(\mathfrak{o}_0-r)\rho_{2,1}\right)_{-1}$$

$$+ \frac{\beta^2}{2}\left(\frac{\gamma-1}{\gamma}\rho_{2,1}^2 - 1\right)_{-1}^2 = 0 \tag{10.58}$$

Equations (10.57) and (10.59) are solved by (quadratic formula)

$$_0 = \frac{-(\alpha + \frac{\gamma-1}{\gamma}\beta\lambda_s\rho_{2,1}) \pm \sqrt{(\alpha + \frac{\gamma-1}{\gamma}\beta\lambda_s\rho_{2,1})^2 - \beta^2(\frac{\gamma-1}{\gamma}\rho_{2,1}^2 - 1)\frac{\gamma-1}{\gamma}\lambda_s^2}}{\beta^2(\frac{\gamma-1}{\gamma}\rho_{2,1}^2 - 1)} \tag{10.59}$$

$$_{-1} = \frac{1}{\beta^2(\frac{\gamma-1}{\gamma}\rho_{2,1}^2 - 1)}\left(-\left(\frac{\beta^2}{2} - \mathfrak{s}_0\alpha + \frac{\gamma-1}{\gamma}\beta(\mathfrak{o}_0-r)\rho_{2,1}\right)\right.$$

$$\left.\pm \sqrt{\left(\frac{\beta^2}{2} - \mathfrak{s}_0\alpha + \frac{\gamma-1}{\gamma}\beta(\mathfrak{o}_0-r)\rho_{2,1}\right)^2 - \beta^2\left(\frac{\gamma-1}{\gamma}\rho_{2,1}^2 - 1\right)\frac{\gamma-1}{\gamma}(\mathfrak{o}_0-r^2)}\right) \tag{10.60}$$

Caution is advised when deciding about the sign $\pm$ in (10.59) and (10.60), ie, the selection of the appropriate solution pair $\{_0, _{-1}\}$ of (10.57)–(10.59), among four possible choices (see Stojanovic (2005b), 2006a,b) for more details). We note that if $\gamma = 1$, ie, if the logarithmic utility of wealth is employed, (10.57) and (10.59) have a trivial (appropriate) solution: $_0 = _{-1} = 0$ ("logarithmic utility is trivial"). We also note that if $\mathfrak{o}_0 = r$, Equation (10.59) is solved by $_{-1} = 0$ (ie, $_{-1} = 0$ is the appropriate solution of the quadratic Equation (10.59) in the case $\mathfrak{o}_0 = r$). So, if $\mathfrak{o}_0 = r$, only (10.57) needs to be solved, and $h(\mathfrak{s}) = _0$. This also suggests why $\mathfrak{o}_0 = r$ is a much easier case, which can also be solved without the perpetuity simplification (see Liu (2007) and also Stojanovic (2006b)).

Risk premium (variance swaps)

We consider now the issue of computing the risk premium (and its mathematical intuitive meaning). Applying formula (10.27), the risk premium (vector) is equal to

$$(\mathbb{I}_2 - \sigma_s^T \cdot (\sigma_s \cdot \sigma_s^T)^{-1} \cdot \sigma_s) \cdot c^T \cdot \nabla g_\gamma(t, Y, s, \mathcal{I})$$

$$= \left(\mathbb{I}_2 - \begin{pmatrix} 1 & 0 \\ 0 & 0 \end{pmatrix}\right) \cdot c^T \cdot \nabla g_\gamma(t, Y, s, \mathcal{I})$$

$$= \begin{pmatrix} 0 & 0 \\ 0 & 1 \end{pmatrix} \cdot \begin{pmatrix} Y\sqrt{s} & \sqrt{s}\,\beta\rho_{2,1} & 0 \\ 0 & \sqrt{s}\,\beta\sqrt{1-\rho_{2,1}^2} & 0 \end{pmatrix} \cdot \nabla g_\gamma(t, Y, s, \mathcal{I})$$

$$= \begin{pmatrix} 0 & 0 & 0 \\ 0 & \sqrt{s}\,\beta\sqrt{1-\rho_{2,1}^2} & 0 \end{pmatrix}$$

$$\cdot \{g_\gamma^{(0,1,0,0)}(t, Y, s, \mathcal{I}), g_\gamma^{(0,0,1,0)}(t, Y, s, \mathcal{I}), g_\gamma^{(0,0,0,1)}(t, Y, s, \mathcal{I})\}$$

$$= \left\{0, \sqrt{s}\,\beta\sqrt{1-\rho_{2,1}^2}\,g_\gamma^{(0,0,1,0)}(t, Y, s, \mathcal{I})\right\}$$

$$= \left\{0, \sqrt{s}\,\beta\sqrt{1-\rho_{2,1}^2}\,g^{(0,1)}(t, s)\right\} \rightarrow \left\{0, \sqrt{s}\,\beta h(s)\sqrt{1-\rho_{2,1}^2}\right\}$$

$$= \left\{0, \sqrt{s}\,\beta\left(\frac{-1}{s} + 0\right)\sqrt{1-\rho_{2,1}^2}\right\} \tag{10.61}$$

where $_0 = \gamma_{,0}$ and $_{-1} = \gamma_{,-1}$ are solutions of (10.57) and (10.59). The formula for the (perpetual) risk premium (10.61) has an intuitive meaning as follows: after as much hedging as possible is performed (via (10.75)), the remaining risk (due to the incompleteness of the market) is priced (substituted, or thought of) as follows (see Stojanovic (2006b) for more details)

$$\frac{dB(t)}{dt} = \left\{\frac{dB_1(t)}{dt}, \frac{dB_2(t)}{dt}\right\} \rightarrow \left\{0, \sqrt{s}\,\beta\left(\frac{\gamma_{,-1}}{s}\right)\sqrt{1-\rho_{2,1}^2}\right\} \tag{10.62}$$

Indeed, as the risk due to the Brownian motion $B_1(t)$ can completely be hedged away (Y is tradable), the white noise $dB_1(t)/dt$ is priced as zero; on the other hand, since the risk due to the Brownian motion $B_2(t)$ cannot be hedged away by means of trading, the white noise $dB_2(t)/dt$ is priced as

$$\sqrt{s}\,\beta\left(\frac{\gamma_{,-1}}{s} + \gamma_{,0}\right)\sqrt{1-\rho_{2,1}^2}$$

In particular, the (relative) risk aversion γ affects the selection of the risk premium. Recall that this analysis was independent of a particular contract payout.

Pricing formula for variance swaps

Having determined the (perpetual) risk premium, we are ready to solve the problem of pricing of variance swaps. The pricing PDE (10.26) becomes

$$V_\gamma^{(1,0,0,0)}(t,Y,s,\mathcal{I}) + \tfrac{1}{2}sV_\gamma^{(0,2,0,0)}(t,Y,s,\mathcal{I})Y^2$$
$$+ \tfrac{1}{2}s\beta^2 V_\gamma^{(0,0,2,0)}(t,Y,s,\mathcal{I}) + s\beta\rho_{2,1}V_\gamma^{(0,1,1,0)}(t,Y,s,\mathcal{I})Y$$
$$+ (r-1)V_\gamma^{(0,1,0,0)}(t,Y,s,\mathcal{I})Y + sV_\gamma^{(0,0,0,1)}(t,Y,s,\mathcal{I})$$
$$+ ((\gamma_{,-1} + s_{\gamma,0})(1-\rho_{2,1}^2)\beta^2 + \alpha(s_0 - s)$$
$$+ (r - \mathfrak{o}_0 - s\lambda_s)\rho_{2,1}\beta)V_\gamma^{(0,0,1,0)}(t,Y,s,\mathcal{I}) - rV_\gamma(t,Y,s,\mathcal{I}) = 0$$
(10.63)

together with the terminal condition

$$V_\gamma(T,Y,s,\mathcal{I}) = \varphi(\mathcal{I}) = \frac{\mathcal{I}}{T-t_0} - K^2 \qquad (10.64)$$

Due to the φ independence of Y, we can hypothesise that $V(t,Y,s,\mathcal{I}) = V(t,s,\mathcal{I})$, and therefore (10.63) simplifies to

$$V_\gamma^{(1,0,0)}(t,s,\mathcal{I}) + \tfrac{1}{2}sV_\gamma^{(0,2,0)}(t,s,\mathcal{I})\beta^2 + sV_\gamma^{(0,0,1)}(t,s,\mathcal{I})$$
$$+ ((\gamma_{,-1} + s_{\gamma,0})(1-\rho_{2,1}^2)\beta^2 + (r - \mathfrak{o}_0 - s\lambda_s)\rho_{2,1}\beta$$
$$+ \alpha(s_0 - s))V_\gamma^{(0,1,0)}(t,s,\mathcal{I}) - rV_\gamma(t,s,\mathcal{I}) = 0 \qquad (10.65)$$

or, similarly,

$$V_\gamma^{(1,0,0)}(t,s,\mathcal{I}) + \tfrac{1}{2}sV_\gamma^{(0,2,0)}(t,s,\mathcal{I})\beta^2 + sV_\gamma^{(0,0,1)}(t,s,\mathcal{I})$$
$$+ (\mathbb{N}_\gamma - \gamma s)V_\gamma^{(0,1,0)}(t,s,\mathcal{I}) - rV_\gamma^{(0,1,0)}(t,s,\mathcal{I}) = 0 \qquad (10.66)$$

with

$$\gamma = \alpha + \lambda_s\rho_{2,1}\beta - \gamma_0(1-\rho_{2,1}^2)\beta^2 \qquad (10.67)$$

and

$$\mathbb{N}_\gamma = \alpha s_0 + \gamma_{,-1}\beta^2(1-\rho_{2,1}^2) - (\mathfrak{o}_0 - r)\rho_{2,1}\beta \qquad (10.68)$$

Equation (10.66) is of course augmented by the terminal condition

$$V_\gamma(T,s,\mathcal{I}) = \frac{\mathcal{I}}{T-t_0} - K^2 \qquad (10.69)$$

Equations (10.66) and (10.69) are solved by $V_\gamma(t, s, \mathcal{I}) = V_{K,\gamma}(t, s, \mathcal{I})$

$$V_{K,\gamma}(t, s, \mathcal{I}) = e^{-r(T-t)}\left(\frac{\mathcal{I}}{T-t_0} - K^2 + \frac{1}{(T-t_0)_\gamma^2}((T-t)\mathbb{N}_{\gamma\gamma}\right.$$
$$\left. + (1 - e^{-(T-t)\gamma})(s_\gamma - \mathbb{N}_\gamma))\right) \quad (10.70)$$

yielding the following.

Theorem 10.2 The fair price $V_{K,\gamma}(t, s, \mathcal{I})$ of a variance swap with strike $K > 0$ (a contract with the terminal payout given by (10.69)), under the assumption of Heston's economy (10.36), and using the perpetual risk premium corresponding to the HARA utility of wealth with the relative risk aversion $\gamma \in (0, \infty)$, is given by (10.70), with $_\gamma$ and $\mathbb{N}_\gamma$ defined by (10.67) and (10.68), and where $_{\gamma,0}$ and $_{\gamma,1}$ are defined by (10.59) and (10.60).

Using again data (10.50), and with

$$\gamma = 5, \quad K^2 = 0.04 \quad (10.71)$$

in Figure 10.2 we showcase the variance swap pricing formula (10.70) and, in particular, that if the (instantaneous) price/volatility correlation is negative ($\rho_{2,1} = -0.5$), variance swaps are more expensive under the "bull" market conditions ($\mathfrak{o}_0 = 0.2$) than under the "bear" market conditions ($\mathfrak{o}_0 = -0.2$).

Fair strike K_F (variance swaps)
The fair strike K_F follows form the pricing formula (10.70), by means of solving for K the equation

$$V_{K,\gamma}(t_0, s(t_0), 0) = 0 \quad (10.72)$$

concluding that

$$K_F = \sqrt{\frac{1}{(T-t_0)_\gamma^2}((T-t_0)\mathbb{N}_{\gamma\gamma} + (1 - e^{-(T-t_0)\gamma})(s(t_0)_\gamma - \mathbb{N}_\gamma))} \quad (10.73)$$

with $_\gamma$ and $\mathbb{N}_\gamma$ defined by (10.67) and (10.68), and where $_{\gamma,0}$ and $_{\gamma,-1}$ are defined by (10.59) and (10.60).

Of course, for $t_0 < t < T$, $V_{K_F,\gamma}(t, s(t), \mathcal{I}(t))$ denoted the price of a volatility swap for which (10.72) holds, ie, the fair-strike volatility swap.

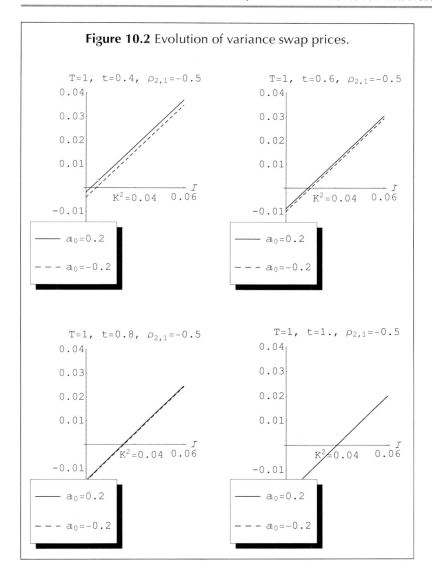

Figure 10.2 Evolution of variance swap prices.

Remark 10.11 Formula (10.73) implies that

$$(T - t_0)\mathbb{N}_{\gamma\gamma} + (1 - e^{-(T-t_0)\gamma})(\mathbb{s}(t_0)_\gamma - \mathbb{N}_\gamma) \geq 0 \qquad (10.74)$$

must hold.

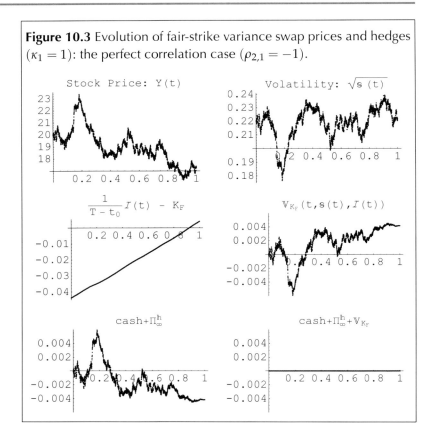

Figure 10.3 Evolution of fair-strike variance swap prices and hedges ($\kappa_1 = 1$): the perfect correlation case ($\rho_{2,1} = -1$).

The most conservative hedging (variance swaps)

Having determined the price of the variance swap, to determine the corresponding hedge is now only an application of the general (most conservative) hedging formula (10.35). Indeed, we have the following.

Corollary 10.3 The most conservative hedging (the cash value to be invested in the tradable) of $\kappa = \{\kappa_1\}$ variance swap contracts with price $V = \{V_\gamma\}$ is given by the formula

$$\Pi_\infty^h(t, Y, s, \mathcal{I}) = \Pi_\infty^h(t) = \left\{ -\frac{e^{-r(T-t)}(1 - e^{(t-T)\gamma})\beta\kappa_1\rho_{2,1}}{(T-t_0)\gamma} \right\}$$
(10.75)

where γ is given by (10.67), and where $\gamma_{,0}$ is defined by (10.59).

Proof Using (10.35),

$$\Pi^{h}_{\infty}(t, Y, s, \mathcal{I})$$
$$= \Pi^{h}_{\infty}(t, A) = -(\sigma_s \cdot \sigma_s^T)^{-1} \cdot \sigma_s \cdot c^T \cdot (\nabla V)^T \cdot \kappa$$
$$= -(\sigma_s \cdot \sigma_s^T)^{-1} \cdot \sigma_s \cdot c^T \cdot \{\nabla V_\gamma(t, Y, s, \mathcal{I})\}^T \cdot \{\kappa_1\}$$
$$= (-Y \quad -\beta\rho_{2,1} \quad 0) \cdot \begin{pmatrix} V_\gamma^{(0,1,0,0)}(t, Y, s, \mathcal{I}) \\ V_\gamma^{(0,0,1,0)}(t, Y, s, \mathcal{I}) \\ V_\gamma^{(0,0,0,1)}(t, Y, s, \mathcal{I}) \end{pmatrix} \cdot \{\kappa_1\}$$
$$= \{-\kappa_1(\beta\rho_{2,1} V_\gamma^{(0,0,1,0)}(t, Y, s, \mathcal{I}) + Y V_\gamma^{(0,1,0,0)}(t, Y, s, \mathcal{I}))\}$$
$$= \{-\beta\kappa_1\rho_{2,1} V_\gamma^{(0,1,0)}(t, s, \mathcal{I})\}$$
$$= \left\{ -\frac{e^{-r(T,t)}(1 - e^{(t-T)\gamma})\beta\kappa_1\rho_{2,1}}{(T - t_0)\gamma} \right\} \quad (10.76)$$

which completes the proof. $\square$

In particular, the hedging position is a function of time t only, ie, independent of all three factors Y, s and $\mathcal{I}$.

The hedging formula (10.75) provides the most conservative hedging possible, yet, due to the market incompleteness, unless $\rho_{2,1}^2$ is close to 1, the remaining risk is significant, as can be verified by further Monte-Carlo experiments.

Except for the price/variance instantaneous correlation $\rho_{2,1}$, we use the same data as before (given in (10.50)). We consider two values for the correlation: $\rho_{2,1} = -1$ and $\rho_{2,1} = -0.9$. The correlation is increased in order to obtain some reasonable degree of hedging success. In Figures 10.3 and 10.4 the kind of simulations showcased in Figure 10.1 were supplemented by:

- the variance swap price $V_{K_F,\gamma}(t, s(t), \mathcal{I}(t))$ evolution;
- the position in cash and the hedging stock position $\Pi^{h}_{\infty}(t)$ evolution: and
- the position in cash, the hedging stock position $\Pi^{h}_{\infty}(t)$, and the position in the variance swap $V_{K_F,\gamma}(t, s(t), \mathcal{I}(t))$ evolution.

We can note that the stochastic process $V_{K_F,\gamma}(t, s(t), \mathcal{I}(t))$ originates at zero (it is the price of a fair-strike variance swap). The total value of the portfolio, ie, cash $+\Pi^{h}_{\infty}(t) + V_{K_F,\gamma}(t, s(t), \mathcal{I}(t))$, is (approximately, since $dt \neq 0$) deterministic in the case $\rho_{2,1} = -1$, as

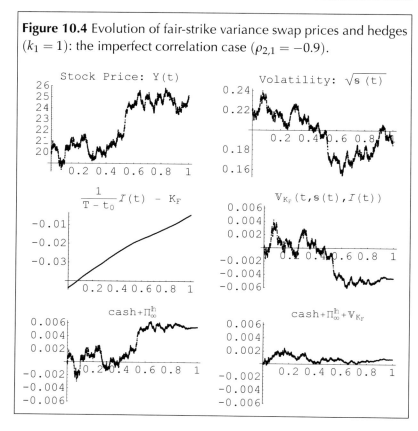

Figure 10.4 Evolution of fair-strike variance swap prices and hedges ($k_1 = 1$): the imperfect correlation case ($\rho_{2,1} = -0.9$).

shown in Figure 10.3, and stochastic, yet significantly less volatile than the variance swap price process $V_{K_F,\gamma}(t, \mathfrak{s}(t), \mathcal{I}(t))$, in the case $\rho_{2,1} = -0.9$, as shown in Figure 10.4.

REFERENCES

Heston, S. L., 1993, "A Closed-form Solution for Options with Stochastic Volatility with Applications to Bond and Currency Options", *The Review of Financial Studies*, **6**, pp 327–343.

Howison, S., A. Rafailidis and H. Rasmussen, 2004, "On the Pricing and Hedging of Volatility Derivative", *Applied Mathematical Finance*, **11**, pp 317–346.

Kallsen, J., 2002, "Utility-based Derivative Pricing in Incomplete Markets", in Geman, H., D. Madan, S. R. Pliska and T. Vorst (eds), *Mathematical Finance – Bachelier Congress 2000* (Berlin: Springer).

Liu, J., 2007, "Portfolio Selection in Stochastic Environments", *The Review of Financial Studies*, **20**, pp 1–39.

Stojanovic, S. D., 2003, *Computational Financial Mathematics using Mathematica*® (Boston, MA: Birkhäuser).

Stojanovic, S. D., 2005a, "Risk Premium and Fair Option Prices under Stochastic Volatility: The HARA Solution", *Comptes Rendus de l'Académie des Sciences. Série I. Mathématique*, **340**, pp 551–556.

Stojanovic, S. D. 2005b, "Higher Dimensional Fair Option Pricing and Hedging Under HARA and CARA Utilities", Working Paper, available at: http://ssrn.com/abstract=912763.

Stojanovic, S. D., 2006a, "The Dividend Puzzle Unpuzzled", Working Paper, available at: http://ssrn.com/abstract=879514.

Stojanovic, S. D., 2006b, *Equities, Derivatives, Risk Premium & Portfolio Optimization*, Lecture Notes (New York: Global Association of Risk Professionals).

Stojanovic, S. D., 2007, "Pricing and Hedging of Multi Type Contracts Under Multidimensional Risks in Incomplete Markets Modeled by General Itô SDE Systems", *Asia Pacific Financial Markets*, **13(4)**, to appear, also available at: http://ssrn.com/abstract=936190.

Swishchuk, A., 2000, "Modeling of Variance and Volatility Swaps for Financial Markets with Stochastic Volatilities", *Wilmot Magazine*, **2**, pp 64–72.

Windcliff, H., P. A. Forsyth and K. R. Vetzal, 2006, "Pricing Methods and Hedging Strategies for Volatility Derivatives", *Journal of Banking and Finance*, **30**, pp 409–431.

11

Corridor Variance Swaps

Peter Carr; Keith Lewis

Bloomberg/NYU; KALX, LLC

It is widely recognised that delta-hedged positions in options can be used to trade volatility. To facilitate volatility trading for their clients, several institutions routinely offer variance swaps. A variance swap is a financial contract that upon expiry pays the difference between a standard historical estimate of daily return variance and a fixed rate determined at inception. As in any swap, the fixed rate is initially chosen so that a variance swap has zero cost to enter. See Demeterfi *et al* (1999) or Carr & Madan (1998) for pricing and Chriss & Morokoff (1999) for risk management issues.

Over the past few years, several institutions have also begun offering corridor variance swaps. These differ from standard variance swaps only in that the underlying's price must be inside a specified corridor in order for its squared return to be included in the floating part of the variance swap payout. As in a standard variance swap, the fixed payment is made at maturity and is initially chosen so that the corridor variance swap has zero cost to enter. In the corridor variance swap considered in this chapter, the fixed payment is independent of the occupation time of the corridor. However, variations exist in which the fixed payment accrues over time at a constant rate only while the underlying is in the corridor.

A corridor variance swap is a generalisation of a standard variance swap in that the latter results from the former when the corridor is extended to all possible price levels. An upside variance swap uses a corridor extending from a fixed barrier up to infinity, while a downside variance swap uses a corridor extending from a fixed barrier down to zero. From the speculator's perspective, the advantage of a corridor variance swap over a variance swap is that it allows the expression of a view on volatility that is contingent upon the price level. For example, an investor who thinks that returns are likely to be more negatively skewed than predicted by the market might buy a downside variance swap and sell an upside variance swap. From the hedger's perspective, the advantage of a corridor variance swap over a standard variance swap is that the hedge involves fewer initial positions and less frequent revision over time.

Carr & Madan (1998) showed how to synthesise continuously monitored variance and corridor variance swaps when the underlying price process is assumed to be continuous. The purpose of this chapter is to show how to accurately approximate the payout to discretely monitored variance and corridor variance swaps under no assumptions about the underlying price process. Given the increasing recognition of the importance of jumps and that all swaps are monitored daily in practice, these extensions are long overdue. We show that with frictionless markets and deterministic interest rates, the payout to a corridor variance swap can be accurately approximated by combining at most daily trading in the underlying with static positions in standard European-style options maturing with the swap and struck inside the corridor. In particular, the approximation error is third order and, hence, the strategy replicates well if third and higher powers of daily returns sum to a negligible amount.

The structure of this chapter is as follows. In the next section we define the payouts to upside and downside variance swaps. Then we give a section showing how to approximate the payouts to these swaps by combining static positions in options struck inside the corridor with at most daily trading in the underlying futures. In the subsequent section we show the results of a Monte Carlo simulation of our payout definition and hedging strategy. In the penultimate section we discuss corridor variance swaps when the corridor is defined by two positive finite constants. We summarise and suggest extensions in the final section.

STRUCTURING UPSIDE AND DOWNSIDE VARIANCE SWAPS

Here, we define the payouts to upside and downside variance swaps. For an upside variance swap, the corridor needed to define the payout is the semi-infinite interval (L, ∞), where the fixed constant $L \geq 0$ denotes the lower bound. Upside variance swaps can be used to create other corridor variance swaps. For example, when $L = 0$, the payout to an upside variance swap will degenerate into the payout from a standard variance swap. For a downside variance swap, the payout will be given by the difference between the payout to a standard variance swap and an upside variance swap. To create a corridor variance swap whose supporting corridor has a positive lower bound and a finite upper bound, we can take the difference of two upside variance swaps with different lower bounds, as will be discussed in the penultimate section.

Consider a finite set of discrete times $\{t_0, t_1, \ldots, t_n\}$ at which the path of some underlying is monitored. In what follows, we use a futures price as the underlying and we take the monitoring times to be daily closings. Let F_0 denote the known initial futures price and let $F_i \geq 0$ denote the random futures price at the close of day i, for $i = 1, 2, \ldots, n$. For an upside variance swap, the futures price is said to start in the corridor on day i if $F_{i-1} > L$ and it is said to stop in the corridor on day i if $F_i > L$. The opposite inequalities hold for downside variance swaps. For an upside variance swap, the futures price is said to enter the corridor on day i if $F_{i-1} \leq L$ and $F_i > L$. In contrast, it is said to exit the corridor on day i if $F_{i-1} > L$ and $F_i \leq L$. For a downside variance swap, entry occurs on days when the futures price exits the upside corridor. Likewise, exit occurs on days when the futures price enters the upside corridor.

The exact specification of the payout to a corridor variance swap differs from firm to firm. Our specification of the payout to a corridor variance swap is chosen so that the hedging error can be made third order without imposing a model for price dynamics. We also insist that the payouts to upside and downside variance swaps be defined so that they sum to the payout of a standard variance swap. To begin specifying the payout of a corridor variance swap, let $F_{i-1} \in R_{i-1}, F_i \in R_i$ denote the indicator function, which is one when F_{i-1} is in region R_{i-1} and F_i is in region R_i, but is zero otherwise. An upside variance contract is defined to be a financial security that has the following non-negative payout at the fixed time t_n:

$$Q_n^u(L) \equiv \sum_{i=1}^n \left\{ \mathbb{1}_{F_{i-1}>L, F_i>L} \left(\ln \frac{F_i}{F_{i-1}} \right)^2 + \mathbb{1}_{F_{i-1}\leq L, F_i>L} \left(\ln \frac{F_i}{L} \right)^2 \right.$$

$$\left. + \mathbb{1}_{F_{i-1}>L, F_i\leq L} \left[\left(\ln \frac{F_i}{F_{i-1}} \right)^2 - \left(\ln \frac{F_i}{F_L} \right)^2 \right] \right\} \quad (11.1)$$

The first term in the summand is due to the days in which the futures price starts and stops inside the upper corridor, while the last two terms are due to the entry and exit of the corridor, respectively. If the futures price starts and stops below the upper corridor on day i, then that day's move is ignored. If the futures price starts and stops in the corridor on day i, then that day's percentage change is squared. If the futures price enters the corridor on day i, then only the percentage change from L is squared. If the futures price exits the corridor on day i, then the square of the percentage change outside the corridor is subtracted from the square of the total percentage change.

Our formulation in (11.1) treats entry and exit asymmetrically. Under our asymmetric formulation, there exists a model-free hedging strategy whose error is only third order, as shown in the next section. In contrast, suppose that the exit payout was defined symmetrically to the entry payout to be $(\ln L/F_{i-1})^2$. Then, there does not exist a model-free hedging strategy whose error is only third order.

A second reason for our asymmetric treatment of entry and exit is that we want the sum of the payouts from an upside variance contract and a downside variance contract with the same barrier L to equal the payout from a standard variance contract. A downside variance contract is defined to be a financial security that has the following non-negative payout at the fixed time t_n:

$$Q_n^d(L) \equiv \sum_{i=1}^n \left\{ \mathbb{1}_{F_{i-1}\leq L, F_i\leq L} \left(\ln \frac{F_i}{F_{i-1}} \right)^2 + \mathbb{1}_{F_{i-1}>L, F_i\leq L} \left(\ln \frac{F_i}{L} \right)^2 \right.$$

$$\left. + \mathbb{1}_{F_{i-1}\leq L, F_i>L} \left[\left(\ln \frac{F_i}{F_{i-1}} \right)^2 - \left(\ln \frac{F_i}{F_L} \right)^2 \right] \right\} \quad (11.2)$$

The payouts in (11.1) and (11.2) sum to the following payout of a standard variance contract:

$$Q_n(L) \equiv \sum_{i=1}^n \left(\ln \frac{F_i}{F_{i-1}} \right)^2 \quad (11.3)$$

From (11.2), our treatment of entry and exit on the downside variance contract is also asymmetric. In contrast, suppose that the exit payout for a downside variance contract was defined symmetrically with the entry payout to be $(\ln L/F_{i-1})^2$. Then the payouts to upside and downside variance contracts with symmetrically defined exit and entry would not sum to the payout (11.3) of a variance contract. The reason is that while the total return decomposes into the returns to and from the barrier,

$$\ln \frac{F_i}{F_{i-1}} = \ln \frac{F_i}{L} + \ln \frac{L}{F_{i-1}} \qquad (11.4)$$

the squared total return differs from the sum of squared returns to and from the barrier by twice the product of these returns,

$$\left(\ln \frac{F_i}{F_{i-1}}\right)^2 = \left(\ln \frac{F_i}{L}\right)^2 + \left(\ln \frac{L}{F_{i-1}}\right)^2 + 2\left(\ln \frac{F_i}{L}\right) \ln\left(\frac{L}{F_{i-1}}\right) \qquad (11.5)$$

Hence, if entry and exit are defined symmetrically for both upside and downside variance contracts, the payout to a portfolio of an upside and downside variance contract would miss the payout to a variance contract by the last term in (11.5).

The asymmetry of our payout definition in (11.1) vanishes if one assumes continuous price processes, continuous path monitoring and the ability to trade the underlying continuously. Under these assumptions, the hedging strategy we propose in the next section works perfectly. It should not be too surprising that the relaxation of these idealised conditions necessarily introduces replication error. What is perhaps surprising is that the replication error can be kept to third order provided that one is willing to treat entry and exit asymmetrically.

By definition, a corridor variance swap is a swap with a single payment at maturity given by the difference between a floating part and a fixed part:

$$VS_n^c(L) = Q_n^c(L) - F_0^c(L) \qquad (11.6)$$

The floating part is the payout $Q_n^c(L)$ to a corridor variance contract, where the superscript c takes on the value u for an upside variance swap and the value d for a downside variance swap. The fixed payment $F_0^c(L)$, $c = u, d$ is chosen at time t_0 so that the corridor variance swap has zero initial cost of entry. Suppose that $Q_0^c(L)$

is the known initial cost of creating the terminal random payout $Q_n^c(L)$, where $c = u, d$. Then the fair fixed payment to initially charge on the corridor variance swap is simply given by

$$F_0^c(L) = \frac{Q_0^c(L)}{B_0(t_n)}, \quad c = u, d \tag{11.7}$$

where $B_0(t_n)$ denotes the initial price of a pure discount bond paying US\$1 at t_n. As a result, the next section focuses on determining an accurate approximation to $Q_0^c(L)$.

APPROXIMATE REPLICATION

Assumptions

For the rest of this chapter, we assume frictionless markets and deterministic interest rates. We also assume that one can trade futures at the same frequency (for example, daily) with which marking-to-market and swap monitoring occur. Finally, we assume that one can take static positions in the continuum of European-style futures options with strikes inside the supporting corridor and maturing with the swap. Note that we make no assumptions regarding the stochastic process followed by futures or option prices. In particular, jumps are allowed, volatility can be stochastic and the process parameters do not need to be known. Under the above assumptions, this section shows that the payouts on upside and downside variance swaps can be well approximated by combining static positions in standard options with at most daily trading in the underlying futures.

The market that probably best approaches the above idealised conditions is that for S&P500 derivatives, where one has liquid trading in both futures and in European-style options. Although the S&P500 index options are written on the cash index, they often mature with the futures and, hence, in those cases can be regarded as European-style futures options. Furthermore, as our replication error will be related to third and higher moments of the underlying's return, the reduction in these moments arising from diversification in the index is attractive. We next review the approximate replication of a variance swap payout before tackling the harder problem of approximately replicating the payout to a corridor variance swap.

Variance swap

It is well known that the geometric mean of a set of positive numbers is never greater than the arithmetic mean. It is also well known that the larger the variation in the set of numbers, the greater the disparity between the two means. The approximate replication of the payout to a variance swap exploits this basic property.

By Taylor series expansion of $\ln F$ about $F = F_{i-1}$, we note that

$$\ln F_i - \ln F_{i-1} = \frac{1}{F_{i-1}}\Delta F_i - \frac{1}{2F_{i-1}^2}(\Delta F_i)^2 + O\left(\frac{\Delta F_i}{F_{i-1}}\right)^3, \quad i = 1, \ldots, n \tag{11.8}$$

where $\Delta F_i \equiv F_i - F_{i-1}$ denotes the change in the futures price over day i. Rearranging implies that the squared daily return is just twice the difference between the daily compounded return and the continuously compounded return, up to terms of order $O(\Delta F_i/F_{i-1})^3$:

$$\left(\frac{\Delta F_i}{F_{i-1}}\right)^2 = 2\left[\frac{\Delta F_i}{F_{i-1}} - \ln\left(\frac{F_i}{F_{i-1}}\right)\right] + O\left(\frac{\Delta F_i}{F_{i-1}}\right)^3, \quad i = 1, \ldots, n \tag{11.9}$$

Squaring both sides of (11.8) implies:

$$\left(\ln \frac{F_i}{F_{i-1}}\right)^2 = \left(\frac{\Delta F_i}{F_{i-1}}\right)^2 + O\left(\frac{\Delta F_i}{F_{i-1}}\right)^3, \quad i = 1, \ldots, n \tag{11.10}$$

Substituting (11.10) in (11.9) implies that the squared continuously compounded return is just twice the difference between the daily compounded return and the continuously compounded return, up to terms of order $O(\Delta F_i/F_{i-1})^3$:

$$\left(\ln \frac{F_i}{F_{i-1}}\right)^2 = 2\left[\frac{\Delta F_i}{F_{i-1}} - \ln\left(\frac{F_i}{F_{i-1}}\right)\right] + O\left(\frac{\Delta F_i}{F_{i-1}}\right)^3, \quad i = 1, \ldots, n \tag{11.11}$$

Summing over i gives a decomposition of the sum of squared returns:

$$\sum_{i=1}^{n}\left(\ln \frac{F_i}{F_{i-1}}\right)^2 = \sum_{i=1}^{n}\frac{2}{F_{i-1}}\Delta F_i - 2\sum_{i=1}^{n}(\ln F_i - \ln F_{i-1}) + \sum_{i=1}^{n} O\left(\frac{\Delta F_i}{F_{i-1}}\right)^3$$

$$= \sum_{i=1}^{n}\frac{2}{F_{i-1}}\Delta F_i - 2\ln F_n + 2\ln F_0 + \sum_{i=1}^{n} O\left(\frac{\Delta F_i}{F_{i-1}}\right)^3 \tag{11.12}$$

due to telescoping. Thus, up to third-order terms, the sum of squared returns decomposes into the payout from a dynamic futures strategy and a function $f(F_n) = -2 \ln F_n + 2 \ln F_0$ of just the final futures price. As a static position in bonds and options can be used to create this final payout function, approximate replication is feasible.

There is some flexibility in choosing the composition of the replicating portfolio since any linear function added to f can be offset by the appropriate position in bonds and futures. As our ultimate goal is to approximately replicate the payout to a corridor variance swap, we will add a linear function to f so that it becomes U-shaped with the minimum occurring at L. Hence, for any $L > 0$, suppose that we subtract and add $2 \ln L + 2/L \times (F_n - F_0)$ to the right-hand side of (11.12):

$$\sum_{i=1}^{n}\left(\ln \frac{F_i}{F_{i-1}}\right)^2 = \sum_{i=1}^{n} \frac{2}{F_{i-1}}\Delta F_i - \frac{2}{L}(F_n - F_0) + u(F_n) - u(F_0)$$

$$+ \sum_{i=1}^{n} O\left(\frac{\Delta F_i}{F_{i-1}}\right)^3 \qquad (11.13)$$

where

$$u(F) \equiv 2\left[\frac{F - L}{L} - \ln \frac{F}{L}\right] \qquad (11.14)$$

As shown in Carr & Madan (1998), any continuous payout at t_n of just the final futures price can be spanned by the payouts from a static position in bonds and European-style options maturing at t_n. To determine the replicating portfolio for the payout $u(F_n)$, note that the function $u(F)$ is U-shaped with zero value and slope at $F = L$. The second derivative $u''(F) = 2/F^2 > 0$. Hence, a Taylor series expansion with second-order remainder of $u(F_n)$ about $F_n = L$ implies

$$u(F_n) = \int_0^L \frac{2}{K^2}(K - F_n)^+ \, dK + \int_L^\infty \frac{2}{K^2}(F_n - K)^+ \, dK \qquad (11.15)$$

Now,

$$F_n - F_0 = \sum_{i=1}^{n} \Delta F_i$$

and substituting this and (11.15) into (11.13) implies

$$\sum_{i=1}^{n}\left(\ln \frac{F_i}{F_{i-1}}\right)^2 = \sum_{i=1}^{n}\left(\frac{2}{F_{i-1}} - \frac{2}{L}\right)\Delta F_i + \int_0^L \frac{2}{K^2}(K - F_n)^+ dK$$
$$+ \int_L^\infty \frac{2}{K^2}(F_n - K)^+ dK - u(F_0) + \sum_{i=1}^{n} O\left(\frac{\Delta F_i}{F_{i-1}}\right)^3$$
(11.16)

Thus, the payout to a variance swap is well approximated by summing the payouts from a dynamic position in futures and a static position in options and bonds. For the dynamic component, (11.16) indicates that one holds $e^{-y_{in}(t_n-t_i)}(2/F_{i-1} - 2/L)$ futures contracts from day $i-1$ to day i, where y_{in} is the continuously compounded yield on day t_i to maturity t_n. For the static component, (11.16) indicates that one holds $(2/K^2)\,dK$ puts at all strikes below L, $(2/K^2)\,dK$ calls at all strikes above L and one shorts $u(F_0)$ bonds. If the initial cost of the approximate hedge is financed by borrowing, then the repayment at t_n is

$$\int_0^L \frac{2}{K^2} \frac{P_0(K, t_n)}{B_0(t_n)} dK + \int_L^\infty \frac{2}{K^2} \frac{C_0(K, t_n)}{B_0(t_n)} dK - u(F_0) \qquad (11.17)$$

where $P_0(K, t_n)$ and $C_0(K, t_n)$, respectively, denote the initial prices of puts and calls struck at K and maturing at t_n. If there is no charge for the third-order approximation error, then (11.17) is the fair (non-annualised) fixed payment for a variance swap on US$1 of notional. This fixed payment is actually independent of the choice of L, since it only depends on the convexity of the payout.

One can interpret the dynamic component of our approximate replicating strategy as a Black (1976) model dynamic hedge to the static portfolio described above. By the Black model dynamic hedge, we have in mind that the hedger trades futures continuously under the belief that the futures price process is continuous with constant volatility σ. As is well known, the number of futures held at any time in this model is given by the first partial derivative of the value function with respect to the futures price. To show that the dynamic component of our hedge can be interpreted as a Black model dynamic hedge, let

$$U(F_n) \equiv \int_0^L \frac{2}{K^2}(K - F_n)^+ \, dK + \int_L^\infty \frac{2}{K^2}(F_n - K)^+ \, dK - u(F_0)$$

$$= u(F_n) - u(F_0) = 2\left[\frac{F_n - F_0}{L} - \ln\frac{F_n}{F_0}\right] \tag{11.18}$$

be the U-shaped payout created by the static position in bonds and options. Since $u(L) = 0$ by (11.14), U takes its minimum value of $-u(F_0)$ at $F_n = L$. The Black model value at time t_{i-1} of this payout is given by

$$V(F_{i-1}, t_{i-1}) \equiv e^{-y_{i-1,n}(t_n - t_{i-1})} 2\left[\frac{F_{i-1} - F_0}{L} - \ln\frac{F_{i-1}}{F_0}\right]$$
$$- \sigma^2(t_n - t_{i-1})$$

Hence, the Black model delta at time t_{i-1} is

$$\frac{\partial}{\partial F} V(F_{i-1}, t_{i-1}) = e^{-y_{i-1,n}(t_n - t_{i-1})} \left(\frac{2}{F_{i-1}} - \frac{2}{L}\right) \tag{11.19}$$

which differs from the number of futures needed to hedge a variance swap only by a small present value factor. Surprisingly, the Black model delta in (11.19) is actually independent of σ, that is, $\partial^2 V / \partial\sigma\partial F = 0$. Put another way, the static portfolio is chosen so that its Black model vega is independent of the futures price. Of course, the Black model dynamic hedge of this portfolio only works perfectly under continuous trading, continuous price paths and constant volatility. Since the approximate replicating strategy actually involves only discrete trading at prices that can reflect jumps and stochastic volatility, one would anticipate that this attempt at a Black model hedge would fail. However, for the particular static portfolio described above, the hedging error approximates the payout to a variance swap with fixed payment $\sigma^2(t_n - t_0)$.

Upside and downside variance swaps
The previous section showed that the payout to a variance swap

$$\sum_{i=1}^n \left(\ln \frac{F_i}{F_{i-1}}\right)^2 - \sigma^2(t_n - t_0)$$

could be approximately replicated by forming a static portfolio of options and bonds that has the U-shaped payout $U(F_n)$. This portfolio is delta-hedged daily with the Black model delta for each option calculated using the fixed volatility rate σ. It follows that if we just wish to create the payout to a variance contract

$$\sum_{i=1}^{n}\left(\ln\frac{F_i}{F_{i-1}}\right)^2$$

we could delta-hedge each option at $\sigma = 0$.

To approximate the payouts to upside and downside variance contracts, suppose that we guess that the approximate hedge just involves delta-hedging options struck above and below the barrier, respectively, where each option is delta-hedged at zero volatility. Hence, for the upside variance contract, the static component of the proposed hedge has a payout that is constant for $F_n \leq L$ and is given by the right half of the U-shaped payout $U(F_n)$ defined in (11.18) for $F_n > L$:

$$U_r(F_n) \equiv u_r(F_n) - u_r(F_0), \quad \text{where } u_r(F) \equiv u(F)_{F>L} \qquad (11.20)$$

To create the payout $U_r(F_n)$, we would only hold the $(2/K^2)\, dK$ calls at all strikes K above the lower bound L and we would also short $u_r(F_0)$ bonds. No puts would be held.

Similarly, the proposed hedge for the downside variance contract has a static component payout that is constant for $F_n \geq L$ and given by the left half of the U-shaped payout $U(F_n)$ defined in (11.18) for $F_n < L$:

$$U_\ell(F_n) \equiv u_\ell(F_n) - u_\ell(F_0), \quad \text{where } u_\ell(F) \equiv u(F)_{F<L} \qquad (11.21)$$

Hence, we hold $(2/K^2)\, dK$ puts at all strikes K below L and we short $u_\ell(F_0)$ bonds. No calls are held. We note that the sum of the static positions in options in the proposed hedges for the upside and downside variance contracts is just the static option position in the hedge for the variance contract.

For the dynamic components of the proposed hedges, recall that we delta-hedge each option at $\sigma = 0$. Hence, for the dynamic component of the proposed hedge for an upside variance contract, one holds $-e^{-y_{in}(t_n-t_i)}(2/L - 2/F_{i-1})^+$ futures contracts from day $i-1$ to day i, since out-of-the-money call deltas vanish under zero volatility. For the dynamic component of the proposed hedge for a downside variance contract, one holds $-e^{-y_{in}(t_n-t_i)}(2/F_{i-1}-2/L)^+$ futures contracts from day $i-1$ to day i, since out-of-the-money put deltas also vanish under zero volatility. We again note that the sum of the dynamic futures positions in the proposed hedges for the upside and downside variance contracts is just the dynamic futures position in the hedge for the variance contract.

If the futures price opens and closes below L, then in the proposed hedge for the upside variance contract, no futures are held and there is no gain in the bonds or out-of-the-money calls marked at zero volatility. Likewise, the intrinsic value of the upside variance contract does not change in this case, so the proposed hedge works perfectly in this case. Furthermore, the proposed hedge for a downside variance contract must also work in this case since this hedge is just the difference in the successful hedges of a variance contract and an upside variance contract.

If the futures price opens below L and closes above, then no futures are held in the proposed hedge for the upside variance contract, and the intrinsic value of the call portfolio rises from zero to $u_r(F_i)$. Figure 11.1 shows u_r as a function of F when $L = 1$. The first derivative is $u_r'(F) = (2/L - 2/F)^+$, which is continuous at $F = L$. The second derivative is $u_r''(F) = {}_{F>L}2/F^2$, which is discontinuous at $F = L$. By a Taylor series expansion of $u(F_i)$ about $F_i = L$:

$$u_r(F_i) = \left(\frac{\Delta F_i}{L}\right)^2 + O\left(\frac{\Delta F_i}{F_{i-1}}\right)^3 \tag{11.22}$$

for $F_i > L$ since $|F_i - L| \leq |\Delta F_i|$. On days when the futures price enters the upper corridor, the intrinsic value of the upside variance contract rises by $(\ln F_i/L)^2$. From (11.10), this differs from $u_r(F_i)$ by $O(\Delta F_i/F_{i-1})^3$, so the proposed hedge is sufficiently accurate in this case as well. Furthermore, the proposed hedge for a downside variance contract must also work in this second case for the same reason as in the first case.

If the futures price opens and closes above L, then the analysis of the previous section implies that the proposed hedge of the upside variance contract has a profit and loss of $(\Delta F_i/F_{i-1})^2 + O(\Delta F_i/F_{i-1})^3$, while the intrinsic value of the upside variance contract rises by $(\ln F_i/F_{i-1})^2$. From (11.10), the proposed hedge has

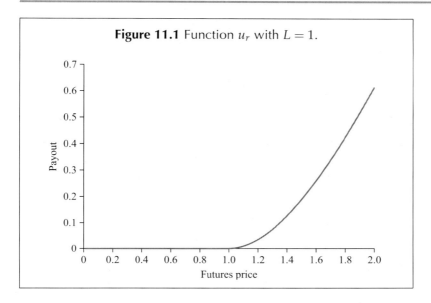

Figure 11.1 Function u_r with $L = 1$.

sufficient accuracy in this third case. Furthermore, the proposed hedge for a downside variance contract must also work in this case.

If the futures price opens above L but closes below it, then the analysis of the profit and loss from the proposed hedge of the upside variance contract is complicated by the fact that $u_r(F)$ defined in (11.20) is not an analytic function of F. However, we note that exit of the upper corridor is equivalent to entry of the lower corridor. If the futures price enters the lower corridor from above, then no futures are held in the proposed hedge to the downside variance contract and the intrinsic value of the puts held rises from zero to

$$u_\ell(F_i) = \left(\frac{\Delta F_i}{L}\right)^2 + O\left(\frac{\Delta F_i}{F_{i-1}}\right)^3, \quad F_i < L \qquad (11.23)$$

from a Taylor series expansion of $u(F_i)$ about $F_i = L$. When the futures price enters the lower corridor, the intrinsic value of the downside variance contract rises by $(\ln F_i/L)^2$, which only differs from $u_\ell(F_i)$ by $O(\Delta F_i/F_{i-1})^3$. From (11.10), the proposed hedge to the downside variance contract has sufficient accuracy in this last case. It follows that the proposed hedge for the upside variance contract must also work in this case since this hedge is just the difference in the successful hedges of a variance contract and the downside variance contract.

We have just shown that the payout $Q_n^u(L)$ of the upside variance contract is well approximated in all cases:

$$Q_n^u(L) = \int_L^\infty \frac{2}{K^2}(F_n - K)^+ \, dK - u_r(F_0)$$
$$- \sum_{i=1}^n \left(\frac{2}{L} - \frac{2}{F_{i-1}}\right)^+ \Delta F_i + \sum_{i=1}^n O\left(\frac{\Delta F_i}{F_{i-1}}\right)^3 \quad (11.24)$$

If the initial cost of the approximate hedge is financed by borrowing, then the repayment at t_n is

$$\int_L^\infty \frac{2}{K^2} \frac{C_0(K, t_n)}{B_0(t_n)} \, dK - u_r(F_0) \quad (11.25)$$

If there is no charge for the third-order approximation error, then this is the fair (non-annualised) fixed payment for an upside variance swap on US$1 of notional. The corresponding entity for a downside variance contract is

$$\int_0^L \frac{2}{K^2} \frac{P_0(K, t_n)}{B_0(t_n)} \, dK - u_\ell(F_0) \quad (11.26)$$

MONTE CARLO SIMULATION

This section reports the distribution of hedging errors arising from simulating the hedge of an upside variance swap over 250,000 paths. We considered the errors arising from hedging the sale of an upside variance swap with daily monitoring, a three-month term and a lower barrier of US$90. We first assumed that the underlying futures price starts at US$100 and follows geometric Brownian motion with 5% real-world drift and 30% volatility.

Figure 11.2 shows the density function of the hedging errors. The units on the x-axis correspond to the fixed leg price of $900 = 10{,}000(30\%)^2$. The curve designated symmetric corresponds to an upside variance swap payout where exit and entry are treated symmetrically. The curve designated asymmetric uses the asymmetric upside variance swap payout proposed in this chapter. The asymmetric profit and loss has mean -0.0097 and standard deviation 0.01 while the symmetric profit and loss has mean -0.042 and standard deviation 0.069. Note that the symmetric profit and loss has a fat tail for losses.

We next assumed that the underlying futures price follows the jump diffusion process suggested by Merton (1976). The initial

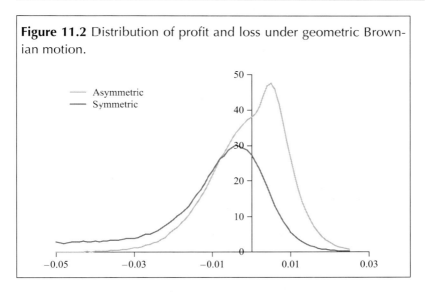

Figure 11.2 Distribution of profit and loss under geometric Brownian motion.

futures price start at US$100, has 5% real-world drift and a 30% diffusion coefficient as before. We set the arrival rate equal to one, so that jumps arrive once a year on average. The jump in the log price is normally distributed with mean zero and standard deviation of 10%. Figure 11.3 summarises the results of the previous simulation but now using the Merton model. The hedges corresponding to the asymmetric payout definition continue to perform well, while the same hedges coupled to a symmetric payout definition are actually "short jumps". The asymmetric mean is -0.0037 with standard deviation 0.094 while the symmetric mean is -0.08 with standard deviation 0.3.

These simulation results clearly suggest that the complications arising from an asymmetric payout definition are outweighed by the improved hedge effectiveness.

INTERIOR CORRIDOR

In this section, we generalise our results on upside and downside variance swaps to corridor variance swaps with an interior corridor. Let $\mathcal{C}$ denote the interior corridor (L, H) where $L > 0$ and H is finite. The futures price is now said to enter the corridor on day i if $F_{i-1} \notin \mathcal{C}$ and $F_i \notin \mathcal{C}$. In this case, define the entry price N_{i-1} as $N_{i-1} \equiv L$ if $F_{i-1} < L$ and $N_{i-1} \equiv H$ if $F_{i-1} > H$. The futures price is now said to exit the corridor on day i if $F_{i-1} \in \mathcal{C}$ and $F_i \notin \mathcal{C}$. In this case, define

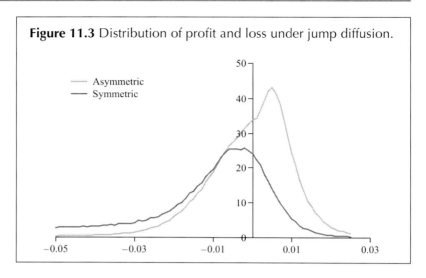

Figure 11.3 Distribution of profit and loss under jump diffusion.

the exit price X_i as $X_i \equiv L$ if $F_i < L$ and $X_i \equiv H$ if $F_i > H$. The payout on the corridor variance contract is now defined as

$$Q_n(L, H) \equiv \sum_{i=1}^{n} \left\{ F_{i-1}\in C, F_i \in C \left(\ln \frac{F_i}{F_{i-1}} \right)^2 + F_{i-1}\notin C, F_i \in C \left(\ln \frac{F_i}{N_{i-1}} \right)^2 \right.$$

$$+ F_{i-1}\in C, F_i \notin C \left[\left(\ln \frac{F_i}{F_{i-1}} \right)^2 - \left(\ln \frac{F_i}{X_i} \right)^2 \right]$$

$$+ [F_{i-1}<L, F_i>H + F_{i-1}>H, F_i<L]$$

$$\left. \times \left| \left(\frac{F_i - L}{L} \right)^2 - \left(\frac{F_i - H}{H} \right)^2 \right| \right\} \qquad (11.27)$$

The first three terms in the summand correspond to the three terms in the summand in (11.1). The last term arises from the possibility of jumping over the corridor in either direction. In either case, the squared return from the exit price is subtracted from the squared return from the entry price.

To create the payout in (11.27), consider the following function:

$$\phi(F) \equiv \begin{cases} F>L u(F) & \text{if } F \leq H \\ 2\left[\dfrac{H}{L} - 1 - \ln\left(\dfrac{H}{L}\right) \right] + \left(\dfrac{2}{L} - \dfrac{2}{H} \right)(F - H) & \text{if } F > H \end{cases}$$

$$(11.28)$$

where $u(F)$ is defined in (11.14). Thus, $\phi(F) = u_r(F)$ for $F \leq H$ and is the tangent to u_r at $F = H$ for $F > H$. Figure 11.4 graphs ϕ against F.

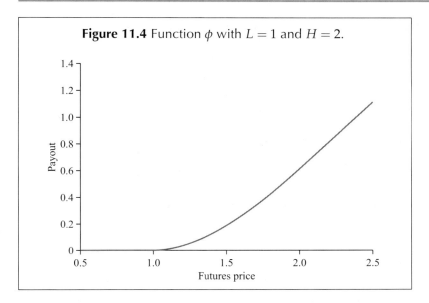

Figure 11.4 Function ϕ with $L = 1$ and $H = 2$.

The function ϕ is continuous and differentiable everywhere, but it is not twice differentiable at L and at H.

We can use calls maturing at t_n to create the payout $\phi(F_n)$:

$$\phi(F_n) = \int_L^H \frac{2}{K^2}(F_n - K)^+ \, dK \qquad (11.29)$$

Using an analysis similar to that in the last section, we conclude that

$$Q_n(L, H) = \int_L^H \frac{2}{K^2}(F_n - K)^+ \, dK - \phi(F_0)$$
$$- \sum_{i=1}^n \left(\frac{2}{L} - \frac{2}{F_{i-1} \wedge H}\right)^+ \Delta F_i + \sum_{i=1}^n O\left(\frac{\Delta F_i}{F_{i-1}}\right)^3 \qquad (11.30)$$

Thus, the desired payout is again well approximated by the sum of the payout from a static position in calls and bonds with the payouts from a dynamic position in futures. For the static component, one holds $(2/K^2)dK$ calls at all strikes in the corridor (L, H). One also borrows $\phi(F_0)$ pure discount bonds paying US\$1 at t_n. For the dynamic component, one holds $-e^{-y_{in}(t_n - t_i)}(2/L - 2/F_{i-1} \wedge H)^+$ futures contracts from day $i - 1$ to day i. When $F_{i-1} \leq L$, no futures are held, as in the last section. When $F_{i-1} > H$, the number of futures contracts held is independent of F_{i-1}, so that the number of contracts held hardly changes while the underlying remains above the corridor. If the initial cost of the approximate hedge is financed by borrowing, then the repayment at t_n is

$$\int_L^H \frac{2}{K^2} \frac{C_0(K, t_n)}{B_0(t_n)} \, dK - \phi(F_0) \qquad (11.31)$$

If there is no charge for the third-order approximation error, then this is the fair (non-annualised) fixed payment for the interior corridor variance swap on US$1 of notional.

SUMMARY AND EXTENSIONS

We defined the payout to a corridor variance swap in such a way that the payout could be well approximated by the payout from combining static positions in options and bonds with at most daily trading in the underlying futures. Although our payout definition treats entry and exit asymmetrically, it treats entry for a downside variance swap symmetrically with entry for an upside variance swap. Exit for the two swaps is also treated symmetrically. As a result, the sum of a downside variance swap and an upside variance swap is a standard variance swap, which does not remain true when exit and entry are treated symmetrically.

There are at least seven extensions to this work. First, one can further analyse our small approximation error to see whether it can be at least partially spanned. For example, a simple linear regression of the error on a constant and the change in the futures price can be used as a guide to how to account for this error in determining the fixed rate for the corridor variance swap and the dynamic component of the hedge. Using ordinary least squares, one finds that the return skewness affects the fixed rate, while the return kurtosis affects the futures position. Second, one can try to relax our model assumptions such as continuum of strikes, deterministic interest rates and frictionless futures trading, or at least try to determine their effect. Third, one can attempt to determine the effect of small perturbations in our definitions. For example, (11.10) makes it clear that the hedge has the same order error if daily returns are discretely compounded rather than continuously compounded. One can also try to determine the effect of demeaning the daily returns as some (corridored) variance swaps have this feature. Fourth, one can adapt our approach to make it more applicable to the corridor variance realised from individual stock returns.

If stocks replace single-name futures as the underlying, then stock dividends become relevant. Also, if listed options are used in the hedge, then American-style options must be handled. Fifth, one can supplement the approximation developed here by also developing bounds on the fair fixed payment via super- and sub-replication of the corridor variance. Sixth, it would be interesting to extend this work by characterising the entire class of path-dependent payouts that can be approximated or bounded in this way. Finally, one can also try to develop a theory of model-free approximate hedging that would in general allow semi-dynamic trading in both futures and options. In the interests of brevity, these extensions are best left for future research.

REFERENCES

Black, F., 1976, "The pricing of commodity contracts", *Journal of Financial Economics*, 3, pp 167–179.

Carr, P. and D. Madan, 1998, "Towards a theory of volatility trading", in R. Jarrow (ed), *Volatility*, (London: Risk Books), pp 417–427. Reprinted in Musiella, Jouini and Cvitanic (eds), 2001, *Option Pricing, Interest Rates, and Risk Management* (Cambridge University Press), pp 458–476. Available at www.math.nyu.edu/research/carrp/papers.

Chriss, N. and W. Morokoff, 1999, "Market risk for volatility and variance swaps", *Risk*, October, pp 55–59.

Demeterfi, K., E. Derman, M. Kamal and J. Zhou, 1999 "A guide to variance swaps", *Risk*, June, pp 54–59.

Merton, R., 1976, "Option pricing when underlying stock returns are discontinuous", *Journal of Financial Economics*, 3, pp 125–144.

Index

absolute risk aversion (CARA), 260
arbitrage, 245
asymmetric treatment of entry and exit, 290
ATM volatilities, 21, 24, 35

barrier variance, 146, 148–151, 177
barrier variance contracts, 149–151
basket, min and max options, 116
Black model dynamic hedge, 295
Black option model, 246
Black–Scholes, 62, 177
    case, 151
    formula, 3
    implied volatility, 142, 158, 166
    measure, 145, 163
    model, 51, 96, 150, 152, 177
    theory of pricing, 259
    type PDE, 269
    variety, 144
bootstrap procedure, 115
bootstrapped distributions, 128
bootstrapping correlation matrixes, 114
Brownian bridge techniques, 99
Brownian motion, 301

Carr and Madan's approach, 220
Carr and Madan's formal pricing approach, 195
CBOE Futures Exchange (CFE), 234
CBOE VIX options, 244
CFE realised variance futures, 248
CFE VIX futures, 238
Chicago Board Options Exchange (CBOE), 141, 233
Chicago Mercantile Exchange (CME), 145
CME futures options, 156
complete and incomplete markets, 261
conditional variance swaps, 78

Conquest Managed Futures Select (MFS) fund, 86
Conquest MFS programme, 87
conservative hedging, 282
consistency, 5
constant-maturity two-year Treasury rate, 71
contour plots, 117
copula methods, 102
corridor implied volatility (CIV), 144
corridor variance contracts, 146
corridor variance swap, 78, 224, 287, 289
corridor variances, 164
covariance matrixes, 118
CPI report, 63
cross gamma hedge, 107
cross-gammas, 104
curve spread, 73

DAX, 120, 122
defining volatility, 187
delta of an option, 6
delta-hedge, 185
delta-hedged option trading, 76
delta-hedging options, 188
derivatives pricing and hedging, 260, 267, 268
deterministic interest rates, 292
discretisation errors, 155
dispersion trading, 224
down corridor variance swaps, 227

equity, 213
equity market, 24
equity market volatility, 198
euro/US dollar exchange rate, 20
euro–yen exchange rate, 125

fair strike K_F, 280
fair value, 244
Fisher Black's formula, 135
fixed income, 64, 67, 68, 70

INDEX

forecast performance, 165
forward-start variance swap, 200, 210, 214
  pricing, 201
frictionless markets, 292
future return of the stockmarket, 255
futures price, 289, 298
FX market, 21

gamma, 223
gamma swaps, 78, 220, 222, 224
greeks, 100

hedge funds, 237
hedging error for longer expiries, 48
Heston (1993) model, 8, 33
Heston's economies, 264, 271
hyperbolic absolute risk aversion (HARA), 260

implied average correlation matrix, 112
implied correlation, 108
implied correlation surface, 113
implied estimation of the correlation, 110
implied risk-neutral density, 50
implied volatilities, 13, 14, 25, 34, 246
implied volatility $\varsigma(K)$, 15
implied volatility surface, 26, 28, 29, 32, 33
implied volatility's term structure, 16
index variance swaps, 207
interest rates, 72
interior corridor, 301
intuitiveness, 5
investment strategies, 254
IUG, 248

jump diffusion, 302

Korean market, 251
Kurtosis, 203

limit, 12
local volatility model, 98
log-returns, 111
log-volatility regressions, 169
long bond exposure, 62
long volatility, 83

managed futures returns, 85
Marcenko–Pastur law, 119
maturity, 192
mean-reverting property, 69
Merton's model, 84
Merton's problem, 262, 263, 266
MFS breakout sub-systems, 90–92
MFS versus drift diffusion, 89
Mincer–Zarnowitz regression, 165
"model-free" implied volatility (MFIV), 141
Monte Carlo, 100
Monte Carlo simulation, 275, 300
"Mountain Range" products, 96
multivariate variance gamma model, 102

neutral derivative pricing, 259, 265, 266, 268, 271
"new economy" bubble, 95
Nikkei225 quanto euro forwards, 126
no-arbitrage, 12
notional, 192

one-month forward-start one-month variance swaps, 218
one-year variance swaps, 228
option-implied volatility, 66
option-portfolio variance vega, 221
Options Clearing Corporation, 236
options tricks, 136
out-of-the-money volatilities, 36

parsimony, 5
portfolio theory, 260, 262, 264
price densities, 118
price distributions, 123, 124
pricing, 193
pricing formula, 264, 279, 280

realised volatility, 143, 241
realised volatility measures, 151
risk, 203
risk and return of forward-start variance swaps, 208
risk and return of one-month and one-year variance swaps, 205
risk and return of one-year S&P500 index forwards, 205
risk premium, 65, 74
risk premium (variance swaps), 277
risk premium PDE, 263, 264, 274, 275
RUG, 248

S&P500 derivatives, 292
S&P500 futures, 156
S&P500 futures portfolio performance, 215–218
S&P500 futures portfolio risk, 215–218
S&P500 implied volatility index, 83
S&P500 index, 160, 206, 227
S&P500 option data, 158
S&P500 options (SPX), 233
S&P500 six-month forward-start six-month variance swap returns, 212
S&P500 variance swap term structure, 209
SABR (stochastic alpha, beta, rho) model, 8
Sharpe ratio, 134, 214, 219
shorting variance swaps, 204
six-month forward-start six-month variance swaps, 217
smile asymptotics, 50
smile consistent pricing, 55
smile interpolation, 10
smile interpolation among expiries, 16
speculation, 245
standard deviation bonds, 255
sticky absolute rule, 4

sticky delta rule, 4, 23
sticky strike rule, 3
stock markets, 252
stock price = stock value ± noise ± information, 135
straddle, 188, 189, 196
strangle profiles, 189, 196
strangles, 188
strike price, 192
swaption, 43
swaption ATM volatility surface, 40
swaption market, 34
swaptions butterfly surface, 42
swaptions risk reversal surface, 41

Taylor series expansion approximation, 155
term structure, 69, 72
Theta of an option, 19
three-month variance futures, 249
time-series correlation, 108
time-series estimators, 129
trading equity correlation, 112
trend following, 93
truncation errors, 155

up and down conditional variance swaps, 226
up and down corridor variance swaps, 225, 228
upside and downside variance swaps, 288, 296
US dollar variation, 243

value at risk, 134
Vanna–Volga (VV) method, 4
variance gamma process, 103
variance regressions, 170
variance risk, 190
variance swap, 55, 76, 185, 191, 200, 202, 215, 216, 222, 223, 227, 260, 272–274, 279, 280, 293
variance swap prices, 281, 284
variance swap replication, 230
variance swap returns, 204

variance vega of three-month options, 194
vega risk, 190
VIX futures, 240, 242, 247
VIX options, 247
VIX Volatility Index, 71, 73
VIX–MFS correlation, 87
volatility, 61, 64, 67, 68, 70, 134, 213, 241
  as an asset class, 187
  cap, 193
  clusters, 198
  contracts, 238
  derivatives, 234, 260, 271, 272
  forecasts, 167
  index, 233, 251–254, 256
  investing, 186
  measures, 154, 157–159, 161, 162, 165

path dependency risk, 191
regressions, 168, 171
risk premium, 75
smile, 20
surface, 3, 7
swaps, 76
traders, 237
volume-weighted average price (VWAP), 137
VV approach, 10, 31, 33, 39
VV method, 9, 40
VV option price, 46
VV price, 11
VV risk-neutral density, 51
VV weights, 44

weighted Monte Carlo (WMC), 101
world basket, 124